EX LIBRIS

AD MORTEM FIDELIS

C. T. CHANDLER

The
TREASURY *of*
ANGLING

by Larry Koller

SPECIAL PHOTOGRAPHY BY
George Silk

A Ridge Press Book

Golden Press ❧ New York

The
TREASURY *of*
ANGLING

by Larry Koller

A Ridge Press Book
Golden Press ⚓ New York

ATLANTIC SALMON

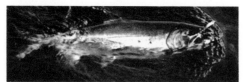

PACIFIC SALMON

LANDLOCKED SALMON

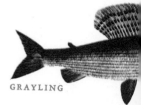

GRAYLING

BROWN TROUT

RAINBOW TROUT

CUTTHROAT TROUT

DOLLY VARDEN

GOLDEN TROUT

Editor-in-Chief: JERRY MASON
Editor: ADOLPH SUEHSDORF
Art Director: ALBERT A. SQUILLACE
Associate Editor: EVELYN HANNON
Associate Editor: RUTH BIRNKRANT
Art Associate: LEON BOLOGNESE
Art Production: DORIS MULLANE

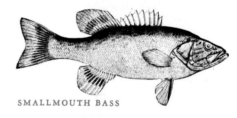

SMALLMOUTH BASS

PAN FISH

PERCH

WALLEYED PIKE

PREPARED AND PRODUCED BY
THE RIDGE PRESS, INC. PRINTED IN THE
UNITED STATES OF AMERICA BY
WESTERN PRINTING AND
LITHOGRAPHING COMPANY
PUBLISHED BY GOLDEN PRESS, INC.
850 THIRD AVENUE,
NEW YORK 22, NEW YORK.
PUBLISHED SIMULTANEOUSLY IN CANADA
BY THE MUSSON BOOK
BOOK COMPANY, LTD., TORONTO.
© 1963 BY GOLDEN PRESS,
INC. AND THE RIDGE PRESS, INC.
LIBRARY OF CONGRESS CATALOG
CARD NUMBER: 62-15425

STEELHEAD

BROOK TROUT

LAKE TROUT

MUSKELLUNGE

PICKEREL

LARGEMOUTH BASS

PIKE

CONTENTS

Angling is the art of catching fish with a rod, a line, and a hook. It is an ancient and honorable sport; its roots lie deep in the past, a tradition intangible but persistent governs its conduct. The tradition, which received its form and best expression from Izaak Walton and Charles Cotton, permits the angler to be guileful and deceptive, and to bring to bear on the contest whatever wisdom and experience he has been able to accumulate—for so will the fish. But it urges that the fight be fairly fought, and that the fisherman show a lively curiosity about—and a decent respect for—the natural equilibrium of life in lake and stream. Fishing, of course, may be done by other methods and with other motivations. But it seems to be true that applying the art in terms of the tradition yields the maximum of satisfaction and is most soothing to the spirit.

Belief in these verities has motivated
this book. I do not consider myself an elite fisherman or a purist, but I am
convinced that any fisherman who aspires to be better than he is will do
well to follow a traditional course. For a man
fishes to catch fish, and a thorough angling education can teach him many
things that will serve him in his quest.

The fisherman who has learned his craft is a many-sided man.
He is an ichthyologist of sorts, aware of the
life cycle, feeding habits, and temperament of the game fish he seeks. He is an
amateur entomologist, a keen and knowledgeable observer
of the seasonal insect life of the water he fishes. If he has learned his

lessons well he will know something of hydrochemistry and be enough of a meteorologist to have a feeling for weather. He will be a mechanic who knows his tools: he will be able to deliver an intelligently selected lure or fly to a chosen spot, and will know the capacities of rod, line, and leader under strain when his maneuvers have successfully raised a fish.

Beyond these tactical considerations, however, are the sensory perceptions the angler gathers unto himself. He responds to the ever-changing moods of rivers and lakes, and to the interrelated lives of the creatures that inhabit the environment. His eye detects the microsecond gleam of a trout flashing at his fly in the depth of a turbulent run. His ear is tuned to the faint flip of the rise, even above the tumult of running water. He cannot be indifferent or dispassionate toward his place in this natural world and call himself an angler.

In "The Treasury of Angling," I
have undertaken to discuss fishing as a blend of all these elements.
The book is impartial as to the fisherman's techniques,
but it feels strongly about what it means to be a fisherman. No one will ever
know all there is to know about angling, but the angler's
pleasure will always be in direct proportion to his understanding.
Like all worth-while efforts, angling
gives back in the degree to which it is given.

LARRY KOLLER

The author and the editors wish to express
special appreciation to Mr. James T. Babb and Miss Marjorie G. Wynne, of the
Sterling Memorial Library of Yale University, for their generous
assistance in providing illustrations from the resources
of the Rare Book Room and the justly famous Wagstaff Collection of angling
materials, and to Evelyn Luscher for her aid in editorial research.

ceste despr [illegible] occident en orient.

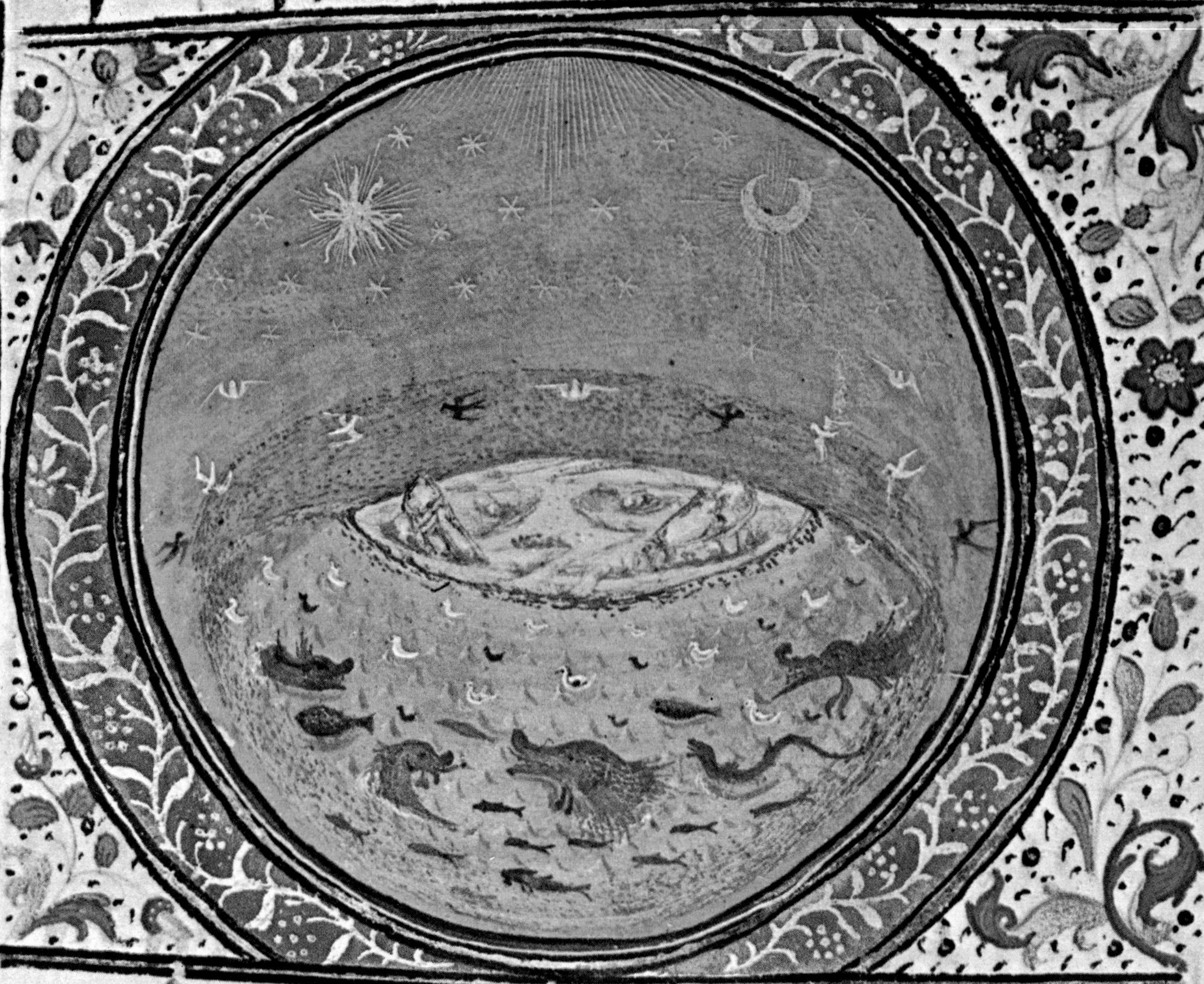

De louurage du cinquiesme Jour selon la bible.

De rechief dist dieu
les eaues donnent
poissons et volatilles
sur terre dessoubz le firmament
Dont crea dieu grans ballaines
et toutes ames vivans et mou
vans lesquelles les eaues [illegible]

Angling in ANTIQUITY

"They fasten red wool around a hook and fix to the wool two feathers that grow under a cock's wattles, and which in color are like wax. The rod they use is six feet long and the line of the same length. Then the angler lets fall his lure. The fish, attracted by its color and excited, draws close and...forthwith opens its mouth, but is caught by the hook, and bitter indeed is the feast it enjoys, inasmuch as it is captured."

DE ANIMALIUM NATURA

T h e Roman rhetorician Claudius Aelian wrote this description of fishing with an artificial fly more than seventeen centuries ago. The anglers were Macedonians. Their stream was the river Astraeus. And, judging by other hints Aelian gives us, the quarry appears to have been a species of trout.

It is not clear from the account whether the Macedonians were fishing for food or for sport, although we may infer it was sport because food fishermen, like Simon Peter of Galilee, always go for quantity and use comprehensive equipment, such as the net or the trap, to get it. The rod, the line, and the artful lure generally bespeak the angler in the patient exercise of his craft, seeking to beguile one fish.

In any event, Aelian's Macedonians of about 200 A.D. are certainly the first fly-fishermen of record.

Of fishermen before them we have tantalizing glimpses, but no coherent history. We know, however, that the angler's tackle—rod, line, and hook—has an ancient heritage and that it appears among the earliest evidence of human society on earth. Archaeologists at

On the Fifth Day, the
Lord created the fishes of the waters—
depicted (left) in illumination from "Historiaux de la Bible,"
by Peter Comestor, France, 1460.

the site of Ur of the Chaldees, in the valley of the Euphrates, have unearthed fishhooks—well made and not unlike those in use today—nearly five thousand years old. The Egyptian wall painting reproduced on page 12, the earliest known picture of a rod fisherman, dates from about 2000 B.C. The rod or, more precisely, the pole, resembles a billiard cue, but its function is unmistakable. Very likely it was a length of cane from Abaris, in Lower Egypt.

Since food was the principal objective, however, it was the net, the spear, and to a lesser extent the hand line that predominated in the misty morning of fishing history.

Primitive man used a gorge. Not a hook, really, the gorge was simply a slender piece of stone, shell, bone, or wood an inch or two long and needle sharp at each end. A groove was cut around the middle of the gorge to seat the line—probably a length of vine—and keep it from slipping. The gorge was buried in a piece of meat or fish flesh and dropped into a pool or river to attract fish. When the bait was taken, the angler—like today's still-fisherman—gave his victim enough time to swallow it, then yanked on the line. The gorge cleared the bait and imbedded itself, crosswise, inside the fish. If the line was strong enough to take the strain, the angler would haul out his catch.

The oldest gorge known was found buried more than twenty feet down, along a bank of the river Somme, in France. It was estimated to be at least seven thousand years old and possibly as much as thirty thousand. Yet this most ancient of angling tools is still employed by fishermen in many parts of the world and especially in the South Seas.

Fishermen in Biblical times favored the net or a hand line, as is still the case in Mediterranean and Middle Eastern areas today. Netting—or seining—was

Earliest known picture of a rod fisherman
(top) from Egyptian wall painting done in 2000 B.C.
is reproduced from Percy Newberry's
"Archaeological Survey in Egypt, Beni Hasan."
Above: An Assyrian hand-lines in his
ancient lake, from "The Monuments of Nineveh," by
Austin Henry Layard. The Greek angler of
about 500 B.C. (right) does his
rod fishing nude, from "Die griechischen
Meisterschalen," P. Hartwig.

12

generally done from boats, but the hand-line technique was shore-based. The angler on the bank threw out a number of weighted lines, each with a single baited hook. The lines were tied to notched sticks imbedded in the bank, and in due time if all went as expected, hauled in for removal of the catch.

The Bible itself contains many references to fishing, although most of them are metaphorical and only a few at all specific. Habakkuk, lamenting the ascendancy of the Chaldeans over his people, says: "They take up all of them with the angle. They catch them in their net. And gather them in their drag." Job asks: "Cans't thou fill his skin with barbed irons? or his head with fish spears?" And, again: "Cans't thou draw out Leviathan with an hook? or his tongue with a cord which thou lettest down?" The Prophet Isaiah said: "The fishers also shall mourn, and all they that cast angle in the brooks shall lament and they that spread nets upon the waters shall languish." Hooks, spears, and nets, but no word about the rod, or pole.

However, Plato and Aristotle mention angling in the centuries before Christ, and Plutarch has some advice for us about fishing lines which survives from the early second century A.D. The line should be braided horsehair, he says, and that used next to the hook should be taken from a white horse. He believed a stallion's tail hairs were the strongest and the best, the gelding's next, and the mare's least good because of the weakening effect of her urine upon them.

True angling for sport apparently was not unknown, but seems to have been confined to the higher echelons of society, those privileged few with wealth, leisure time, and confidence that their next meal would arrive promptly. Early Egyptian picture writing shows the no-bility fishing with rods in large fish tanks. Wealthy Romans built special fish ponds—a beginning of fish culture?—to provide themselves an easy catch for the table and some angling sport, as well. This is not un-like the practice of pond and stream stocking in private waters for the exclusive use of club members. The well-heeled salmon fisherman working his fly over a leased pool on the Restigouche is today's descendant of the ancient angler in the upper income brackets.

One other fundamental aspect of fishing was also well established by this time. This is the angler's itch to deceive brother fishermen as well as fish. In Plu-tarch's life of the noble Roman Mark Antony we find one of the first of that classic genre, the fish story.

It seems that Antony and Cleopatra boarded a boat and went fishing one day. Antony got not so much as a nibble, which is always embarrassing in the presence of one's lady. So he secretly instructed some servants attending the royal party—probably to bait the hooks—to slip over the side and attach some fish that had already been caught to his hook. He promptly caught so many fish that Cleopatra became suspicious. But she praised Antony highly, as a woman will, and told her courtiers who'd missed the show that they should come out on the morrow to see the great angler at work.

Next day, however, it was Cleopatra's divers who were paddling about under water. And to Antony's hook they attached "a salted fish from Pontus," very dead. Feeling the tug on his line, Antony hauled in, and general merriment ensued.

Antony must have been grinding his teeth, but Cleo-patra's charm evidently was overwhelming enough to risk a laugh at her lover. Some accounts say that Antony rallied with the remark that although the fish was not as large as he had expected, it was certainly the oldest caught that day.

By and large, however, the ancient angler remained an ancient angler in method and purpose for many centuries. Better fishing gear evolved very slowly, but patience has always been a fisherman's virtue. No one major invention transformed his world overnight. He was not so fortunate as the hunter, whose craft was revolutionized by the invention of gunpowder and tools for its use. The fisherman's art progressed at a snail's pace, the only notable change coming in the length of the rod. Since the reel was unknown in an-tiquity (except for the sticks on which the Egyptians wound their hand lines), fishermen simply tied their lines to the tip of their rods, like the barefoot boy with his cane pole. To cast farther out, they merely cut a longer pole and affixed a longer line.

Thus, by painful evolution, the rod had reached some fifteen feet or more in length by the late fifteenth century, when modern fishing history really begins.

Now, for the first time in English literature, we en-counter a full description of a rod for angling in a remarkable essay entitled "A Treatyse of fysshynge wyth an angle." It is part of the second edition of *The*

Boke of St. Albans, printed in 1496 in England by Wynkyn de Worde, an Alsatian associate of the great printer William Caxton.

Although the work is unsigned, it is generally ascribed to Dame Juliana Berners, the prioress of the Benedictine nunnery of Sopwell, near St. Albans. It is curious, and disturbing to male chauvinists, that a lady should be the fountainhead of fishing wisdom, and since the good Dame is a shadowy figure at best, recurrent efforts have been made to prove the author was a masculine Julyans Bernes or Barnes. There is also some evidence that the Treatyse was written a long time before it was printed, perhaps as early as 1450, which would remove it from Juliana's age span. And there is a fragmentary French literature on angling which some scholars feel Dame Juliana may have had access to. All this is conjectural, however. No one has really been able to authenticate another writer or earlier sources for the work.

I find the Treatyse not only of great interest, but packed with extremely good advice.

Dame Juliana deals at length with the rod. She suggests that for the butt section, or "staffe," the angler begin with a piece of green "hasyll, wyllowe or ashe." The wood, she advises, is best cut in winter, between Michaelmas (late September) and Candlemas (early February). The piece should be nine feet long and as big around as one's arm. It should be hollowed by burning out the core and then shaved down to a convenient weight and size. The tip section, or "croppe," is best made of hazel, or perhaps "black thornn, crabbe tree . . . or juniper," and of a length to bring the total to fifteen feet. The tip is joined to the butt by multiple hoops of "yron" or "laton" (tin), and the whole

massive affair finished off with a removable spike at the butt end, which seems to have served the same function as the modern surf caster's sand spike — to fix the rod erect in the bank or shore when it became tiresome to hold. For ease of carrying, the tip section could be telescoped into the hollow butt.

For at least one hundred years, this fearsome rod underwent no change. Dame Juliana's prescription for rod making prompted no argument from Leonard Mascall, author of *A Booke of fishing with Hooke & Line,* which was the next major contribution to angling literature. It appeared in 1590 and copied substantially from the Treatyse, although it also proposed some pioneering notions on the subject of fish culture.

No objections were heard either from Gervase Markham, whose book, *The Pleasures of Princes* (one of which was angling), appeared some twenty years later. Markham was a dashing and colorful fellow who served as a soldier in the Low Countries and as a captain under the Earl of Essex in Ireland. He is also supposed to have imported the first Arabian horses to England and to have sold one to King James I for £500. He likewise seems to have been scorned in his own time as a plagiarist, although it is unclear how much of this was deliberate and how much the more or less accepted practice of incorporating parts of old books into one's own. In any event, Markham accepted Juliana's precepts, adding only that rods could be made in one piece, two pieces spliced together, or three telescoping pieces. The last should have a flexible tip of hazel and a butt of two pieces of cane, probably bamboo.

Perhaps the most fascinating of Dame Juliana's instructions, however, concern artificial lures. She had observed—or learned—that the insects which swarmed

Angler (right) and device for twisting horsehair line (below)
illustrate Dame Juliana's "A Treatyse of fysshynge wyth an angle," 1496.

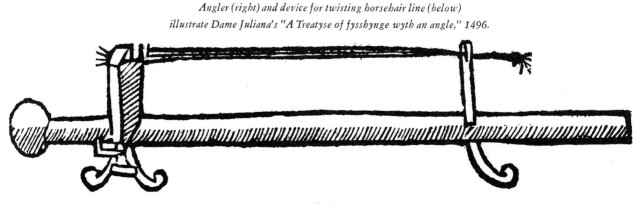

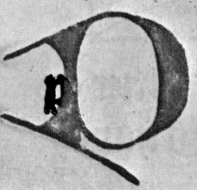

over a stream came and went according to a consistent seasonal cycle. It followed that there was a relationship between this cycle and the feeding habits of fish, and that the successful angler would be the one whose lures most closely approximated the insect in season. In other words, he who could best "match the hatch" would take the most fish.

Interestingly enough, the fly Dame Juliana describes first is the same red hackle that Aelian's Macedonians used on the Astraeus. Whether she had read Aelian or not, we don't know, but she is most specific in recommending a body of "roddy wull" and wings of "redde capons hakyll." It is most effective, she says, at the "begynning of Maye." As, indeed, it is.

To match the hatch more carefully, she goes on to develop a set of twelve patterns, one for each month of the year. Her descriptions are precise enough so that copies can be readily made today. The Angler's Club of New York has a set of this famous dozen tied by Dr. Warren Coleman and mounted on parchment in the fifteenth-century manner by William Vreeland of the Metropolitan Museum of Art.

Dame Juliana's precepts were the basis of angling knowledge in England for a hundred and fifty years. The writers who followed her made small contributions, but by and large were content to rework or plagiarize the Treatyse. Meanwhile, through great and turbulent times, Englishmen fished their placid streams

eſcam inhamatam
n et trincha intuen
bāt Hz lucius īge-

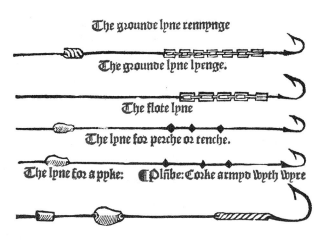

*Left: First known
representation of an angler
with float is found in "Dialogus
Creaturarum Moralisatus," 1460.
Various ground and float
lines (above) also appear in
Dame Juliana's Treatyse.*

and the art of angling meandered on its gentle course oblivious of kings.

It was a vastly different England that greeted the first edition of *The Compleat Angler* in 1653. Dame Juliana was a subject of Henry VII, who had wrested his crown from Richard Crookback at Bosworth Field in the sunset of the Middle Ages. Her Treatyse appeared only four years after Columbus' first voyage. In 1653, Henry VIII and the age of Elizabeth were past, and dour James I was best remembered for the most glorious Bible in the English language. Silky, sad-eyed Charles I had been beheaded, and a fitful civil war was being fought between fiercely righteous Oliver Cromwell and the Cavalier supporters of Charles II.

It was the world of John Milton, John Donne, Samuel Pepys—and Izaak Walton.

Strangely little is known of Walton's life, although it seems clear that he was a kind and amiable man with a great capacity for friendship and a vast love for the subjective pleasures of angling. He was born in Stafford, established himself in London sometime before 1613, and was engaged in business—the nature of which has never been determined—in Chancery Lane for many years. He was married twice, but both wives and all but one of his many children died before him. He enjoyed the companionship of churchmen and had a wide circle of friends among them. And politically he was a Royalist.

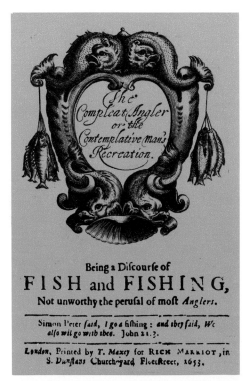

But all of this is of little consequence. It clothes the man with the substance of fact, but adds no dimension to the gentle spirit that pervades the pages of *The Compleat Angler*. In his quaint and elegant dialogues, in the breadth of his philosophy, in his modest and gentlemanly manner, old Ike reveals himself completely as an angler and as a man.

He was sixty years old when *The Angler* appeared, a sport fisherman to the bone, with a preference for bait fishing and trolling, but with generosity enough to grant that artificial flies could also be effective. He deals little with the mechanics of tackle and equipment, and we learn almost nothing of rods and lines that had not already been said elsewhere.

But in the areas of method and approach he is masterful, and it is here that he established the pattern of angling as we know it today. Walton's experience was confined to the slow chalk streams of England—only one of many types of trout water—yet his observations and deductions about fish, their feeding habits, and their life cycle are uncommonly thorough. So keen are his analyses of the angler's problems that no contribution of any value was made to this phase of fishing for another hundred years.

Finally—or perhaps primarily—he fixed for all time the position of the angler as a man who fishes for the love of fishing. Walton's own preference, as with most anglers, was the trout family, but he also angled for pike, carp, tench, bream, and other of the so-called coarse fish, in a day when these species were regarded purely as food and were generally taken in the most expedient manner possible. Ike firmly believed that outwitting any fish was a pleasure if the fisherman had the noble spirit of sport fishing rather than the mundane manner of the fishmonger.

In 1676, when Walton was eighty-three, the fifth edition of *The Compleat Angler* was issued with a new section titled, "Instructions How to Angle for a Trout or Grayling in a Clear Stream." It was written by Charles Cotton, old Ike's fishing companion of many years' standing, and concerned the use of artificial flies.

Although Walton seems to have been a bait fisher-

Izaak Walton (far left) and Charles Cotton with frontispiece from the first edition of "The Compleat Angler."

man by preference, he was no stranger to fly-fishing and had some wise and engaging things to say about it. Observe the insect life of the stream, he advised, and be prepared to match it on the spot with an artificial made from materials carried along in a kit bag.

But about the ritual of a specific fly pattern for each of the twelve months, he had a caution:

"I say," said Ike, "he that follows that rule shall be as sure to catch fish, and be as wise, as he that makes hay by the fair days in an almanac, and no surer; for those very flies that use to appear about and on the water in one month of the year, may the following year come almost a month sooner or later, as the same year proves cooler or hotter." Which are words to live by in this much later day.

There was no one whom Walton would have welcomed more warmly into the pages of his book than Charles Cotton—and none who more properly belongs there. For fishing had made close and abiding friends of this oddly matched pair. Cotton was a younger man than Ike by some thirty-seven years. He was an aristocrat, a spendthrift, a writer of bawdy verse—and an able translator of Montaigne into English. He was clever, dissipated, and a first-class fly-fisherman.

His instructions are a splendid job. His scientific detail is keenly observed and he pays a satisfactory amount of attention to method and to terminal tackle. "I shall divide Angling for Trout or Grayling," says Piscator to his pupil, Viator, "into these three ways: At the Top; at the Bottom; and in the Middle. . . . That which we call Angling at the Top, is with a fly; at the Bottom, with a ground-bait; in the Middle, with a minnow, or a ground-bait."

We would not say it this way anymore. Important advances in flies, tackle, and stream knowledge since Cotton's time have expanded the fly-fisherman's technique to embrace all three angling levels. Yet they were perfectly good ground rules when they were written.

With the philosophies and methods of these two pioneer anglers finally combined, *The Compleat Angler* became truly complete. Still, the feeling Walton and Cotton had for angling as a sport did not cross the Atlantic for a long time. The respect for fish and for angling that prevailed among generations of European sportsmen brought up on the *Angler* did not penetrate America's consciousness until it was almost too late.

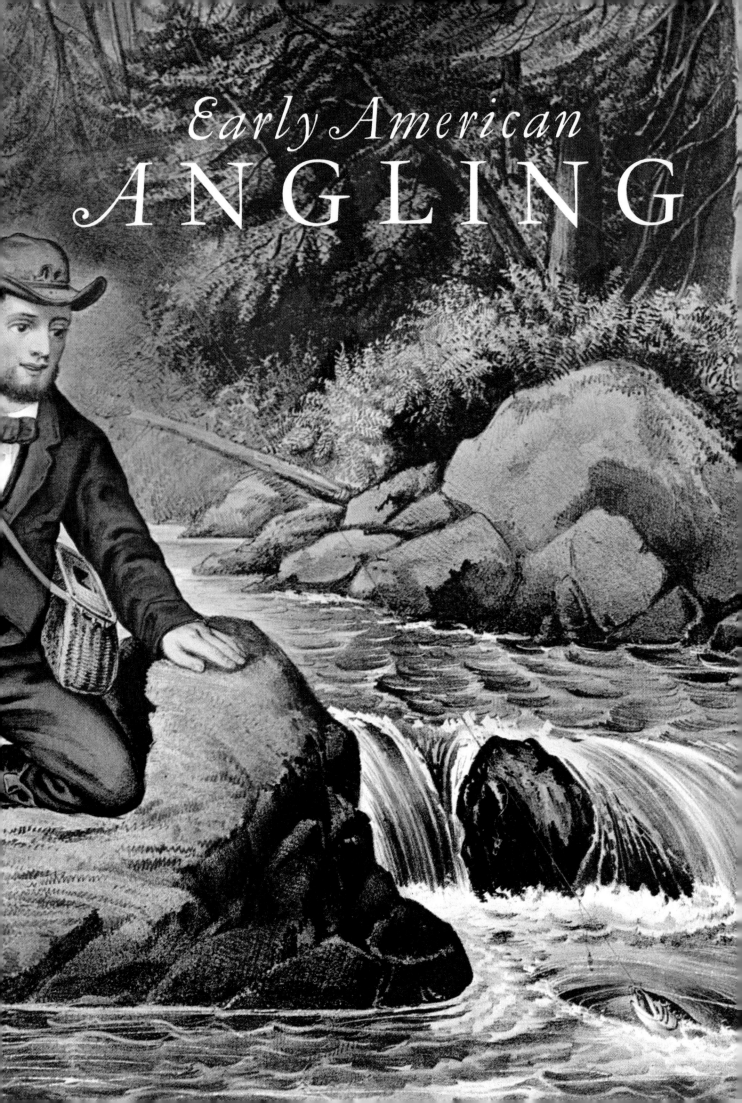

Early American
ANGLING

There was much ado in the village of South Hadley, Massachusetts, one pleasant spring day in 1783. Since dawn a procession of deep box wagons had been clattering along the main street. Clouds of dust fogged the street between the low, square houses as the hoofs of the horses spurted dry earth at every step. The teams moved in two lines, empty wagons toward the river, loaded wagons homeward toward the outlying hills, creaking under the weight of their silvery haul.

The dust rose higher with the sun, but through the haze could be seen the bright bonnets and aprons of housewives, and the glint of the knives with which they dexterously slit and gutted great piles of fresh fish.

The empty wagons moving toward the river stopped below the roaring falls. Men, wading up to their necks in the big pool, dragged coarse-meshed nets through the water and out to the banks, dumping hundreds of flopping, bright, big fish onto flattened weeds now slick with slime. Their helpers clubbed the fish to death, barely keeping up with the hauls of the seines. Other men, covered with blood and scales, tossed the fish into the wagons.

The salmon run was on in the Connecticut River.

Anson Smith left his small, gray house on the riverbank at dawn. He moved up to the foot of the big pool below the falls just as the first of the wagons rumbled down the deep-rutted road from the village. He watched the big fish leaping into the rush of water pouring over the rocks at the foot of the falls. Many attempted to ascend the cascade, but only now and then did Anse see one make it. The others fell back into the pool, where they gathered their strength for another try. This would be a good day for fishing, Anse thought, and he turned back to get his one-man scoop net.

To Anse, these hordes of migrating salmon moving up the river each spring and blocked temporarily at the falls by the hand of Providence offered a welcome change in diet and a food supply for coming months—nothing more. He caught enough in a few days to fill half a dozen barrels, shoveling salt between the layers of fish until the natural brine rose enough to cover them. They would keep until the last one was eaten, well into the hunting season.

He welcomed the chance to stop his regular work at the mill to lay away the season's catch, even though

it was an arduous chore. He could have bought the fish, as the local housewives did, for about a penny a pound and been money ahead. But for Anse the week spent on the river was a holiday. He scooped out the big salmon in twos and threes, pulled the thrashing forms from his net, and clubbed them. Then, with half a dozen—all he could carry—strung on a slim sapling, he labored up the path to his little house where he cleaned the fish and packed the rich red flesh in brine in the storage barrels.

Not like that wastrel, Eben Potter, his neighbor down river. Eben was too lazy to put in a hard week on the river for a catch of salmon. In fact, Anse reflected, Eben didn't even own a net. Instead, he spent the evening hours of spring and summer poking along the rocky riverbank, looking for a pitiful few salmon

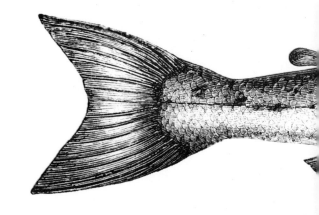

lying in a shallow run where he could reach them with his twenty-foot ash pole and a rod length of horsehair line. He'd hook out one fish, or maybe two, in a couple of hours on the river—and a devilish time he had of it once he got fast to one. Might take him a quarter of an hour to land it and, often as not, the fish got clean away.

Anse figured that Eben had some special kind of hook that found its way into the wide mouths of the fish in some mysterious fashion, for he had occasionally seen Eben hauling on a fish and it was always caught in the head. Eben was pretty secretive about that special hook he used and would always grab it in his closed fist after taking it out of the fish—the few times Anse had been close enough to see the fish landed. Every now and then, though, Anse had watched Eben tossing the hook over the water and, in the final rays of the setting sun, he thought it had a fuzzy look, as though Eben were fishing with a small bunch of dead grass. Anse dismissed the whole thing from his mind, for he always had more fish in his barrels at the end of a week during the spring run than Eben gathered all summer and fall.

Thus, two American fishermen. Anse had never heard of Izaak Walton; Eben cherished one of the few copies of *The Compleat Angler* to make its way across the ocean to America in the eighteenth century. Even if Anse had seen a copy, it would have made little difference; like many South Hadley residents he could

Thus, like Anse, you caught fish when you wanted fish to eat, and spent as little time as possible at the job.

This had its logic. Certainly during the seventeenth and early eighteenth centuries, the sheer physical labor of building a life in a new and undeveloped country left little time for diversions. Even for men of English stock and heritage cozening a few fish in the course of a hot afternoon must have seemed an extravagant and time-wasting exercise.

Still, the sporting spirit would not be downed and occasional references may be found in which the writer's enthusiasm overcomes his discretion. Doughty Captain John Smith was such a one. Visiting New England in 1614, he became fascinated with fishing in both salt and fresh water and wrote in his journal: "What pleasure can be more than to recreate them-

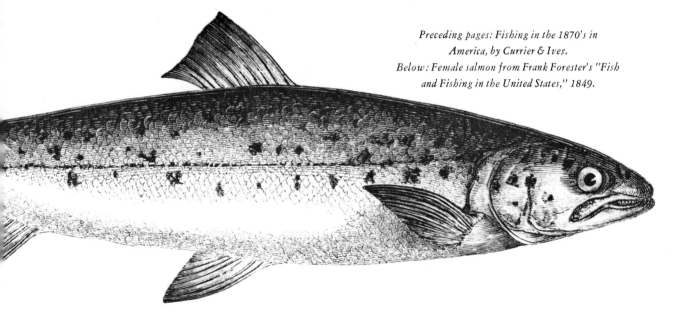

Preceding pages: Fishing in the 1870's in America, by Currier & Ives.
Below: Female salmon from Frank Forester's "Fish and Fishing in the United States," 1849.

not read. But more important, he would have been unsympathetic in any case to Ike's reflections on the subjective pleasures of angling. Fish were food and that was that.

(They were so abundant and so frequently served that farm laborers along salmon rivers such as the Connecticut sometimes stipulated, before hiring on, that they would not accept more than one fish dinner a week. Along the Delaware River, one of the first efforts at unionism was made by factory workers surfeited with an unchanging diet of fish. They refused to carry on unless management limited fish to two servings a week.)

selves before their owne doores, in their owne boates, upon the Sea, where man, woman, and childe, with a small hooke and line by angling, may take diverse sorts of excellent fish, at their pleasure?" And then, to justify the effort in more understandable terms for the colonials: "And is it not pretty sport to pull up twopence, sixpence, or twelvepence, as fast as you can hale and veare a line?" It is not certain, however, that the captain was observing sport fishing.

Cotton Mather, never a figure of fun, discovered some home truths about fishing and promptly registered his disapproval in 1721. "Alas!" he wrote, "the Ministers of the Gospel now *fish,* not with *Nets,* but

GUDGEON.

PERCH.

BARBEL.

TROUT.

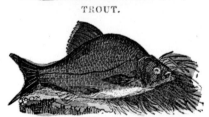

ROACH.

BREAM.

PIKE.

GREYLING.

CHUB.

with *Rods;* and after long *angling,* and *baiting,* and *waiting,* how few are taken!"

Actually, the implacable Mather voiced a prevailing clerical attitude toward sport fishing. Both in England and America there had been, and would continue to be, bleak debate on the morality of inflicting pain on one of the Lord's creatures when there was no useful purpose—such as eating it—in view.

The first American publication to strike a small blow in behalf of the sport fisherman appeared in 1743. Its title was *Business and Diversion Inoffensive to God and Necessary for the Comfort and Support of Human Society: A Discourse utter'd in Part at Ammauskeeg-Falls, in the Fishing-Season, 1739.* It took as its text John xxi: 3—"Simon Peter saith unto them, I go a-fishing." This rather begged the question of sport, but there was no doubt a deep-dyed fisherman was pleading the case, for the quiet pools in New Hampshire's Merrimack River, near Amoskeag Falls (as they are now known), always have provided pretty fair fishing. The book was published anonymously, but in time it came to light that the author was one Joseph Seccombe, another rebellious minister.

By then the opposition was crumbling, however. Wherever the wilderness had been pushed back far enough for settlers to relax a little, fishing for fun became a pastime. The Schuylkill Fishing Company was founded in 1732, the first of a number of recreational groups which sprang up in Pennsylvania. And elsewhere the institution of the fish fry came into vogue. This was not serious angling. Mostly the folks went for perch, striped bass, catfish, and shad, which they cooked on the riverbanks in the early evening. The ladies were permitted to fish, too, and there were distractions such as singing and bird watching and bathing in the stream. It might curl a true angler's lip, but it was sporty, after a fashion.

True sport fishing also gained acceptance through its popularity with significant people. Daniel Webster went after the big trout of the Cape Cod area. Henry Ward Beecher, another incorrigible clergyman, was an enthusiast. And a biographer lent charm to his picture of the youthful Patrick Henry by describing him as a

frivolous type who usually could be found "over the brook with his angle-rod."

Even so, the formal development of angling knowledge and technique did not advance very far until the 1830's and did not attract many devotees among American sportsmen until the 1840's and '50's. Anson Smiths far outnumbered Eben Potters.

In tracing the evolution of sport fishing in America in the first half of the nineteenth century, it is important to keep several factors in mind. Not only did the degree of dedication vary among fishermen, but the fishing conditions differed from region to region and from time to time. A settled area, emerging from the harshness of frontier life and hankering for a few luxuries to lighten the days, might be receptive to angling ideas and equipment from abroad. By the same token, however, the factories of a thriving town might be killing the fish of a once virgin stream with dyes or other manufacturing wastes discharged into the water.

On the other hand, in a wilderness area of the same period there might be an abundance of fish, but no time or inclination to catch them sportingly.

Most importantly, it cannot be forgotten that fishing methods depended in large part on the fish to be caught. The salmon of the East Coast aside, the game fish most Americans hooked in the early days were the native brook trout, whose habits, attitudes, and responses were vastly different from those of the English brown trout. After the brown was imported to the United States in the 1870's, there was a greater coincidence between the fishing problems of Americans and Englishmen—although by that time there were also developing marked differences in both equipment and technique.

Left to their own devices, Americans found original, indigenous solutions to the question of how to catch fish sportingly. They did not reject the philosophy of Walton and Cotton, but *The Compleat Angler* was not necessarily their starting point. For many of them awareness and appreciation came late, but certainly by the end of the nineteenth century, the serious American angler—whether fly-fisherman or bait caster—was willing to accept the honorable tradition and high standards Ike and his friend prescribed for the complete angler.

In the wilderness waters of the early 1800's, few

"The Trout Stream" (above left) by Currier & Ives.
Frontispiece (left) from "The Modern Angler," c. 1830.

Americans felt the need for a fishing technique. The fish—principally the brook trout—would rise to almost any object resembling an insect that came to their attention. This being so, fly-fishermen relied on "attractor" patterns, the more brilliantly colored the better. A three-fly cast of Red Ibis, Parmachenee Belle, and Silver Doctor, the gaudiest, most unnatural trout flies in the book, stood a fine chance of producing a creel full of fish. The trout evidently could see them better, and the fisherman certainly could see them on the stream.

Interestingly enough, it was the bass fisherman who discovered that lavish color was a successful lure. Trout fishermen quickly adopted the notion and achieved equally satisfactory results.

Fishing with nonnatural lures was in its infancy, however, and all flies were fished wet. Practitioners of the art were considered "scientific anglers" by bait fishermen, but the term meant less then than it does now. For although the fly-fisherman of the 1830's might be said to have advanced beyond his bait-fishing neighbor as a student of the stream and its residents, the important developments and refinements in tackle and method were yet to come.

A discernible change in angling attitudes and techniques began with the appearance of Alfred Ronalds' treatise on British stream insects, *The Fly-Fisher's Entomology,* in 1836. This pioneer work was the first of the major nineteenth-century contributions to angling literature. It challenged fishermen to learn the natural science of their craft and triggered off theorizing, discussion, and experimentation that continue to this day.

A decade later, in 1846, another Englishman, George Philip Rigney Pulman, wrote *The Vade Mecum of fly-fishing for trout,* which suggested, among other good notions, that since trout eagerly picked freshly hatched insects from the surface, the fisherman might do well to offer them a *floating fly.* A floating fly, of course, would be a dry fly; Mr. Pulman was modestly proposing to revolutionize the art of angling. His idea was ahead of its time, however, and given little heed. Better luck was enjoyed by William C. Stewart, whose volume, *The Practical Angler,* first appeared in 1857 and convinced American fly-fishermen that the upstream method of fishing was superior to all others. And Thaddeus Norris, the greatest American fisher-

man of the century, won enormous respect for his monumental *American Angler's Book* in 1864.

Fishing methods were bound to advance in any case. Sophistication of technique lends flavor to any endeavor and slowly but surely the growing body of nineteenth-century sportsmen became an interested audience for the growing library of angling literature. Yet in America the refinements came none too soon, for fishing conditions were changing drastically under the impact of the industrial invasion of virgin land.

In a most colorful book, published in the Civil War period, Mary Orvis Marbury, one of the first American flytiers of note, said: "As streams have become depleted and fish more shy, they need to be fished with greater caution and skill, and there is therefore a greater demand for smaller flies delicately tied in colors less gaudy than those now needed for the flies used in the wild, unfrequented rivers and lakes."

It must be said that Mrs. Marbury was referring to the speckled brook trout, a fish that still exhibits a greater fondness for bright colors in flies than the other stream species in eastern waters. Yet even the "native" trout was becoming more sophisticated as his numbers diminished and interest in angling developed. With the importation of the brown trout in the 1870's, "attractor" patterns as a mainstay of the trout fly-fisherman came to an end.

The successful fisherman now had to be an accomplished fisherman. Many of nature's creatures were finding their accustomed habitats intolerable. Salmon already had disappeared from southern New England waters by the 1850's, and brook trout were rapidly being depleted.

Another blow to the game-fish species was struck inadvertently. As various food fish became less readily available, live carp were imported from Europe, presumably to be maintained in private ponds or pools for personal or commercial use. One such importer was a Captain Robinson, who got his carp from Holland in the 1840's and placed them in his ponds near the banks of the Hudson River, in Orange County, New York. His carp flourished until one season when the river rose, carried away his dams and floodgates, and released the fish. Unfortunately, the carp was held in excessively high regard at the time and the state legislature passed a bill to prohibit taking carp from the Hudson

River for five years. The intent was to protect the fish until they were established as a new source of food.

Henry W. Herbert, the great sporting writer known as Frank Forester, took the legislators to task for this foolishness in 1849. "I cannot here . . . control myself," he wrote, "but must invoke the contempt and indignation of every gentle sportsman, every reasonable thinking man, upon the heads of that ignorant, motley, and *destructive* assemblage, which is entitled

Woodcut from T. F. Salter's "The Angler's Guide," London, 1830.

the Senate and Assembly of New York . . . that it was found impossible to induce those learned Thebans to do anything to prevent American Woodcock from being shot before they are fledged, and American Brook Trout from being caught upon their spawning beds; but that no sooner is a coarse, watery, foreign fish accidentally thrown into American waters, than it is vigorously and effectively protected. . . ."

Forester wrote better than he knew. Current efforts to eliminate carp from American waters as destructive to the growth and welfare of game fish have cost hundreds of thousands of dollars, with no real hope of success yet in sight.

By far the greatest impact on the fly-fisherman, however, was made by the Englishman, Frederick Halford. In 1886, *The Dry-fly Man's Handbook* appeared to convert the fly caster finally from the sunken fly to the floater. Halford combined the best of Pulman and Stewart with some strong notions of his own, and he had a profound effect on fishermen around the world. The angler now had a wider approach in presenting his fly—either upstream or downstream—with the advantages of upstream fishing on his side. The dry fly, wrote J. W. Hills, a noted entomologist, "altered both the practice and the temperament of the angler. It called different qualities into request. It has a charm and allurement which the older sport did not possess. In what does its charm lie? Partly in the fact that all the moves in the game are visible."

Angling now had come a long way from the days of

Eben Potter. Fly-fishing, in particular, was just a step away from final establishment of the methods practiced today. This step would be taken by Theodore Gordon in the twentieth century—and will be discussed in Chapter Four.

Meanwhile, another group of anglers, fishing mostly in ponds and lakes, was developing its tackle and techniques with game fish other than the trout and salmon. These were the bait casters, and one of their prime objectives was the pike.

Walton also made quite a business of catching pike, although he accepted the classical view of spontaneous generation of the species: "'Tis not to be doubted but that they are bred, some by generation, and some not; as namely, of a weed called Pickerel-weed . . . this weed and other glutinous matter, with the help of the sun's heat in some particular months, and some ponds adapted for it by nature, do become Pikes." Ike's mystification has been cleared up in the ensuing centuries.

One of Walton's preferred methods of fishing for

Frontispiece from Gervase Markham's "The Young Sportsman's Delight," [1712].

the "Tyrant of the Fresh Waters" comes down to us in the practice of jug fishing on Midwestern rivers. He used natural baits, of course, either a live fish or frog, and recommended that they be "thus fastened to bladders ... or bottles of hay or flags, to swim down a river, whilst you walk quietly along on the shore, and are still in expectation of sport."

Walton apparently feared the pike and tells many tales of their ferocity, true to some degree today. He also disdained to fish for them with a rod, preferring a strong hand line—as did Dame Juliana. The Treatyse instructs the angler to "put a plumbe of lede upon your line a yarde longe from your hoke, and a flote in mid way between; and cast it in a pytte where the pyke usyth; and this is the beste and moost surest crafte of takynge the pyke."

Early American pike fishermen were equally unconcerned with the caliber of rod used in taking the big, fierce fish. Brown's *American Angler's Guide* (1849) recommends "a stiff rod of ash or bamboo, about 12 feet long, accompanied with a reel containing from 50 to 100 yards of strong flax or grass line, with a small fish, or the leg or hinder part of a frog for bait." Yet Brown also quotes Delabere Blaine, an English authority of the period, "that if your hook and line be good, you may make shift with an indifferent rod... he [Blaine] has often put a ring on his walking stick and with his line thus mounted, has killed his pike."

In any case, rods used for pike fishing in the middle 1800's were, by present standards, enormous. Blaine

again, this time quoting T. F. Salter, a contemporary: "The length of the rod for live-bait fishing and trolling, may vary from 15 to 17 feet, according to circumstances; if its wood and workmanship can be depended upon, 16 feet is in no case too much; and where extensive streams are fished over, one of 16 or 18 feet is convenient." The obvious conclusion is that the art of casting a bait was sadly lacking during these times. The length of the rod alone became the mechanical means for dropping a live minnow or frog over the fish.

"In a very wide water," Blaine continues, "considerable length of rod is necessary for the purpose of reaching the probable haunts of the fish, and making a cast over the reeds or hedges which frequently skirt the banks and edges of some waters." Blaine would have been confounded by the ease with which a modern bait caster can reach his fish with a modern five-foot rod and multiplying reel. Yet the early pike fisherman worked wonders. Although his tackle was of outlandish proportions and his method—"skittering" (drawing the lure across or through the water at or near the surface)—is one now reserved almost exclusively for pickerel, he caught many big fish.

Bass were unknown to the English angler. This genus is strictly American and has remained so. And from the earliest days of American angling, bass have taken second place only to the trout and salmon family as a fighting adversary. The fisherman of the early nineteenth century was often confused between the two species of bass: the smallmouth or true black bass, and the largemouth or, as it is often called, the Oswego bass. Brown's *American Angler's Guide* of 1849 was not convinced that two species existed and quotes, with some timidity, a description of the smallmouth as against the largemouth furnished by a Buffalo, New York, fisherman, who would certainly know of the two species and be well aware of the physical differences. The significant thing is that anglers were already holding both bass species in high regard as game fish before the Civil War.

Again the dearth of proper tackle made the fishing suffer. Bass fishing was done with live bait of many kinds, mostly minnows, frogs, or "lobsters," which are now better known as the fresh-water crayfish. Long rods were used both for still-fishing and for trolling, which was considered far more sporting. There was also some use of artificial flies, usually bright patterns that were trolled at the end of a long line.

The important advances in bass and pike fishing, however, did not occur until the development of the multiplying casting reel—the "aristocratic winch" that enabled anglers to make long casts with a short rod.

Technique, of course, always requires the equipment to execute it properly. This discussion has concerned the evolution of method, although, as we shall see in the next chapter, there was a parallel development of the tools of angling throughout the nineteenth century. In fact, the American genius for invention devised so much equipment that from 1850 on the angler's problem was one of glut rather than famine.

Today the flood of American tackle, plus the avail- ability of fine English products, lulls many fisher- men into neglecting the natural history of fish and stream which could augment their angling skills. Instead of following Ike Walton's still-valid precepts on knowing the stream, many Americans prefer to rely on the efficiency of their equipment, to wring from technology the solutions to angling problems better found through patiently accumulated knowledge. The world around us is filled with interesting things, no less intriguing than they were centuries ago. The fish of our fresh-water streams, rivers, and lakes are far better known to the sincere angler than ever before. The twentieth-century scientist has disclosed a world of life underwater that was hardly more than guessed at by early fishermen.

Woodcut from T. F. Salter's "The Angler's Guide," London, 1830.

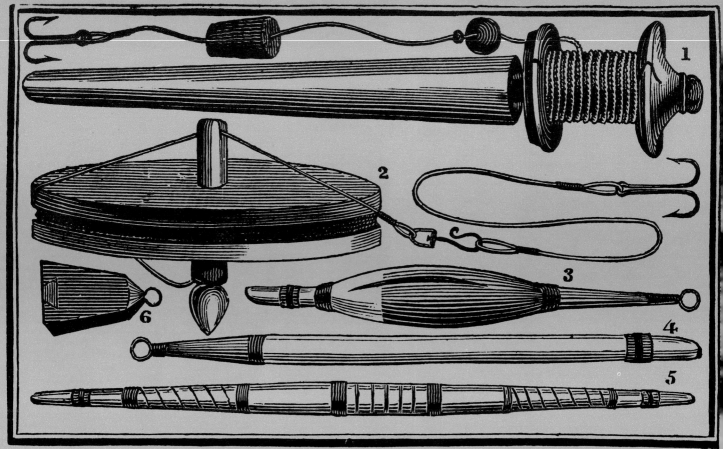

1. Bank runner.
2. Cork or man-of-war trimmer.
3. Cork float.
4. Plug float.
5. Tip-capped float.
6. Plummet to take the depth.

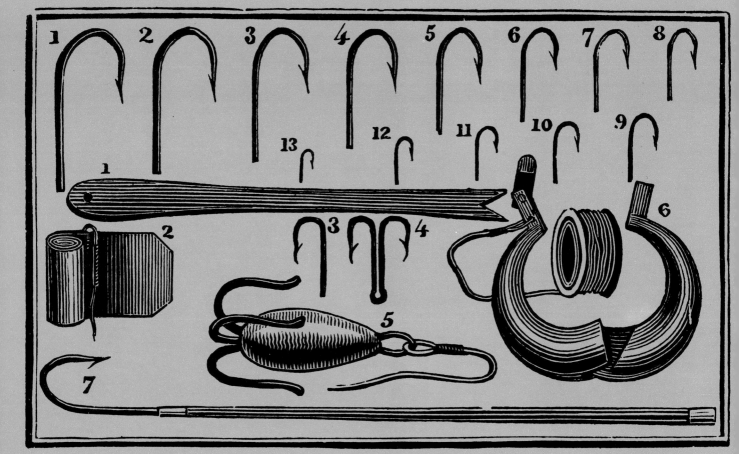

Kirby Hooks.—Sizes from No. 1 to 13.
1. Disgorger.
2. Folding Plummet, to take the depth.
3. 4. Eel Hooks.
5. Drag Hooks.
6. Brass Clearing Ring, Line and Thumb Winder.
7. Landing Hook and Rod.

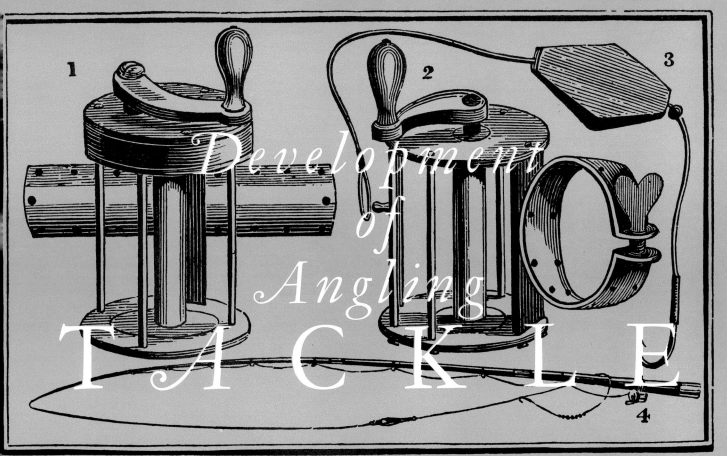

Development of Angling

TACKLE

1. Multiplying Winch.
2. Common Winch.
3. Leger Line and Hook.

4. Rod, Winch, Running Line, Float and Hook, for Barbel, Perch, Carp, &c.

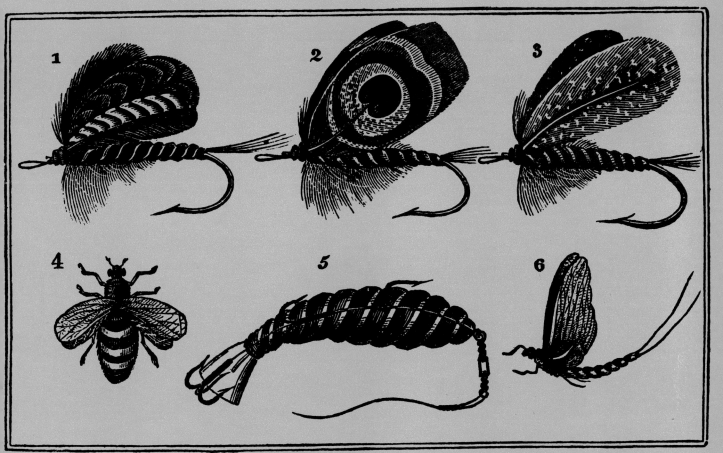

Three artificial Salmon Flies.

1. Jay Fly for Salmon.
2. Peacock Fly for Salmon.
3. Silver Pheasant for Salmon.

4. Bee, a natural Bait for a Chub.
5. Devil, an artificial Bait for Trout.
6. A natural May Fly, or Green Drake, a killing Bait in Dapping for Trout.

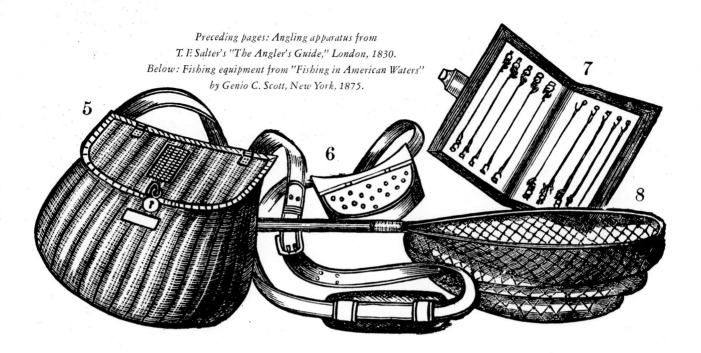

As the French and Indian Wars came to an end, Sir William Johnson cast a trout hook into the unsullied waters of Kenyetto Creek in the southern foothills of the Adirondacks. His mission as His Majesty's superintendent of Indian affairs had been completed. Now he sought relaxation with the wild brook trout of his newly adopted land.

Sir William was one of a rare breed—the gentleman angler in eighteenth-century America. His tackle and tradition derived from Walton and Cotton, and he knew how to catch fish. He had been raised as a member of the Irish sporting gentry; in his background was a great manorial house surrounded by kennels for grouse dogs and stables for hunters. A vast hunting preserve bordered the estate and through it ran trout and salmon streams carefully patrolled by wardens with a hard eye out for poachers. Here the elite anglers of Sir William's boyhood had caught their fish, judiciously selecting a fly from a bristling book, tying it carefully to the tapered horsehair line, and flicking it over the water. A one-handed rod served for trout, a two-handed rod for salmon. Each gentleman also had his gillie standing by, patient and wise, to bait a hook, land a fish, or cook a lunch.

Now, on the banks of the Kenyetto, Sir William lacked only his gillie. Otherwise, he was the British tradition transplanted.

He found the handsome brook trout of America even more eager than their cousins in his native Ireland. In fact, the fishing was so good that in 1769 he acquired property at Sacandaga, New York, and built an elaborate lodge he named "Mount Joy." Later called "Summer House Point," the lodge is said to have been burned during the Loyalist raids of 1781. The site now lies under the waters of Sacandaga Reservoir. Sir William also built a lodge at Northampton, New York, near the headwaters of Kenyetto Creek. In time it was acquired by Major Nicholas Fish and, not illogically, came to be called "Fish House"—although many anglers have preferred to think the name derived from the lodge's proximity to trout. In any event, these were among the first of the fishing lodges so dear to the British sportsman's heart to be established in America.

The Revolutionary War, however, dealt angling a severe blow. Many wealthy Loyalists were on the run by the time the fighting ended, leaving behind them thousands of acres and miles of favorite fishing streams. These private preserves entered the public domain and anyone who cared to could fish them. But angling in the grand manner came to a halt with the wholesale disappearance of the English-reared gentry.

Sport fishing also suffered from the postwar financial depression and, within a generation, from the War of 1812. Few men had money for tackle, and those who did had to buy imports from the hated British, for no tackle of any quality was yet manufactured in the United States. The fact that many Americans were nonreaders kept them from becoming familiar with the classic literature of angling, which, of course, was also British. It is likely that many a back-country fisherman using spear, net, or baited hand line to catch fish for his larder had never heard of an artificial fly or of proper angling tackle. Sport fishing—indeed, all angling—awaited a healthy economy and a new culture.

According to Austin S. Hogan, historian on the State of New York, the earliest written reference to fly-fishing in America dates from 1775. Fly-fishing was known before this time, but the documentary record begins there. It is also certain that sport fishing was dormant from the time of this early reference until the 1830's, when Long Island and the Adirondacks began to arouse the interest of anglers seeking trout.

By 1840, Delmonico's Restaurant in New York was famous for its fat brook trout and lakers taken in Adirondack waters. William T. Porter, editor of *The Spirit of the Times,* a sporting weekly of New York, made trips to Hamilton County in the Adirondacks and published descriptions of the most effective flies. They all were gay in color, large in size, and generally rowdy in character.

But fly casting as we know it now—indeed, all an-

Frontispiece from "The Art of Angling," Brookes, London, 1770.

gling with artificials—awaited the creation of new ideas in tackle, particularly in rods. It is not easy to imagine today how "Adirondack" William Murray, the author of *Adventures in the Wilderness,* could write of an epic struggle with a brook trout in the years just before the Civil War. The fight went on through half a dozen pages of his book until eventually he landed a trout *seventeen inches and three quarters* (his italics) with a rod weighing *nine ounces* (my italics). In fairness, it must be said that this was a light rod for those times. Most of Murray's contemporaries lifted a fly rod anywhere from twelve to twenty feet long. It was made in three sections—butt of ash, middle of hickory, tip of lancewood—and it weighed pounds rather than ounces. A cumbersome staff like this would certainly put Murray's rod in the lightweight class, although today we would consider it suitable only for the bigger salmon, tarpon, and other large salt-water species.

When anglers discussed the fine points of their sport at this time, they compared the merits of various woods for rods. Even into the 1860's, authorities wrangled over greenheart, bethabara, lancewood, and other favorites. Robert Barnwell Roosevelt, T. R.'s uncle and a noted writer on fish and fishing who later became New York State Fish Commissioner, held out for the superiority of cedar. "Cedar rods can only be obtained in America," he said, "and then only on compulsion, but this wood makes the most elastic rods in the world. They spring instantly to every motion of the hand and never warp. They are delicate. The wood is, like woman, cross-grained but invaluable if carefully treated."

Delicacy in fly-fishing did not come until Samuel Phillippe, a gun- and violinmaker of Easton, Pennsylvania, conceived the idea of laminating the tough outer shell of bamboo cane into strips. Bamboo in its natural state, had been used in rod making for many years,

Early aristocratic winch.

but the ideal in rod design did not begin to evolve until about 1846, when Phillippe split, planed, and glued together strips of bamboo to make rod sections. He experimented with tip sections first, then with middle joints, using two and then three strips of cane. He found, however, that neither of these designs cast true. His first success came with a rod made of four strips of cane—always with the hard enamel outside—and, finally, he made the present conventional form with six strips. Sometimes, after gluing together the four sections of cane, he would plane or lathe turn the square corners to make the rod perfectly round in

All prints by Bunny & Gold, London, 1801, and reprinted in "The Complete Angler," London, 1830.

Brass clearing ring for freeing fouled hook.

cross section. One of these classic rods is in a showcase at The Anglers' Club in New York City.

The laminated bamboo rod was a creation of tremendous importance, and one destined to make all other materials obsolete.

At first, of course, production was slow and costly, and distribution was limited. Some time elapsed before all anglers wanted them—or could have them. But from the moment of their appearance, their future was assured. No other natural material could match the elasticity, strength, and casting power provided by the hard outer surface of the cane.

Phillippe sold a few rods of laminated bamboo to the New York tackle firm of Andrew Clerk & Co. before 1850. Charles Orvis of Manchester, Vermont, made his first glued-up bamboo rods before 1855, with results that led him to build a factory in 1856 which still exists and puts out some of the finest bamboo rods made today. He was followed by Hiram Leonard of Bangor, Maine, whose first six-strip (hexagonal) rods appeared before 1860 and whose fine craftsmanship probably earned greater acceptance for the split-bamboo rod than the work of any other maker.

Charles Murphy went into the split-bamboo rod business in Newark, New Jersey, in 1860, with a four-strip rod. He followed this with a special salmon rod in 1865; the next year he marketed the first rod specifically designed for black-bass fishing. E. A. Green was also turning out three-strip bamboos in Newark in 1860. At Clerk's in New York, a buyer could choose from among Phillippe, Murphy, and Leonard rods.

These early bamboos were made of Calcutta cane imported from India, which differs somewhat in character from the bamboo used in rod making today. Calcutta cane is the kind now commonly associated with the barefoot boy—long, slender, with relatively short spaces between the joints or leaf nodes. While far superior to the natural woods mentioned earlier, it turned out to be inferior in several respects to a cane imported from the Tonkin district of Indochina. This was the discovery of William Mitchell, who had been experimenting with canes imported from several sources. The Tonkin cane was considerably harder than the Indian variety, and a rod made from it had far greater casting power and a very responsive action. In

Artificial minnow for still-fishing.

time, Tonkin cane came to be used exclusively for the finest dry-fly rods.

As materials and the process of lamination improved, the fly rod became shorter and lighter, while still retaining enough casting power to put out a line for practical fishing. The early Phillippe rods, although made of split bamboo, closely followed the pattern of solid wood rods. Dr. James A. Henshall, a famed angler especially noted for his success with black bass, had a trout rod made by Phillippe that was eleven feet, four inches in length, and weighed eight ounces. This is not much different from "Adirondack" Murray's eleven-foot rod of lancewood, which weighed nine ounces. But it did not take long for the sporty trout angler to discover that he didn't need this much weight and power to cast a good line or handle a heavy fish. The bamboo was just that much better.

Toward the end of the century, fly rods shrank to something under ten feet in length and a maximum

of seven ounces in weight. This slight decrease in weight does not seem of much importance, but in Dr. Henshall's words: "Like the fraction of an inch applied to a man's nose, it makes a very great difference in practice and reality." In current usage, a nine-foot, six-ounce rod is adequate for bass and salmon fishing and is considered a fairly heavy, powerful stick. The five-ounce rod — six inches shorter — then becomes a medium-action trout rod.

After the turn of the century, acceptance of the dry fly as a firmly established angling technique increased the demand for still lighter rods, with the power and speed to make fifty- or sixty-foot casts. A premium came to be put on lightness, since a dry-fly caster makes countless false casts to whip the water from his fly before again presenting it on the surface. With a heavy rod, this could be a tiring procedure. A standard finally was established with the eight-foot rod weighing four ounces, which had a stiff butt and middle section, and a fast tip. This standard still obtains.

The roster of rod builders of the past century contains many of the great names of angling. Orvis, Leonard, Thomas, Payne, Edwards—all fine anglers—spring immediately to mind. Their rods were a byword for the critical fly-fisherman until the sad day when the Korean War cut off supplies of the proper bamboo. Now most of them are gone, although new generations carrying on the great names of Leonard and Payne are still turning out a few rods from a limited supply of material within a few miles of this writer's home.

Metal jig for pike trolling.

The tradition of fine rod making, which never did serve a mass market, persists today, but for the majority of anglers in the United States, bamboo now has been replaced by fiberglass—tough, resilient, almost fractureproof, and possessing nearly all the casting qualities of fine cane. The critical angler still holds with tradition, but I feel his devotion to bamboo is often more esthetic than practical. I own at least a dozen of the fine "name" rods, but I am holding them as heirlooms. I fish almost exclusively with hollow fiberglass rods in all lengths and weights, from a fairy wand five and a half feet long to a ten-foot, detachable-butt model for salmon and steelhead.

A fly rod must perform within certain limits, depending on its function as part of a specific angling technique. Ideally, a fly caster should own a rod for each class of fly-fishing. He should have one for small streams, where the casts are short and restricted by overhanging brush and trees. There should be a rod exclusively for dry-fly fishing, a fairly stiff one for use on medium-sized waters where fish are not likely to be large. A four-ounce, eight-footer fills these requirements nicely. For wet-fly fishing, it is desirable to have a rod with a softer action to permit more sensitive manipulation of the sunken fly or nymph. This might be an eight-foot-six rod, weighing about four ounces. For casting the larger bucktail and streamer flies, bass bugs, and hair-wing steelhead flies, a more powerful rod is needed. A nine-footer, weighing five and one half ounces, is about right, and such a rod will do a better job of handling the larger fish that will probably be encountered. Finally, of course, there should be rods for salmon: a nine-footer in the six-ounce class for dry-fly fishing and, perhaps, a ten-footer with detachable butt, weighing about seven ounces, for the larger

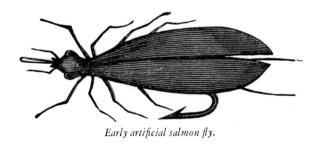
Early artificial salmon fly.

wet flies. On some of the big salmon rivers—the St. John in New Brunswick, for example—a two-handed rod up to twelve feet long is desirable for the wading fisherman who may have to cast a fly up to one hundred feet to put it over a lie of fish.

This line-up includes every desirable rod the North American fly-fisherman will need, for all game species from the small brook trout and grayling to the powerful, long-running salmon and steelhead. All these rods are still obtainable in bamboo, and with the ex-

ception of the largest size, are readily available in hollow fiberglass.

Most fishermen settle on one rod for trout, and a heavier rod for casting larger flies, depending on the occasion and the method used. An eight-foot rod will handle most trout-fishing needs, a nine-footer the heavier flies and fish. Modern fishermen tend to fit the rod to the method of fishing the fly, choosing the lightest tackle that can reasonably do the job. Some skillful extremists—Lee Wulff, for example—successfully take large Atlantic salmon on dainty rods weighing only two ounces. For most anglers, however, such refinement is unnecessary.

It is a curious fact that although present-day rods are made in many types and sizes, and for purposes almost without number, all stem from the same basic fly-rod design. The early bait-fishing rods were simply fly rods with the reel seat mounted above the hand instead of below it. The subsequent evolution of this design into the short bait-casting—or "plug"—rod of today is part of the story of the only broad, general fishing method that America can claim as a "first."

Actually, the story of bait casting as we know it began not with a rod, but with a reel. In 1803, George Snyder, a Pennsylvania watchmaker, joined the westward migration and moved from Bucks County to Paris, Kentucky. There, in the famous Bluegrass region, he found black bass, a fish then unknown in his native Pennsylvania. Snyder, a skillful trout fisherman, immediately noted that bass usually demanded a mouth-filling bait rather than the tiny tidbits that successfully lured a trout. He tried first to catch his bass with a long fly rod and standard single-action reel, using minnows and frogs for bait.

But it was not long before he was discontented with this rig. He could not cast much beyond the length of his rod, and a great deal of fertile bass water could not be reached. After struggling with the problem for a year or two, Snyder turned his watchmaking talents to the design of a new reel that would permit casting directly from the spool. The best guess is that he built his first geared, quadruple-multiplying reel about 1810. The fact that few changes have been made in his basic concept over the past hundred and fifty years is proof enough that he designed it well.

The principle of Snyder's reel, as every fisherman

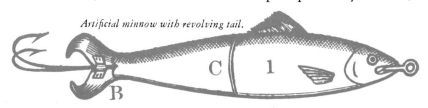
Artificial minnow with revolving tail.

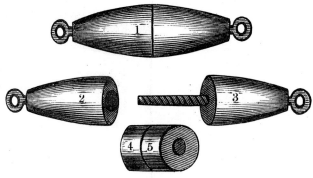

knows, is that the weight of the bait tossed by the rod will pull line from the freely rotating spool of the reel. No longer would the length of the rod limit a fisherman in lofting his bait. The distance obtainable on a cast was governed only by the weight of the bait, the diameter of the line, and the free-running characteristics of the reel. A new technique in angling had been born. Further, it had immediate appeal for Snyder's neighbors among the old Kentucky gentry, whose interest in horses and hunting was soon matched by their enthusiasm for this sporty angling.

Snyder's reel was eminently suited to bait casting in America. Yet the "Kentucky reel" remained in Kentucky for much of the next generation, and did not spread nationally until after the Civil War, when production and distribution increased.

About 1833, another watchmaker, Jonathan Meek, turned to reel making and he, in turn, was followed by J. W. Hardman, Benjamin Milam, Beverly Noel, and J. L. Sage, all of them watchmakers, all of them operating in Kentucky, all of them contributors to the evolution of the bait-casting reel.

The first bait casters used long rods—the fly-rod length—with the reel mounted on top of the rod above the hand, so that the spool could be controlled by the angler's thumb. Natural baits were lobbed in what was called an underhand cast, a slow, steady swing of the rod to toss the bait and to provide momentum enough to carry line from the reel. Dr. Henshall is generally considered the first to have tried designing a special rod for use with the multiplying reel.

In 1875, the old *Forest & Stream* published Henshall's initial recommendations for a bass bait-casting rod. Henshall argued that long rods were not necessary with the multiplying reel. He held for a rod under ten feet that could be used with one hand, a departure from the long, heavy bait rods that demanded two. "As a comparatively long, pliant rod is best for casting a fly, so is a short, stiffish rod best for casting a minnow. With a rod of this character, and a free-running, multiplying reel, it is an easy matter to cast from thirty to forty yards." The suggestions for the new design were applied at once by C. F. Orvis, who made and marketed a shorter, stiffer rod in Manchester, Vermont. The road toward the nationwide use of the shorter rod had begun.

This new approach was only a partial step forward. Henshall's first "standard" rod was all of eight feet, three inches long and weighed about eight ounces. Its butt section was ash and the other two joints were lancewood. Apparently, Henshall did not prefer split

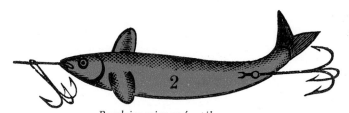

Revolving minnow for pike.
Prints from "Fishing in American Waters," 1875.

bamboo for his first rod (since he had made it himself), although later, and for many years after, he did use a similarly designed bamboo rod by Leonard, which weighed only six and a half ounces and was just over eight feet long.

Henshall's conservatism in rod length was sound. He fished almost exclusively with natural baits at this time. The softer action afforded by the rod's new length did not strip off the soft minnow in casting, as would the stiff, five-foot rods that came into use later for casting heavy spoons and wooden lures.

Actually, Henshall was critical of these short, stiff sticks and termed them "frog rods," unsuited to sport fishing. Conceding that they were accurate for casting and had some advantage for playing a heavy fish in weedy waters, he nonetheless protested: "This mode of angling does not appeal to one who has a just appreciation of the amenities of the gentle art and...is disposed to give the fish a chance."

Most bass fishermen of the late 1800's were not

London, Published by T. McLean, Jan.ʸ 1. 1820.

PIKE FISHING.

Top: Pike fishing.
Left: Salmon fishing. Both from Henry
Alken's "National Sports
of Great Britain," London, 1821.

disposed to give the fish a chance. The era of huge artificial lures of wood and metal had begun, and a short, unyielding stick was needed to toss these heavy objects over the fish.

The first commercial bait-casting lure was probably the Buel spoon, made in Whitehall, New York, more than a decade before the Civil War. This was a triangular piece of metal that spun on a shaft adorned with a treble hook covered with red and white feathers. This "skittering" lure took pike, bass, and other game fish in trolling and when cast with a long pole. In casting, however, the amount of water that could be covered was not great.

A number of spoon lures were marketed in the late 1800's: the Skinner spoon, the Lowe Star bait, the Four Brothers Spinner, to name a few that are still around. These were all underwater lures which became famous for bait casting with the development of the shorter rods. But, incredibly, it was not until the end of the century that fishermen discovered bass to be avid surface feeders, and the floating wooden plug made its first appearance.

Jim Heddon is generally credited with devising the first commercially successful top-water bass lure shortly before the turn of the century. Legend says he was sitting on a log and whittling while waiting for a fishing pal one fine summer day along the banks of Michigan's Dowagiac River. By the time his friend came along, Jim's whittle stick had been chipped to the size and shape of a cigar. Jim tossed the bit of wood into the slow-moving current and watched it float away. It whirled in an eddy for a few seconds, then suddenly disappeared as a big bass exploded under it and seized it momentarily before spitting it out.

Heddon quickly took the hint. In no time at all he was making the first of the "dowjack" plugs, a corruption of the name of his pet river. This floater came out in true American colors in 1898—white body, red collar, blue nose—and was rigged with three treble hooks. It was an instant success and most assuredly furthered the cause of the short-rod bait caster. This early surface lure, when fished slowly and provocatively, with the collar throwing lively ripples on the surface, is still a killing bait for bass.

In the great sport-fishing period that began with the horseless carriage, lures were produced in all sizes, shapes, colors, and actions. Tackle manufacturers sprang up everywhere and all of them featured bait-casting rigs. Reels improved as level-winds and anti-backlash devices made their appearance. Rods became shorter and stiffer after the appearance of the six-foot "frog rod" in the Chicago area just before Teddy charged up San Juan Hill. The big plugs and spoons tossed by these powerful, stubby sticks did well with bass until eventually the fish became sophisticated.

Today, big plugs aren't the killers of bass they used to be. After the angler's car made most of the productive waters easily accessible, bass became harder to catch. By the end of World War I, fishermen were looking for more effective lures and more refinement and sport in bass fishing.

Now the fly rod was called into action to cast hair bugs and cork-and-feather lures which simulated much of the bass' natural food. Bait casting for bass went into eclipse for a few years, until a group of Pennsylvania anglers, headed by Charles Fox, applied delicacy to the art.

Fox felt that the bait-caster's lures were overly large, little short of hideous, and nowhere close to the true appearance of natural food. He began to whittle surface, diving, and sinking plugs—midget reproductions of foods that formerly had served as successful baits. These weighed as little as one quarter ounce, approximated the food the fish normally fed upon, and could be cast with artistry—if a man had the tackle.

This was a problem. Most of the existing bait-casting gear demanded a fairly heavy lure (at least half an ounce) to flex the rod and pull line from the reel. It was clear that light-lure bait casting required a rod flexible enough to bend under the weight of a small bait, a reel that ran with exceptional freedom, and a line that would move without friction and drag as the bait flew out.

Fox took a lead from the tournament caster, whose special competition equipment could throw weights of three eighths of an ounce. For light lures a return to a longer, whippier rod of about seven feet was necessary. Reels were made with aluminum spools fitted with cork arbors to encourage quick starting on the cast; and a final refinement came with the free-spool model, a reel design in which the spool is disengaged from the turning gears and handle, thus reducing fric-

*Gentleman angler of the
late nineteenth century is assisted
by his gaffer, from
"Fishing in American Waters," 1875.*

delightful fishing technique after a century and a half of experimentation and development.

Closely related to light-lure bait casting is spinning—the method Americans borrowed from Europe only two decades ago. The term *spinning* is an old one in this country, but it formerly meant trolling with spinners or a fish-shaped lure that revolved through the water when under way. (The British salmon angler also uses this term for a method of fishing with a prawn or minnow, cast with a long, whippy rod—à la Henshall.) Currently, however, spinning in America refers specifically to casting a light lure, attached to light line, from a reel having a fixed spool. This principle, of course, is ideal for casting all lightweight lures and natural baits, since it does away with the problem of reel inertia. Also, happily, there is no backlash or bird's nest to mar the pleasure of casting.

Actually, spinning as we now know it did not gain significant acceptance until extruded monofilament line was invented after World War II. Successful spin casting with very light lures rests, of course, upon a line limp enough to be very flexible, smooth enough to offer almost no friction as it peels over the end of the spool and passes through the guides, and light enough to offer little or no resistance to the lure as it travels out.

As a matter of history, the spinning principle was conceived centuries ago. The Siwash Indians of the Northwest are known to have had the idea of winding line around a wooden frame, which was held in one hand and pointed toward the area he wanted to fish. Bait, hook, and sinker were tossed over the water with the other hand, so that line whipped off the end of the frame. The Spaniards, early in the eighteenth century, used much the same idea in their bird-cage reel, which was held in one hand while the bait was tossed with a rod held in the other. At this same time, Scotsmen were using a belt basket to hold their line. The basket was strapped, or belted, to the waist, the line coiled neatly within. As the bait was cast with a rod, it pulled the coils of line from the basket. The Swiss came up with a belt reel that combined features of the Scotsman's basket and the Spaniard's bird cage. With guides mounted on the rod, this gadget proved fairly successful.

These ingenious devices solved some of the problems of getting the bait out to the fish, but retrieving

tion and overcoming inertia. If such a reel is wound with lightweight line of nylon braid or monofilament, friction is reduced to a practical minimum and it becomes possible to cast out to respectable fishing distances lures as light as one quarter of an ounce.

Through this final step in the evolution of bait-casting equipment, what was formerly a heavy-handed maneuver has now become artistry. The little lures are, in fact, no larger than some of the bugs and flies used on the fly rod for bass and salmon. The light-lure rod has much of the whippy response of a trout rod, and the breaking strength of the fine line used—often as little as five pounds—puts the angler on equal footing with the fly caster using leader material of similar weight. Bait casting has finally come into its own as a the line was another matter. It had to be rewound, or re-coiled, each time. On the other hand, the angler using a long rod and the single-action fly reel or winch had the better of the retrieve, but could not make as long a cast. The most he could do for some additional yardage was to strip some line from his reel, hold it looped in his hand, and release it with the bait.

Toward the end of the nineteenth century, about the time we were getting around to shortening our bait-casting rods, the Scots invented the Malloch reel. It combined the bird-cage idea with our multiplying casting reel. The reel operated on a pivot. In casting, the spool was flipped around so that the open end faced the tip of the rod. Then, as the bait was tossed, the line peeled off the open end of the spool. To retrieve, the spool was turned back to the conventional position —at right angles to the rod—and the line was cranked in. The trouble was that each cast put twists in the line. These multiplied until the line had to be removed from the reel to be straightened—a miserable chore that discouraged more fishermen than it caught fish.

In 1903, Viscount Henry de France came up with the first fixed-spool reel that faced toward the rod tip. This seems to have performed as well as a modern spinning reel and, like its modern counterpart, was mounted under the rod. However, the Viscount could not devise a mechanical means for retrieving the line, so he had to wind it on by hand, using a large needle that resembled a crochet hook.

Alfred Illingworth came up with the first mechanical reel for thread-line fishing (as it is known in England) in 1905. His model permitted casting from a fixed spool, and had a roller pickup that re-spooled the line. After winning the International Casting Tournament in 1908, he further improved his reel by adding a cross wind to the retrieving device. And almost as soon as this first successful spinning reel was developed, it was promptly banned from most English waters! It was thought to put too deadly a casting weapon in the angler's hands. The argument whether the spinning reel is moral and permissible still goes on.

Deadly weapon or not, early spinning was not all milk and honey. The best lines for casting were made of gut and these had to be well soaked before a good cast could be made. Also, the line could not be allowed to dry out during any pause in the fishing or it would snap like a pretzel on the next cast. These lines also frayed and frequently broke when a heavy fish was on. Nylon monofilament solved all these problems — or most of them—right after World War II.

Never before in the history of fishing has it been as easy for the fisherman as it is today. Rigged with a properly balanced rod, reel, line, and lures, the rankest novice—if he has the strength to whip the rod—can be casting well enough to catch fish within his first hour of practice. Spin tackle has indoctrinated our millions of anglers with the zest for fishing light, for squeezing the last jump out of a fighting fish. The rather narrow province of full fishing pleasure, known formerly only to the fly-fisherman and the light-lure caster, has now been firmly and forever invaded by the man

*Hackett's spinning tackle,
from "Fishing in American Waters."*

with the long, whippy casting rod and the coffee-mill spinning reel.

Many fly-fishermen object to this—and with cause. It is not easy to stand by and watch a teen-aged beginner explore every pool and pocket in a big stream with his spinning outfit, when to cover such water as thoroughly with the fly could well demand a decade or two of rigorous experience—plus some bold and tricky wading. But this is progress.

The tools for taking fish now seem to fulfill every need, although it would be risky to say, as naturalist-angler Louis Rhead once wrote more than fifty years ago, that American tackle is so perfect that it provides everything the angler might desire.

However, there is much more to fishing than merely casting a fly or lure. If the art of angling were all that simple, there would be no art, no sport, no recreation, no challenge. The fish, as we shall see, are the fascinating variables that keep anglers on their toes, always hopeful, forever pondering ways and means to fill the days on lake and stream.

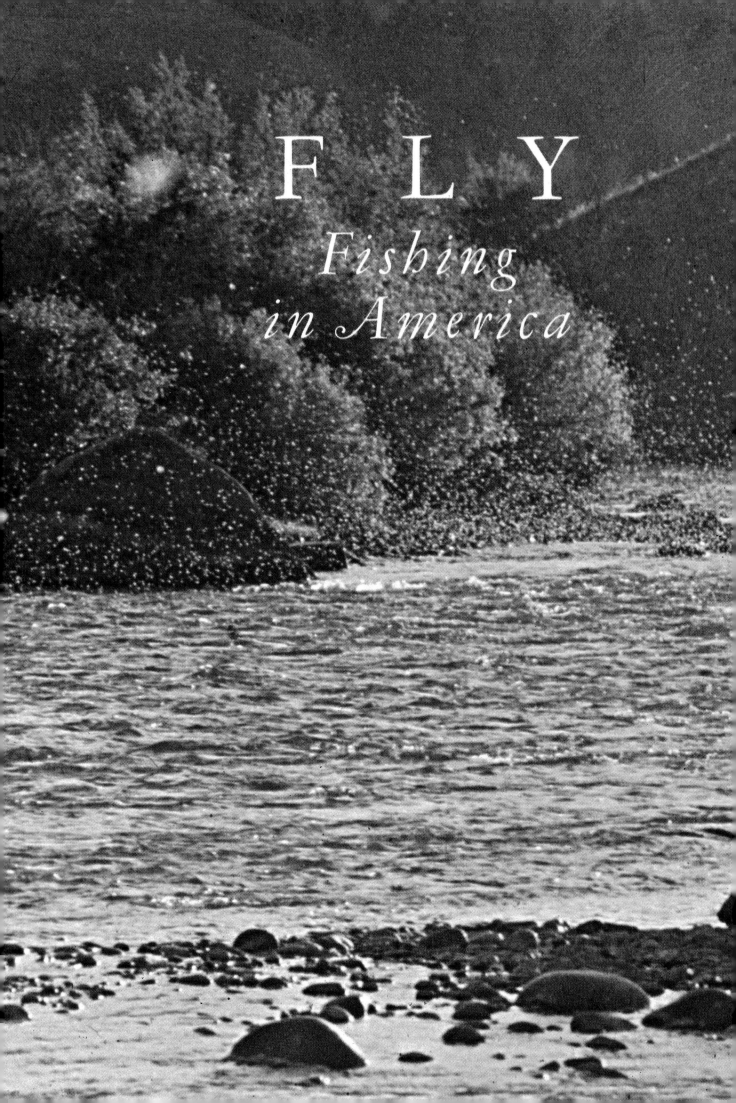

FLY
Fishing
in America

Preceding pages:
Evening hatch of May flies
on a western river.

Frontispiece from John Yonge Akerman's "Spring-tide," London, 1850.

44

B r i g h t sun beat down obliquely on the pool and filtered through the new green foliage of hardwoods along the bank. The water sparkled in the dappled sunlight, then grew dark as it passed under a low hemlock branch guarding the tail of the pool. The afternoon breeze whipped bits of spray from the tips of the white-water caps dancing down on the flow, pouring into deeper water at the head of the hole, but other than the movement of the stream no life stirred. Trout do not show themselves often in early May.

But as the sun moved westward, there were stirrings on the pool bottom. Tiny, dark, flattened shapes moved from crevices between rounded gravelstones and clambered up into the warming sunlight. For although the stream was chill, sun rays made their heat felt and the May-fly nymphs crept up to meet the warmth. One, releasing its grip on a smooth rock, kicked toward the surface. Slowly it rose, struggling and drifting toward the firm current pushing through the middle of the pool. It whirled about, only inches below the surface, then was gone as a spotted, silvery shape swept out of the run, flashed in a quick turn, then disappeared into the fast water, leaving only a faint swirl to mark his passage.

Other nymphs now were drifting free of the bottom, passing the brook trout's feeding station. He came again and again from the fast flow, with now and then a bulge of water or a tail tip showing as he made his rise. Many nymphs escaped him, passing down into the slowing water near the pool's middle. Soon one reached the surface, settled momentarily in the surface film, then wriggled free, into the air. Its three pairs of legs rested tidily on the water. It was no longer a nymph, but a May-fly dun stretching its wings to the sun as its empty, discarded husk drifted away. A sudden breeze tossed the fly aside, into an eddy. Its blue-gray wings now fluttered, drying. Within a few seconds, with the wing creases shaken out, the dun rose from the water in direct flight toward the leafy branches of an alder bush rooted in the edge of the bank. Its incredible transformation into a graceful, diaphanous, air-borne insect had required only moments.

Although this first emerging dun had made a safe escape to the trees, many of its followers were less fortunate. Once the hatch began, the trout of the pool were aroused. A fly would break out, ride the current for a few feet, then disappear in the lip of a swirl—two seconds of adult life extinguished in the feeding of a fish. And as swirls and splashes pockmarked the surface of the pool, the signal was given, mysteriously but immutably, to the birds of the woodland.

First, a redstart fluttered over the pool, darted down to the surface, and picked from the air a dun that had barely risen in first flight. The redstart had the pool to himself only for the space of time in which he could capture two more duns climbing for cover. A wood thrush suddenly appeared in the sunlight over the water, taking a May fly in a swooping dive. Both birds were busy for a time, working up and down the stream, chasing the duns until a kingbird burst in noisily to drive them off. By the time the sun touched the high ridge above the stream valley, the intensity of the hatch had subsided. The surviving duns had found shelter in the trees and the pool became quiet once more.

The first May fly to reach the alders hung from the underside of a leaf. Now completely dry, she crept forward to the edge of the leaf, stretched her forward legs up and over, and moved daintily to its top surface. Her smoky, blue-gray wings were held upright, and her tapered body, pale pink from its store of eggs within, curved upward in a graceful crescent. For a few moments she stood rigidly, then squatted down on the leaf. An almost imperceptible pulsing began at her thorax, where the wings joined the body. She was about to slip off her dun veil, the last evidence of immaturity. The thin skin parted over her back and peeled away in the breeze. Glasslike wings appeared, and as she wriggled free of the last gauzy wisps of skin a new transformation had taken place. Her dull, dun drabness was replaced by brittle shininess. She was now in the final adult stage—a spinner. She took off at once to join the males, already in their mating dance over the pool.

The males, almost invisible in their glassy spinner coats, hovered high over the pool in their ritual flight, climbing almost straight up, then folding their wings and diving down in a short glide. At the end of the glide they paused, climbed again, and dove again in rhythmic, sensual, pulsing flight. For one, the dance ended with the female hovering above him as he reached a peak in his glide.

They came together. He held her from below with

DRY TROUT FLIES

ATLANTIC SALMON FLIES

WET TROUT FLIES

his long forelegs and the tiny caliperlike hooks at the rear tip of his abdomen. The female fluttered furiously to keep both their fragile bodies aloft, but they settled gently down toward the surface of the pool, finally breaking apart just before touching the water. The male flew off in search of another mate, the female began to complete her function.

She flew over the boiling surface of the run, low to the water. Pausing then, she touched the surface lightly, dropping tiny eggs as her body curved downward. Again she rose, flew over the riffle above the pool, dipping and rising as she went. With the bright glow of sunset still strong behind the ridges, she eventually settled wearily onto the quiet waters of the pool, wings outstretched, spent of eggs and strength, destiny fulfilled. She disappeared in a tiny dimple, a final fillip in a trout's feeding for the day.

For hundreds of years the incredible life cycle of the May fly has been fascinating fishermen—and other, more dedicated entomologists. We know that Dame Juliana Berners learned something of the cyclic pattern of these insects and that Ike Walton and Charles Cotton made keen deductions on their importance in the life of fish and, thus, in the tactics of the angler. The earliest artificial fly designs were crude attempts to duplicate some form of the many stream-living insects, particularly the May fly.

When fly-fishing traveled to America, some of the ancient, traditional imitative patterns made the trip, along with English rods, simple reels, horsehair lines, and other trappings, but Americans were not then dealing with sophisticated trout. Giving the fish something big enough and bright enough to see readily was the philosophy of the first American fly caster. It worked well until the trout became wiser.

Colonial fly-fishermen dealt with the somber English patterns, such as the Black Gnat and Cowdung, at first, but soon changed to flies of larger size and more brilliant hues—red predominating. The success of big, bright flies created a new school of anglers that employed "attractor" patterns without regard for any likeness or similarity to natural insects. This led to a wild development of weird fly patterns in the first half

of the 1800's that carries on to this day. It is said that some 25,000 "recognized" fly patterns exist today, although no one has determined just what constitutes a recognized pattern. To this astounding total we can add all the hopeful creations that come from the amateur's vise and arrive at an astronomical figure. Only a tiny segment of this total can conceivably approach natural imitation—despite a good deal of latitude permitted in this direction.

Thad Norris attempted to produce fly patterns that matched native insects. In view of the fact that the relatively few natural patterns in use were copies of English insects, this was a significant effort. In his *American Angler's Book* of 1864, he describes his design of artificial Grannom, a caddis fly common on American streams: "The Grannom has a body of hare's fur; wings of a partridge feather made full; legs of a pale ginger hackle and a short tuft of green floss silk at the tail, to represent the bag of eggs, which this insect carries at the extremity of its body." Norris' description was similar to that in Ronalds' *Fly-Fisher's Entomology* of 1836, and Norris himself had reservations about it. He realized that this indiscriminate use of English patterns would not help the American angler, that Americans would have to learn to observe their own seasonal changes of climate, their own streams, and the native insect life.

The significant point was that an American angler was beginning to think in British terms—close imitation of the natural. By the end of the Civil War, unsophisticated trout were becoming scarce, and the importation of brown trout from Europe in the 70's hastened the education of the fly caster. For the brown was a fish well schooled in the ways of anglers, a shy, secretive fish, with a frustrating ability to discriminate between the real and the false. He rarely succumbed to the lure of flash and brilliance in fly patterns (other than those suggesting minnows), forcing the fly-fisherman of the late 1800's to change tactics if he were to take trout at all. For by this time, the brown had taken over completely in some eastern streams.

The greatest influence on American fishermen, however, was exerted by Frederick Halford, who popularized in 1886 the new approach to fly-fishing: casting a fly, designed and tied to float on the surface, which matched the activity of a recently hatched May fly.

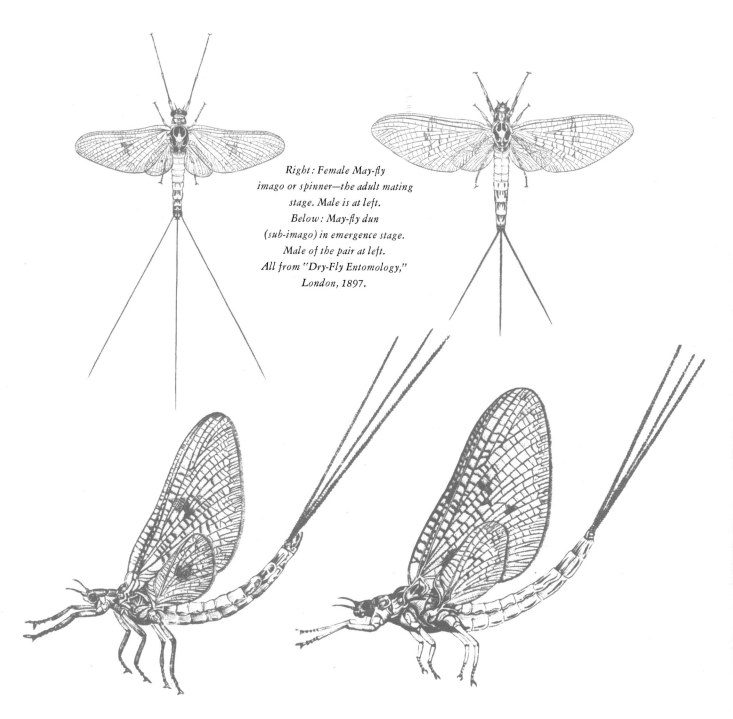

Right: Female May-fly imago or spinner—the adult mating stage. Male is at left.
Below: May-fly dun (sub-imago) in emergence stage. Male of the pair at left.
All from "Dry-Fly Entomology," London, 1897.

In England, Halford's theories had a pervasive effect on trout fishing. Although Pulman had created a basic design for the dry fly more than forty years before, it had gone unheeded. Stewart had followed Pulman with the necessary method—upstream fishing —to make the dry fly practical. Yet it remained for Halford to combine the two radical angling notions, to improve and refine them, to create a new method of fly-fishing. He was fanatical about the exclusive use of his new method on English streams, and for more than a quarter of a century wrote treatise after treatise declaring all other methods unsporting. During this period, he also wrote a great entomology of English flies and imitations, with color plates to standardize the patterns. It would be helpful if we had such a single Bible for all American waters today.

The small, fragile figure of Theodore Gordon now enters the chronology of American fly-fishing. A skillful fly-fisherman on Pennsylvania streams from early boyhood, Gordon had wealth enough to indulge his angling interest. He learned to tie flies from Norris' book, adopted the upstream fishing technique from

Norris and Stewart, then retired to the upper reaches of the Neversink River in New York's Catskills because of ill health. He was a full-time angler, as much as any man can be.

In 1890 he became the American correspondent for the *Fishing Gazette,* published in England, and exchanged ideas on fly-fishing theory, practice, and method with the greats of English angling. The same year he wrote his historic letter to Halford to inquire what fly patterns he used in his new dry-fly method. Halford replied on February 22, enclosing a paper to which were clipped a full set of the original patterns.

Although Gordon was greatly impressed with the set of Halford flies, he was not completely satisfied. For one thing, the flies were not representations of American insects, and he found by experiment that they were smaller than he would have liked them to be and not dressed full enough to float on the fast water of the Catskill streams. Halford himself had had some inkling that the patterns might not be correct, for his letter to Gordon said: "My difficulty however as to advising you of patterns likely to be successful is chiefly due to the fact that I have no knowledge of the streams or lakes nor of the genera and species of natural fly prevalent in them. . . ." He suggested also that he could have flies tied to Gordon's order, if he chose. But Gordon was an expert in this art and he carried on his own experiments to adapt the design principle to his needs.

Up to Halford's time trout flies were "wet"—that is, tied with soft hackles, wings that sloped back and, generally, of materials that would absorb water readily. The Halford concept was to make the fly buoyant by using stiffer hackle and more of it. He also tied the wings in the erect attitude of the newly hatched adult insect. Of course, he strove to imitate, as faithfully as he could, the color, size, and form of the natural May flies found on the English chalk streams.

Gordon accepted the principle of the dry-fly design and matching it to the natural. But from this point on, he found his own way. He had no guide to American stream insects other than his own keen observation. And this, apparently, was enough.

Over the next two decades, Gordon searched endlessly for the right materials to make a buoyant fly of correct color to match the naturals. He continually bemoaned the fact that he could not find natural hackles of the hue and stiffness he wanted. Ten days before his death he wrote to Roy Steenrod, one of his Catskill fishing partners, that he was "trying to fix things so that I can do a little dyeing." He was referring to some "Diamond dyes," recently procured, that he hoped might give him the exact shade of blue dun which he was forever seeking—a problem that still besets the flytier today.

When he died in 1915, Gordon had set the pattern for dry flies in our time. His stiff-hackled, delicate creations, tied on hooks of the lightest wire, persist today in the highest-quality flies. And as he improved the mechanics of the floating fly, he also became our first dedicated angler-entomologist. For a time he struggled to produce flies that would match with great exactitude the insects on which he found trout feeding most avidly. He realized, however, that this was a hopeless task and turned away from the theory of precise imitation of form when it became obvious he could not match the delicate, fairy quality of adult flies in materials of fur, feathers, silk, wool, and steel. Early in the century, he wrote in one of his "Little Talks" in the *Gazette:* "The more I study the imitation of the natural fly and the various books on the subject (or which treat of it), the surer I am that the trout have a wonderful eye for color but a very indifferent notion of form. There is any quantity of evidence; but take your mayfly alone and note the curious buzzards that are mistaken for the natural, particularly hackle patterns that are deadly because so nearly right in color."

It is a curious thing that the one fly pattern which serves as Theodore Gordon's memorial in the world of fly-fishing—the Quill Gordon—does not, in fact, represent a definite species of May fly. Rather, it serves to imitate a group of early season May flies having similar colors, generally a smoky, pale blue-gray. Scientific anglers argue that with this fly, Gordon was imitating *Iron fraudator,* or *Iron pleuralis,* or *Epeorus pleuralis;* indeed, even *Ephemerella invaria* or *E. subvaria.* But which of these it is depends wholly upon the individual's convictions. The hard fact is that a carefully tied, properly fished Quill Gordon takes trout that are rising to any one of the natural flies mentioned, since all are much the same color and virtually identical in form. Gordon believed, with the canny geniality of the professional flytier, that an imitation

Dun of Stenonema fuscum, *the Grey Fox (top); adult form of the Brown Caddis (center); nymph of the Great Stone Fly (lower left); adult stage of the Yellow Stone Fly (below).*

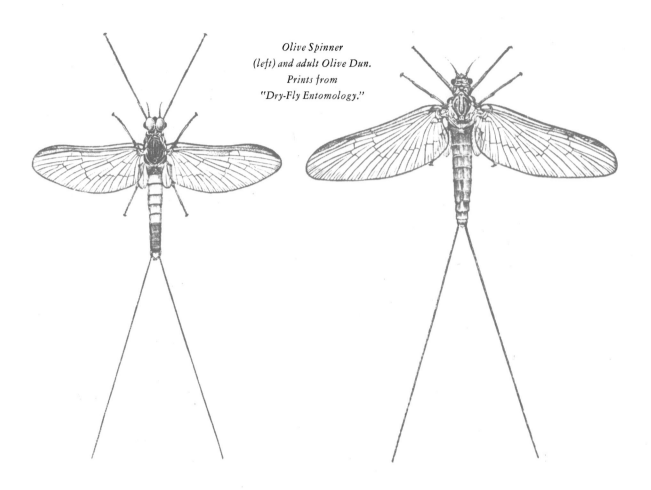

Olive Spinner
(left) and adult Olive Dun.
Prints from
"Dry-Fly Entomology."

covering a group of species would do well enough for the angler, unless the trout were extremely selective.

However, Gordon never decried the use of "attractor" patterns, which he often suggested for "wild waters" where fish were less shy and knowledgeable. He was all for selecting the fly according to the conditions—the current philosophy of the best fishermen.

Philosophies in angling vary enormously. Most fly-fishermen stick to a selection of flies that have a long history of success: Quill Gordon, Cahill, Light Cahill, Grey Fox, Royal Coachman, Red Quill, Hendrikson, etc. And they use a sampling of patterns that embraces the "imitation," "impression," and "attractor" theories. These patterns will take all species of stream trout anywhere in North America—at times. In terms of the "right" fly, these fishermen are the most tolerant and broad-minded.

Farther up the scale are the anglers who discover, by inquiry or observation, the most effective patterns for taking fish in the streams of their particular choice. As a rule, this means talking with successful anglers on these streams, buying flies tied locally, and combining this knowledge with more than casual observation of the natural flies as they appear during a fishing day. The choice of flies here becomes somewhat more specific and will include both "imitation" and "impression" theories in matching the naturals.

At the topmost level are those few scholar-fishermen who investigate the fly life of one particular stream, collecting naturals as they hatch, identifying them precisely, filling notebooks with the emergence dates of each species and the various times of day they appear, and with annotations as to type of weather, wind, humidity, and barometric pressure coinciding with each appearance. Since there are several hundred species of May flies, caddis flies, stone flies, and other insects favored by trout as food, this is an onerous task for all but the dedicated man. Finally, the angler must acquire the skill to tie such flies and, in the normal sequence of creating, amass a multiplicity of materials, for the combinations of fibers, furs, and feathers involved is almost without end.

52

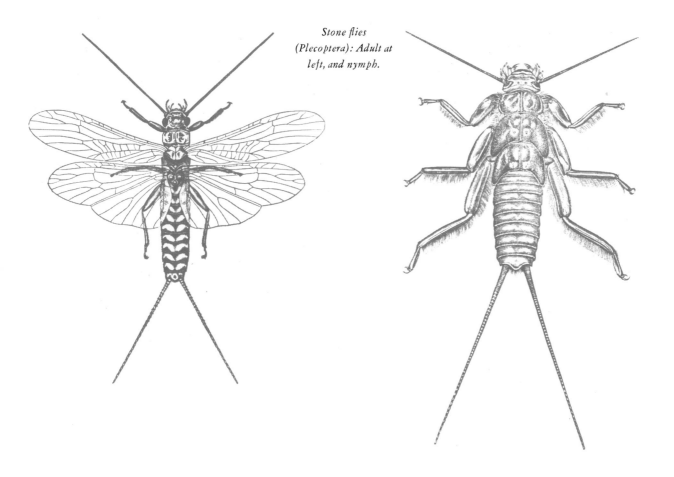

Stone flies (Plecoptera): Adult at left, and nymph.

A fly angler must now decide just how far he cares to go in exploring the intricacies of "matching the hatch." Students of stream insects since Gordon's time —LaBranche, Jennings, Wetzel, Flick, and Schwiebert —carry their search for the perfect imitation to the ultimate. These men and many others strive to produce the perfect match for each species of fly—male and female—they are likely to encounter on any stream. With these scientific anglers, "standard" fly patterns simply do not exist. These men create endlessly to match the hatch in minute detail; they catch trout; they publish their theories in books. For them the challenge of exact imitation is good fun. They spend many winter hours over the tying vise.

In the course of some forty years of fishing, I have not found it necessary to take the ultimate step. For about a decade I tied flies professionally, although I did not produce many—not more than a hundred dozen a year in the most active years. I experimented, as all flytiers do, with many fly designs, following the footsteps of the greats: Gordon and Roy Steenrod, Reub

Cross and Herman Christian, Ray Bergman and Fred Everett, Walt Dette and Harry Darbee. Gordon was before my time. I never knew Christian, but used some of his flies. The others I fished with or knew professionally. During those years we all searched for exactly the right fly designs to take trout consistently when they were surface feeding. It can be stated unequivocally that neither we, nor anyone else, has found them. Probably the closest to this sort of perfection is in flies which in size, color, and form create the most favorable impression of family groups of natural insects. Which was Gordon's conclusion.

The problem is that a fly-fisherman usually must acquire his flies from professionals. From the point of view of practicality and economy, even the most fastidious and conscientious professional must standardize his work. He would like to—and often does—come up with a pattern or series of patterns which can be associated with his name and craft. Yet working with available materials, he is often limited as to what can be done on a continuing basis. The fly-fisherman is therefore forced to accept the professional's best product, even though it may not conform to his notions as to the correct shade of hackle, the taper of the body, the set of the wings, or whatever. Not that anyone can say that any of this really matters.

I remember the years when Reub Cross was tying flies in his house on the banks of the Upper Neversink, an area now flooded by a reservoir created to fulfill, in some small measure, the rapacious demands of New York City residents for water. Reub's great, horny hands turned out some of the most amazingly delicate creations in small dry flies—Quill Gordons, among many others. And as all fishermen do, we swapped flies, as well as fishing lies, hoping, although never really expecting, to come up with the one perfect pattern. Reub's favorite was a fly he called the Cross Special—a pattern now in the limbo of forgotten flies—which was nothing more than a Hendrikson with a Light Cahill body. When I asked what made this so special he gave me his usual straight answer. "Not a damned thing," he said. "I just have the material, it takes fish as well as the Quill Gordon or Hendrikson, and I've got my name on it."

Actually, it is remarkable that a trout should mistake a contrivance of fur and feathers, wrapped around a steel hook, for the wraithlike form and texture of a living, adult May fly. Yet the fish do take such contraptions, for reasons that can only be supposed. Experience suggests that an artificial fly resembling the natural in color and size is generally the most effective in inducing a rise. But when fish become extremely selective, nothing really works.

I have spent hours lying hidden in brush and grass on stream banks, watching at close range while trout were taking natural flies. At times the fish can be maddeningly perceptive. I recall one bright afternoon in May on the Beaverkill when several species of May fly were hatching and the trout were rising—cautiously but steadily. I spent at least an hour casting over rising fish, using every trick I knew: loop casts to bring the fly over the fish before the leader could shy him off; matching the artificial to the natural as closely as possible in color and size; using the finest and longest leaders I possessed; stalking the fish, keeping carefully out of sight and keeping the rod low, to avoid frightening shadows or light flashes from the rod mountings.

Early American FLIES

ROW 1: COLONIAL PERIOD
Black Gnat, Cowdung, Partridge,
and Orange

ROW 2: COLONIAL PERIOD
Red Spinner, Soldier Palmer,
Hackle, and Dun

ROW 3: AMERICAN, 1840
Porter's Piseco Lake fly, his brilliant
Red Hackle, his long Green Drake

ROW 4: AMERICAN, 1845
Yellow Drake, Brown Mealy Moth,
May Fly with detached body, and Blue Jay

ROW 5: AMERICAN, 1850
Dun, Hackle, and Dun with
upright wings

ROW 6: AMERICAN, 1850
Bee, Drake, Red and Green, and lure

ROW 7: AMERICAN, 1865
Roosevelt adaptations of
English dressings: Great Stone Fly,
Blue Dun, and Cowdung

ROW 8: AMERICAN FANCIES, 1870-1890
Seth Green, Reuben Wood, Cheney, and
Oak Stewart (all bass flies)

ROW 9: AMERICAN. ——
Grannom, Scarlet Ibis, and Royal Coachman

ROW 10: AMERICAN, 1890
Adirondack, Montreal, streamer, and
Barnwell (for bass)

ROW 11: AMERICAN, 1900-1925
May Fly, Bivisible, and nymph

ROW 12: AMERICAN, 1890-1925
Mohawk Valley bucktail,
lure by Louis Rhead, streamer fly, and
hackle streamer.

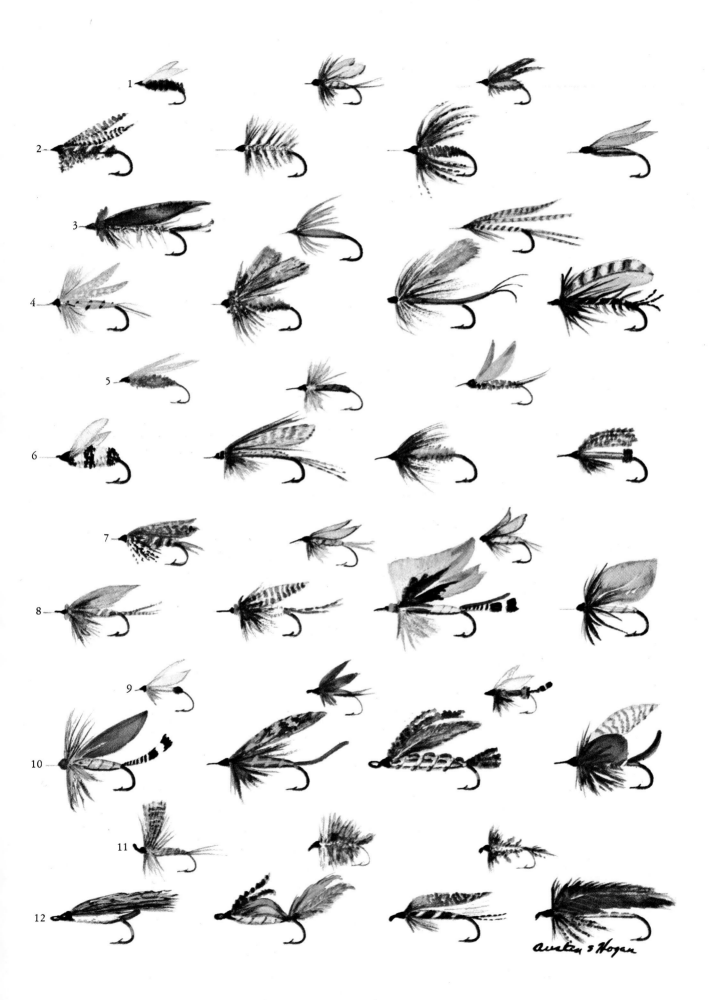

1

2

3

4

5

6

7

8

9

10

11

12

Austin S Hogan

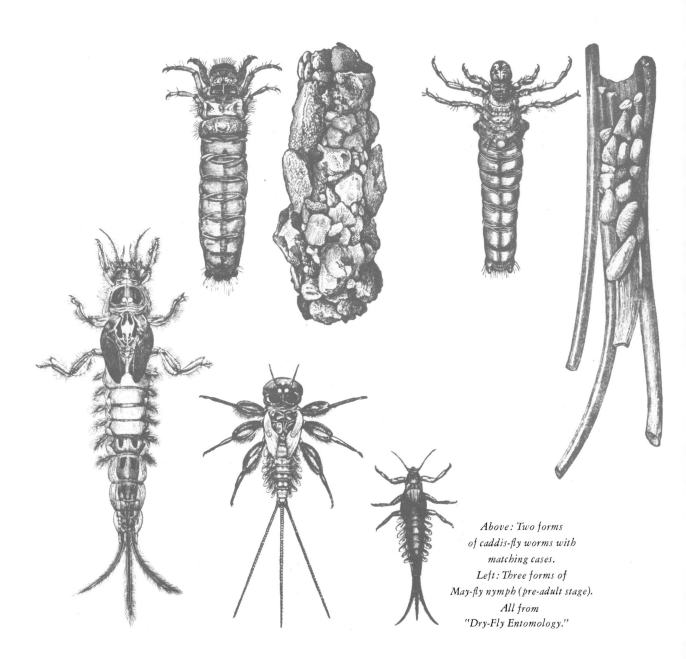

*Above: Two forms
of caddis-fly worms with
matching cases.
Left: Three forms of
May-fly nymph (pre-adult stage).
All from
"Dry-Fly Entomology."*

I could not raise a fish, although they fed steadily on naturals, picking them off the surface within inches of my high-floating dry fly.

Frustrated—as were other fishermen on the stream—but curious, I gave up fishing to watch. I picked a spot where an overhanging bank gave me good vantage directly opposite a point where trout were rising every minute or so. As I peered over the bank I could see five trout, all more than a foot long, lying just under the surface, where the fast water broke into the smooth surface of the pool. Every few seconds duns floated over the fish and with them some tiny yellow-green stone flies that flopped on the surface, beating tiny wings in the effort to take flight. The duns were of two

or three species; it mattered not. The trout were interested only in the little stone flies.

When one of them appeared over the trout, one fish would detach from the group and rise up slowly to look it over, with his head barely an inch from the insect struggling on the surface. He would then drift down with the fly, watching its movements, finning gently, keeping just below and downstream of the fly. After looking it over carefully while it moved some ten feet or more, he would lift up, open his jaws leisurely, and suck it in. With this sort of scrutiny, no angler fools a trout—and these were browns—with a man-made imitation tied to a gut leader.

Fortunately, trout are rarely this cautious and discriminating. Fortunately, too, their moods change swiftly. On this same day, a heavy "duffer" hatch broke out just at sundown. It was *Stenonema fuscum,* a fairly large May fly. Trout went for them diligently right up until dusk. I took a half-dozen good fish on the Grey Fox, which purports to imitate this dun, but other fly casters did as well or better with the Grey Variant, Cahill, and Badger Spider. The rules in imitation, as in other things, are made to be broken.

Trout have keen vision, yet they take artificials that range from precise imitation to the ridiculous. On another Beaverkill evening, trout were dimpling all over the runs to tiny midges that were barely visible on the water. I caught a couple of the insects, hoping to match them. To do so, I would have needed Quill Gordons, or something similar, in size 18. These I did not have. Out of sheer perversity I tied on a #10 Fan-Wing Royal Coachman, and raised and hooked a fish solidly on the first cast. I creeled another four good fish and released half a dozen small ones before darkness called a halt. Certainly the big Royal Coachman is as far from imitating the natural as one can get.

But with exceptions noted, the rational course in choice of flies lies with imitating nature. It may be that the imitation does not deceive with accuracy and, perhaps, it is not needful. My friends Art Flick and Ernie Schwiebert would dissent violently, but this is their privilege. These erudite angler-entomologists are far more dedicated to the exact science of imitation than I, and, for all I know, are better fishermen for it.

Personally, I prefer to meet the fish on more common ground. I know quite well what goes on with the May flies, the caddis, and the stone flies while they live in the stream and after they emerge as adults. I know *Stenonema vicarium* and *Ephemera guttalatta* when I see them on the water and in the air, but I am much more inclined to call them by the names of their artificial counterparts—March Brown and Green Drake —than by their scientific Latin names. The science of entomology may suffer but, I think, not my fishing.

It is enough to know that an adult May fly begins its life cycle as a nymph, and that trout feed far more on May flies as nymphs than as duns or spinners. It's a simple matter of availability. The same can be said for caddis. These, however, do not have a nymph stage, but are taken greedily by the trout as worms, and some-

what less avidly when they become winged adults. The stone fly—large, meaty, and appealing—is appreciated most as a nymph, since he is largely out of reach of the trout after his transformation into an adult.

Nevertheless, the life cycles of stream insects are vitally important to the angler. It is always helpful to know that dark insects—the blue-gray duns, little black stone flies—are early season flies; that the brown flies appear a bit later in the spring; that the pale, light-colored flies come still later and on into the summer. It may be discouraging, however, to realize that much of this discourse on flies and matching the hatch deals largely with floating flies and that only a small proportion of a trout's diet is taken from the surface. Parallel themes can be developed on nymphs, streamer flies, and wet flies, ad infinitum.

The responsibility for *when* to use *what* in angling rests always with the fisherman more than with the fish. Trout—in fact, most fresh-water fish—have cosmopolitan tastes. A fly caster can offer temptation in various ways. When fish are bottom feeding, he may use an imitation caddis worm or a weighted artificial nymph (many types). When the fish are minnow feeding, he may use a streamer or bucktail. He may cast an upstream nymph or wet fly as these insects are moving in the stream, preparing to hatch into adults. Or, finally, he may fish the floating fly to simulate duns, spinners, caddis, crane flies, stone flies, damsel flies, grasshoppers, midges, or any other natural insects. When these possibilities are unsuccessfully exhausted, the "attractor" theory may be explored. Here only the imagination of the fisherman and the flytier imposes limits.

A well-rounded fly-fisherman also attacks the problem of what fly to use by fly types. One day fish will rise—steadily and visibly over much of a stream or lake. The surface fly is suggested. Another day, there will be no sign of surface-feeding fish. Nymphs, wet flies, or streamers may work magic, or if a man is a confirmed dry-fly purist, he may hope to "pound up" fish by repeated casting: creating an artificial hatch which sometimes, not often, arouses attention.

There are no pat answers to taking fish on the fly. This is good. The challenge of luring the fish is—as always—a combination of knowing much about the fish, where it lives, how to find it, and how to feed it the deceptive tidbit it will condescend to take.

The
SALMON

ATLANTIC
Salmon

Th e restless tides over the estuary glimmered in the pale light of a full moon rising from the lip of the sea. Under the breaking waters salmon moved from the ocean's bed, leaving the rich feeding grounds to return to their home river. It was June. The fish were well fed, lusty, and strong, filled with the ardor of spawning, ready to offer themselves in the ineffable act of procreation.

As the moon rose higher, a graceful, powerful form, steel blue above, silvery below, moved purposefully through the shallow waters above the sand bar. Salar, the salmon of the Atlantic, named "the Leaper" by the Romans, tasted the freshness of river water, colder still than the sea, and it was to his liking. Urges timeless as nature herself stirred within him, filling firm muscles, fattened by three years of the sea's bounty. He moved with thousands of his kind into a world almost new, but still remembered from his early years as a parr and a smolt, when this same river carried him to the salt, to grow in length and thickness and to twenty-pound weight—a splendid cock fish, with milt glands filled and the desire to move far up-stream to his assignment upon him.

The journey was not easy. It never has been. Salar spent many days and nights in the estuary, readying himself for the onslaught up river—waiting for the rise of water, with its spring spate, to give him free movement over rocky riffles and along the long, shallow, gravel-filled reaches of the first few miles of the river. These were pleasant days for the most part, spent in final feeding on the schools of minnows hovering at the shoal breaks, but his bright eye was forever turned toward dangers from the sea.

In the misty dawn, as Salar lolled in the green troughs of the breakers, a dark shape, streaming pearl bubbles from its nostrils, darted from deep water and was beside him, its broad snout open and gaping for a hold on his silvery side. But Salar was alerted by the bubbles. His body writhed quickly, a sweep of his broad, forked tail carried him swiftly away, and the marauding hair seal missed its target. A five-pound grilse, a young salmon not so wise as Salar, that had followed the big cock fish into the surf, was not so lucky. The driving flippers of the seal carried him head on into the grilse. He seized it with a deft turn of the head, caught it just forward of the dorsal fin. One crunching bite almost cut the fish in two.

Other dangers surrounded the male salmon during his days in the brackish waters of the river mouth. Finding a resting place near a big underwater boulder, he barely twisted away in terror from a sea lamprey, its sucking mouth filled with a circle of needle teeth, reaching for him from the shadow of the rock. And on this same day he broke away from the ranks of salmon lying in one of the long fresh-water roots of the estuary to escape a rolling, feeding school of porpoises. The herd of beaked mammals snapped and tore at the clustered salmon until they scattered. Salar found safety in a weed bed. But these were natural dangers, to be met on equal terms. The nets of the commercial fishermen were to be feared most.

Only once had he encountered the frenzied fear inspired by the clinging, restraining meshes, and this had been an accident. Driving away from the dark shadow of the netter's boat above him, he had rushed headlong into the loose folds as the thin twine mesh was running out. And again by accident he did not thrust his sharp head within the squares, for he would have "gilled" himself inextricably. But his sudden contact with the strange touch made him writhe and roll, twisting his body within the folds until the stretching of the net freed him as it payed out. This brief engagement left its mark on his broad side where two fine lines of silver scales were ripped out.

And then one gray morning in late June, the rain

Angler locates salmon in
pool, makes selection, hopefully, of the best
fly, casts accurately over the fish.

Pages 58-59: Atlantic salmon.

fell from low, sullen clouds that pressed down over the estuary, seeding the river with fresh, cool water, high in oxygen. Salar frolicked at the mouth of the river, welcoming the change in his element, noting the rising water by the floating leaves and bits of twig carried in the currents toward the sea. He was ready for his assault on the river itself, with its new dangers, its promise at the end.

The river now was runable. The salmon moved up through the deeper channels to tidehead, under iron bridges with the high watermarks of earlier years ringed on the rusted columns parting the swift current. Within two hours he had driven sinuously upstream to the first growth of alders along the bank. True fresh water was now at hand, the river bed clean, its natural banks and pools no longer affected by the ponderous whims of the sea.

The big male salmon now found himself in an element somehow strange, yet still remembered. His years in the sea had not prepared him for vagaries of current, tumbling without form or pattern in the changing form of the stream bed. Behind each boulder he was buffeted by the closing flow of the river's strength. He gained rest and relief only when he fought up the rapids and came into the pool above. But he quickly adjusted to the new movements of his element, quickly learned to slip by the full push of the deeper, faster-flowing flumes and to rest behind a rock in a pocket, where he could support himself gently on his broad, flaring pectoral fins.

With a full head of water in the river, his last irritation—the sea lice—would now disappear. These tiny parasites, carried from the sea on the lower rear half of Salar's body, near the anal fin, had no stomach for fresh water. Without the salinity they liked, they would drop, stunned, from his body, leaving their host with no visible connection with the sea.

The river, now rich with oxygen, invigorated the fish. He leaped playfully, testing himself, perhaps, for the barriers that he must cross upstream. He had moved swiftly during the past two days, covering some twenty miles of the river, and he and his fellow salmon were filled with the zest of travel. Pools up the river cracked every minute or so with their leaps.

On the morning of the third day, Salar rested below one of the boulders in Big Rock Pool. As he

lay with his side supported by the swirling water breaking around the rock, he could see a pair of grilse lying just above him, fighting the swift flow as it broke around the boulder. Below him a two-pound sea-run brook trout had taken a position at the very tail of the rock pocket. Ahead and on either side the gay little salmon parr were dimpling and breaking through the surface.

And now the fish began to take an interest in the insect life of the stream. A hatch of May-fly nymphs was working free of the gravel bottom, drifting aimlessly with the currents, each wriggling within its nymphal shuck to break free and emerge from the river as an adult dun.

The grilse and parr, along with the trout, were taking these drifting nymphs just below the surface. Salar watched with interest, noting the flash of white as the grilse lifted, then opened its jaw, in rising to snatch one of the tiny bits of stream life. And although he was not hungry and felt no desire to take food, he became excited by memories of his first years in the river, when nymphs were fun to chase and big enough to fill his tiny belly. Now a nymph drifted toward him, well below the surface. Salar's fins quivered in anticipation as the hard-shelled insect approached. Then, with an almost imperceptible sweep of his pectorals, he rose just enough to close his jaws slowly over it,

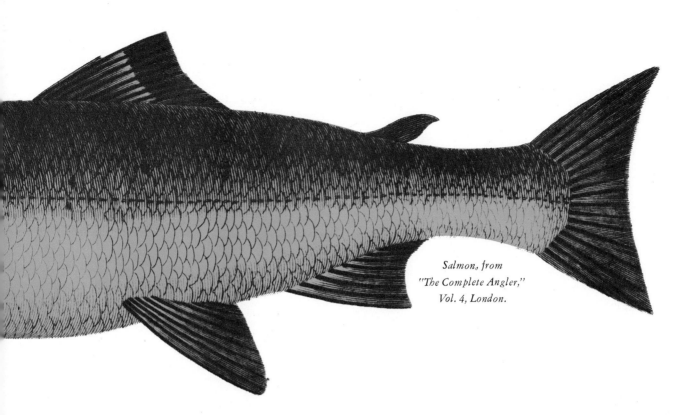

Salmon, from "The Complete Angler," Vol. 4, London.

crushing it, and then ejecting it as he settled back to his hold. Spurred on by the continual feeding of the parr and grilse, he took, crushed, and spewed out a dozen or more of the nymphs until the hatching ended for the morning.

As the last days of June passed, Salar and his fellow travelers moved another dozen miles upstream. But as the river level lowered, after a week of bright, warm days and starry nights, they traveled slower. And the day soon came when they arrived at Forks Pool with too little water to carry them easily beyond. The fish now settled down to await the next rise of water, lying in ranks through the length of the pool, with fish matching each other in size lying side by side. Salar was not aware that, after two weeks in the river, his bright silver was fading and a faint blush of red bloomed on his gill covers. Two weeks away from the salt had taken much of the sheen from his armor. Only the young grilse seemed to be unaffected in color. Perhaps in their immaturity, the pre-spawning changes were slow to show.

Neither was Salar aware that of the two grilse which had stayed close to him in his upstream journey, one was missing. Missing also from the phalanx of fish in the pool were another half a dozen salmon and grilse that had fallen to anglers' flies and night-foraging otter. One had been "jigged" with a heavy treble hook

by a poacher, under cover of darkness. So far, the big cock fish had escaped these dangers, but he was still many miles from his goal near the headwaters.

Salar had not shown interest in the river fly life since his last experience with the nymphs, far downstream. His interest had lagged still more with the passing of each mile and the lowering of the water levels. He seldom leaped now, and then only as he was forced to do by the nature of the stream. For several days he had rested quietly in the warming water, his spirits diminishing.

The salmon rested in Forks Pool for three days before a heavy afternoon thundershower developed into a full, nightlong downpour. When the river lightened at sunrise, its volume had increased notably. The ranks broke and thinned as the salmon moved up river. Salar, invigorated by the fresh, cooler water, pushed upstream six miles to Snag Pool before making any long pause to rest. Now he was within easy striking distance of the clean gravel beds that henfish had chosen for centuries as the spot for digging troughs to catch and hold the pea-sized eggs liberated in spawning.

Since time immemorial, Snag Pool has been a good salmon lie. Further, it is a lie where fish will rise to the fly, for what unfathomable reason no angler knows. Each salmon river has its good lies, or holds, where fish will rest on their upriver journey. Yet only

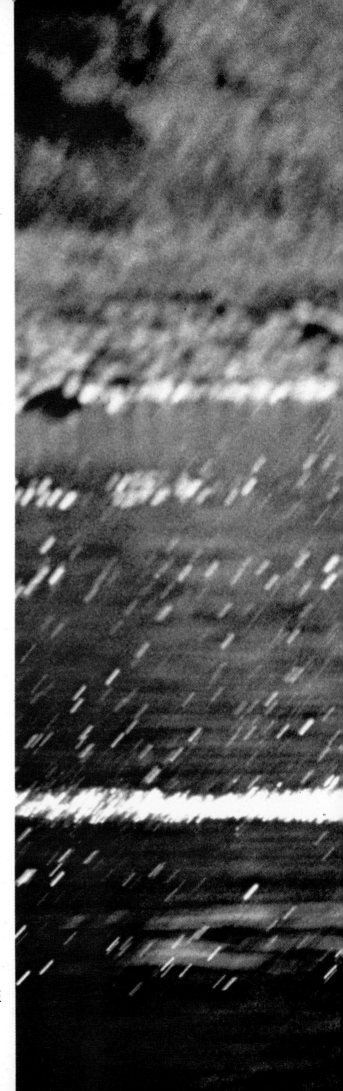

Hooked salmon responds with
wild flurry on the surface, leaps and
tries to eject the fly. Fighting
fish often attempts to break leader by
lashing at it with his tail.

64

Top: Overhand cast, forward position.
Bottom: Dry switch, finish position. Opposite: Underhand
cast, forward position. Prints from "Dry-fly Fishing,"
by Frederick M. Halford, London, 1889.

a charmed few of these lies offer the angler a chance to raise a salmon. From long experience every river guide knows the lies, and also from long experience, most guides shy away from Snag Pool. For many years a huge downed elm has lain diagonally across a good half of the pool's tail, where the flow shallows before breaking into the riffle below. A beaten fish usually comes against the spreading, stubby limbs of the big tree lying half submerged. A simple half roll of the body by a weary, hooked fish is enough to foul the wisp of leader connecting the salmon to the fisherman. Many good fish have found their freedom, even though whipped and ready for the net, at the tail of Snag Pool.

Still more new rain had instilled new vigor in the salmon. They no longer lay in quiet rows in Snag Pool, for only a few fish had decided to remain in this hold. The others had moved further along. Salar, heavier than the rest, did not keep to the pace of the smaller salmon and grilse. He picked a spot behind a sheltering rock at the head of Snag Pool, where the heavy shadow covered him from the bright rays of the sun. But his strength was still great enough to arouse his interest in the feeding antics of the parr, now freely jumping to a new hatch of May flies.

In the many days of his journey, Salar had noted the passing overhead of small creatures, sometimes swinging across his window of vision, sometimes unaccountably moving upstream against the force of fast water. These he ignored, as the summer months passed and

A battle with an eighteen-pound
salmon, from the boiling rise to final tailing,
is first-class angling.

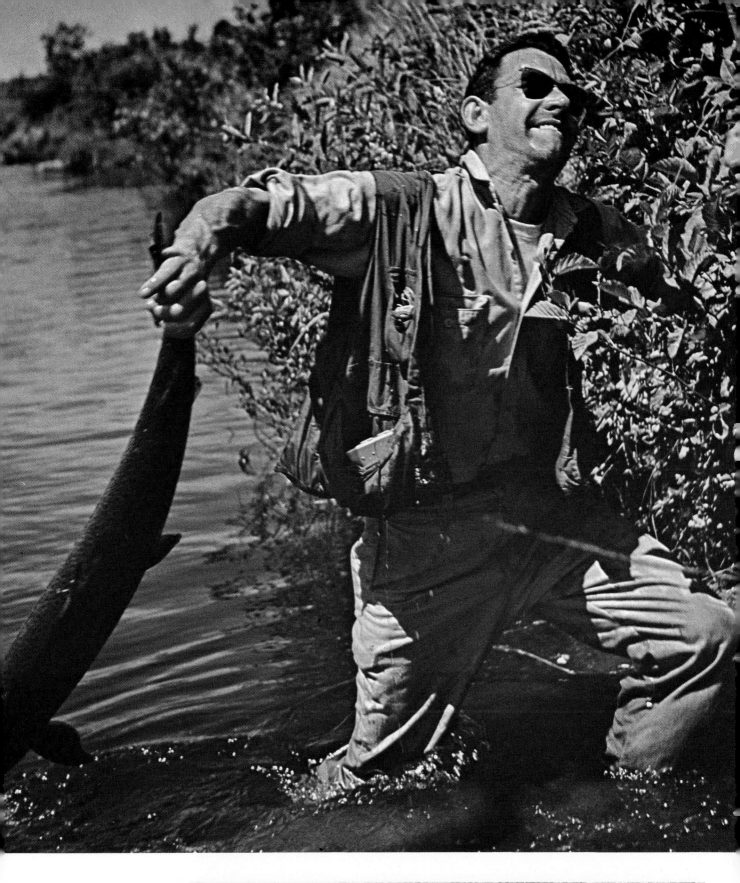

Expert Lee Wulff lands salmon after long fight on two-ounce fly rod.

his desire urged him on. Until his arrival in Snag Pool, he paid scant attention to the fisherman's fly.

Just ahead and to the left of the big salmon, lying in the rock shadow, a sea trout plucked glass-winged May flies from the surface swirl breaking around the rock, dimpling the current in a steady rhythm of rises. Salar, now really alert, watched the trout with his left eye. And then a small, flylike thing, flashing silver from its body, swam across the window of his right eye. The trout saw it at the same instant, twisted toward it, mouth open to seize it, but missed as the current swept it away.

A few seconds later the fly splashed gently through the surface, again kicked across the salmon's view. He

saw it at once with both eyes; then, curious, he pushed his long body up and away from the gravel with a lift of his fins and two sweeps of his forked tail. Deliberately, swiftly, and with great precision he moved ahead of the swimming object to intercept it as it swung across the pocket. His lunge carried him well up to the surface, his thick gray back just breaking through as he rolled down on the fly. His long white-lined jaws closed over it just as his protruding dorsal fin emerged.

Salar swept back toward his lie, readying to crush and taste, then eject, as he had done before with many nymphs. He did not reach the spot, for a sudden restraint kept him from it. Neither did he have time to taste, for the quick sting of the hook point changed

70

his mind. He must rid himself of the sting and the strain at once. Twice he shook his head. The bite was still there. Then the strain became great as the fisherman put his strength into the rod, setting the barb loosely under the salmon's upper mandible.

Surprised, terrified by a pressure new and strange, Salar broke into the air in a straight leap toward the sky, thrashing wildly, bending his body into a full bow before falling heavily into the river on his side. But the torment of fly and line was still with him. He fought to reach his hold near the rock and did, then rubbed his jaw against the roughness of the boulder to force out the fly.

This too, failed him. The strain on his head grew firmer as the fisherman forced the fight, and the salmon drove toward the tail of the pool. He ran forty yards of line from the reel, turned, under heavy pressure from the rod, just before reaching the shallows, then leaped again—high enough to give a solid slap against the leader with his tail.

It was not enough, this frantic strategy. The hook held solidly, although it was tearing a wide rent in the tissues of the salmon's jaw. Salar now moved slowly upstream to sulk in the deep water below his rock hold, and, unwittingly, gave the angler the advantage of position—below the fish, where the salmon must fight both the current flow and the spring of the rod.

The fish was tiring rapidly now. He could not hold his head directly upstream against the pressure from behind. Wearily, he moved across the stream, away from the stress of the line. Again he tried to return to his lie but had not the power to make it. The pull of the line forced him across the river, where, for the first time, he saw the fisherman. This spurred him into summoning the last of his waning power and making another frightened run to the very middle of the pool.

By now his breath was gone. His gill covers worked irregularly as he gulped in fresh water and its feeble mixture of oxygen. He desperately wanted rest but the fisherman gave him none. Wearily then, he turned on his side, fatigued to the end. The guide, with the long-handled, wide-hooped net submerged at the tail of the pool, signaled the fisherman to lead the dying fish over the mesh.

Salar drifted down the slow current toward the guide, his pectoral fin flapping in the sunlight, spent,

beaten. The angler dutifully put on maximum pressure to turn the salmon's twenty-pound body headfirst into the hoop. A yard away from the net, Salar for the first time saw the guide, saw him lunge forward in a quick thrust with the pole. The movement was enough, just enough to spark a half-dozen quick sweeps of the tail, sending the salmon across stream into the waiting, stubby arms of the waterlogged elm. The leader hung for a bare second on a branch, the strain on the fish shifted direction, and the hook slid from beneath his upper mandible. Salar sank slowly from sight into the deep pocket beneath the elm's trunk. He was free.

The big salmon lay quietly through the rest of the day, summoning his strength for another go at the river run. By nightfall he had left, still working on the rise of water, and by dawn he had reached the first of the redds, the spawning grounds that already were furrowed with the efforts of the first females. He spent more than a week in passing from bed to bed, mating with a ten-pound henfish at first, then with a good sixteen-pounder another mile further up the stream.

By now it was autumn and his shape and color had changed. The steel-blue back had turned brownish; traces of pink tarnished his scales that had been so silver-bright. His head had lengthened, his lower jaw was so hooked that his jaws could no longer meet. But he had grip enough to grasp the female on her bed or to nip savagely at any interloping cock fish.

As the last of the leaves fell from the hardwood ridges, Salar had fulfilled his function. His milt was gone, his fins frayed and worn, his body covered with ugly fungus growth. He had mated with at least a dozen henfish in the two spawning months and was now tired, sluggish, waiting only for a rise of water to help his return to the sea. He was a tired old man, now maligned with the name "kelt," a black salmon. He would be corroded and depleted until he went again to salt water to clean himself, to feed mightily on ocean bounty until he could again make the return journey to the redds.

But the winter was dry and the river, in low ebb, remained ice-locked for many months. Not until early April did a freshet open the way to the estuary. Weak and hungry, Salar seized a huge streamer fly played under the iron bridge by a young fisherman. The fish fought to the shore, to be dragged roughly up on the

Landlocked salmon, smaller brother of the Atlantic salmon, likes clear, cold northern waters.

graveled shore line. The youngster, noting with disgust his ragged fins and scarred sides, tossed him into the alders. By morning, stream-side predators had reduced him to a horny head and a bare backbone.

Today Canada has a virtual monopoly on Atlantic salmon and Atlantic-salmon fishing. Three Maine rivers—the Dennys, Narraguagus, and Machias—enjoy a fair run of the fish as a result of diligent cleaning up and restocking programs. But these are about the only American streams that suit the fastidious salmon.

The narrowing of the Atlantic salmon's range has made fishing for him a most exclusive—and expensive—sport. Most of the Canadian rivers are under private lease for a good part of their length. Fishing here means a fee of $35 to $100 per rod per day. With no guarantees. Costs can run up if, because of the uncertainties of the salmon migration, the angler has to wait for the arrival of the fish, or if, because of variations in water levels and temperatures, the fish are not in a taking mood.

Many dedicated salmon fishermen can and do take fish with great regularity when they are in the river, but the salmon is never predictable. Orthodox angling

72

methods, long established by tradition and practice, often fail. The successful salmon angler has digested every trick in the book—and invented some of his own.

The frustration in salmon fishing lies in the fact that the fish is not a feeder in fresh water. After years in the boundless ocean, he finds a fresh-water stream a strange environment; he becomes extremely sensitive to changes and variations in water conditions. The fly-fisherman (for salmon fishing is fly-fishing, both legally and morally) must take this into account. Working in his favor, however, is the fact that as a young parr, the salmon was an insect feeder. If the right fly and a delicate cast can stir the salmon's memory, a rise and a strike will follow.

The fish has no intention of eating, but he will mouth an insect, as he did in his early days in the river, and then eject it. This adult response to a habit fixed in youth gives the fisherman his chance. Early in the spawning run the salmon is likely to accept a wet fly. As the stream level lowers in summer and the water becomes warmer, the dry fly is more effective.

The salmon gives the angler two other small breaks: he is not alarmed by the sight of the fisherman, and he can be induced to rise in fairly shallow water at midday, with a bright sun beating on the stream. In fact, midday is often the most productive fishing hour. Salmon fishermen are notorious late risers.

A strategically located fisherman often can observe whether a fish is interested in the fly. If the fish lifts his head and body slightly as the fly passes over him, and if his front fins move more briskly, he has been aroused. He will almost surely rise if each succeeding cast is carefully made and the fly correctly presented. An hour may be needed to elicit the rise, but it won't be wasted time. A bad cast that slaps the line hard on the surface will usually make a salmon lose interest. His alarm can be seen in the way he settles quickly toward the bottom and changes the rhythm of his tail and fin motion. At this point try for another fish.

The fly used to tempt an Atlantic salmon can be any of the thousands in regular, everyday use. There is almost no standard salmon-fly pattern that makes any sense, since they in no way resemble living insects in either color or form. Wet-fly tradition, carried over from centuries of salmon angling in Scotland and England, calls for heavily dressed flies—bulky bundles of bright feathers from many parts of the world, liberally laced with flashing silver and/or gold tinsel. Some of the old patterns require up to two dozen different materials.

American salmon flies are more sedate. The current trend is toward more modest hues, less flash and gingerbread. On the Lower Miramichi, in New Brunswick, it is said that any fly pattern is a good one, "as long as it's black."

The confusion in fly selection arises from the fact that all these patterns—in a wide range of sizes—do raise fish. It all depends on where you are and at what time of year—and, oddly enough, to some extent on who your guide is. (The guide's influence in salmon fishing is great, justifiably in some instances, too dogmatically in others.) Top-notch salmon anglers seldom rely on a single pattern. The best scheme seems to be to have enough flies on hand, in enough sizes and colors to offer a change of pace to the fish. When a salmon rises and "comes short," refusing the fly, this is the signal to change to another pattern or a different size of the same fly. Then wait a bit on the bank to rest the fish before the next attempt.

The size of the fly apparently has more significance than its color and shape. Salmon on the Lower Miramichi, for example, are best attracted by relatively small flies—#6 and #8. On the Restigouche, in northern New Brunswick, large flies are the order, with #1/0 a fair average.

In fishing the dry fly, size is again the key to raising fish. The temptation is to use a large floater—one that can readily be seen by both the fish and the fisherman—with a large hook to engage and hold the fish. Yet the large dry fly is often disdained by salmon, almost certainly when the water is low and as clear as air. Under these conditions, a smaller fly, even the tiny trout fly, is usually necessary to turn the trick. The small fly offers only a meager hold on the fish and requires a gossamer leader as well, which forces the angler to challenge a powerful fish with tackle offering the slimmest of chances to land him. But this is the philosophy of salmon fishing with the floating fly. It is somehow better to hook and lose a fish than not to engage one.

The salmon's rise to a fly is magnificent. He takes deliberately, without the verve and frivolity of a trout or grayling, but with purpose and power. When he

The first cast, from "The Ristigouche and Its Salmon Fishing," Dean Sage, Edinburgh, 1898.

turns to follow a wet fly sweeping across the current, his long body displaces a heavy bulge in the flow, often pushing a tiny bow wave ahead as he comes to the fly. Water surges up behind the fly. There is a boil as his broad back breaks the surface. And then comes a shocking instant of uncertainty: Does he have it or has he missed? If he has it, the line comes taut within a second or two, and his weight pulls against the rod.

Once the point of the hook is buried in his mouth, the fish makes the action. He may drop to the bottom, shake his head a time or two, then chug a bit around the rocks, hoping to rid himself of the steel. More likely, the sting prompts an immediate and spectacular response. He may wait a moment to gather his wits, but then he breaks from the surface, big and silver, throwing a great spray of glistening drops. His body hangs momentarily in the air, high and gyrating, then smashes flat on the surface. As his broad tail sinks into the water, he surges across and down the stream with full power. No rod can hold him at this stage; he runs line freely from the reel. He may check once, leap again, or sweep wildly down and out of his pool into the quick water below.

The speed of current helps him on the downstream run. If he checks in the pool below, there's a chance to recover some line. If not, it means chasing him down the bank or running after him in the canoe.

Most often a salmon is a gentleman fighter. He gives all he has, tries desperately to rub out the hook on a rock or throw it into the air. But it's rare for a salmon to dive for a hidden snag to foul your line or leader. When it does happen, it seems to lack the sin of intent. He carries the battle to the angler in open water, trusting to his strength and agility to break the maddening restraint of the line and rod. When he sulks he does so quietly and with dignity, his long jaw opens to show a long line of white as he gulps more and more fresh water to build his waning strength.

Once his broad, shining side turns toward the sky, the angler is on top of the fight. A salmon that breaks away from the fisherman most often does so long before this stage is reached.

To take a salmon in the river, as he arrives, clean and strong, from the sea, is an unparalleled delight. The enchantment of angling lives most enduringly in this splendid fish.

L*A*NDLOCKED
Salmon

A f t e r two decades of fairly intensive study of how and where the landlocked salmon lives, I find I have discovered little more about this fish than is necessary to take him. These smaller brothers of Salar, the Atlantic salmon, have such confounding ways it is difficult to calculate their responses. When the mood is upon them, they strike hungrily and swiftly at a fly or lure, and when the mood passes nothing in the world of nature or the angler's tackle box can gain their attention.

In this characteristic the landlocked salmon is kin to the Atlantic, which is notoriously reluctant to rise to a fly during the run up river. This is understandable in the sea-run salmon. He is not a feeder in fresh water. But the fussiness of the landlocked salmon is much harder to explain, since he is a fresh-water resident. On occasion, however, when his appetite has been stimulated, the landlock will feed ravenously. I have killed four-pounders whose bellies were jammed with freshly taken smelt weighing a total of half a pound. To equal this kind of gluttony an average man would have to pack away a whole rib of beef!

As a member of the salmonoid family, the landlock has the normal life pattern of the group. He prefers cool, clean water. He is ready for action when the ice breaks in the lakes. From ice-out time until the lake "turns over," bringing the warmer water to the top, you can expect to take landlocks near the surface. I have taken a good many by casting a streamer fly among floating ice chunks—over the right spot, of course. But as the warmth of the surface water increases with the balmy temperatures of spring, the salmon goes deeper to stay cool. He spends the summer in deep water, where you must try either deep trolling or drifting with bait to get him. In the northern regions, the cool weather that comes with late summer again brings the fish to the surface, readying himself for the spawning run up headwater tributaries.

The secret in catching landlocks, then, seems to rest in knowledge of water temperatures, which can be checked with an angler's thermometer. When we apply the knowledge that the comfort level of the salmonoids is below seventy degrees, it should be easy to locate the fish. But here again the landlock's conduct is paradoxical. For salmon in hatcheries will feed well in water temperatures as high as seventy-six degrees—long after trout refuse to eat. And it is known that in certain hatchery rearing pools, where temperatures are ideal for trout, water must be artificially heated to stimulate salmon to feed.

There are two things that we can say for certain about landlocks: they require a large area of deep water, and their main food is smelt. When we put these facts together, we can combine the right lure with the correct location and—sometimes—catch salmon.

As suggested, their feeding pattern is incomprehensible. A dozen anglers can work over a salmon hole in a deep lake, trolling streamer flies in patterns to match the rainbow's colors, or running the gamut of lures in pearl, gold, copper, or whatever. For hours, perhaps days, the salmon will not hit. Then, for no apparent reason, some mystical being blows a supersonic whistle and leaping silver fish appear, fighting to free themselves of flies and spoons. This activity may last a few minutes or several hours, but when it ends it has ended for everyone. The pattern may be repeated the next day, or it may not happen again for a week. Often as not, it does not occur again for the rest of the season.

Landlocked-salmon fishermen take off at dawn on a northern forest lake.

The angler who kills the most landlocks in any given year may not be the most knowledgeable student of salmon lore, but he is undoubtedly the most persistent angler. He must have kept his lures over the fish from dawn until dusk, in order to be at the right spot at the time the fish was moved to take.

Despite his ambiguous character, the landlocked salmon has his own special charm. There is, first of all, the mystery of his origin. No one knows how this miniature form of the sea-loving Atlantic salmon—and generically he is the same fish—became isolated in fresh water. There is a theory that during the last glacial epoch great ice masses closed off the return of spawning salmon to the sea and that their descendents began a new evolutionary pattern to inhibit their latent taste for salt. This is given some slight support by the fact that landlocks have not been found below the southern limit of glacial movement. But, it can also be argued that the waters south of the glacial limit would not suit the landlocked salmon, anyway. His natural home is the area ranging from central New England north into Canadian waters that flow into the St. Lawrence. Extensive transplanting has broadened the range to include New York state, but most of this effort to put landlocks in new waters has been confined to rivers and lakes of his native area. This sort of geographical isolation is matched only by the golden trout of the High Sierras.

The fish is, of course, beautiful. His form and colors are normally those of the Atlantic salmon bright and fresh from the sea. His black spots are both more numerous and more pronounced, and often assume a "XX" shape among those above the lateral line. His fins and tail are somewhat larger, proportionately, than those of the Atlantic salmon, but in almost all respects he is an Atlantic salmon. In Canadian waters, there is a variety of *Salmo sebago* (named for Lake Sebago, Maine, in which he was first found and classified) called the ouananiche, or *Salmo ouananiche,* that runs somewhat smaller in average size and exhibits more brown in his dark spots than *sebago.* In addition, ouananiche has slightly larger fins and is often tinged with yellow along the lower sides and cheeks.

But these are the superficial differences between landlocked and Atlantic salmon. The important difference, from the angler's point of view, is that the former is a feeder in fresh water, the latter is not. When *sebago* feeds on smelt and other minnows, or rises to nymph or floating flies (which he occasionally will do), he can be lured with some degree of certainty, either by tempting his appetite or by awakening his curiosity.

And if the landlock differs from the Atlantic salmon in fighting ability, it is not unjust to say that the landlock has the best of it. The sea salmon is strong, moves heavily, and is almost deliberate in tak-

77

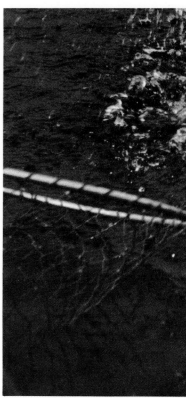

ing the fly and in employing river currents to do battle with the angler. The fresh-water salmon is smaller in size, but nonetheless powerful. He moves with greater speed and vivacity in attacking the lure and in putting on a show of action. A three- or four-pounder hooked on a fly at the surface creates the image of all that a game fish can be. When he strikes it is with a powerful thrust. On a trolled fly or lure he hooks himself before you are aware he is on. Invariably, he jumps at the first restraint of line and rod, and soars upward again and again until he shakes free or spends his power. He will give you half a dozen great leaps — no fish in quiet waters jumps higher or more often — make several rushes that start your reel singing, then bore deep, until your rod tip plunges beneath the surface. As you pressure him, he rolls and twists. When he sees the net, he summons up another burst of energy and speeds off once more in a hopeful dash. He has remarkable stamina; he never quite gives up. I have never reduced a mature landlock to that point of weariness which would allow me to lift him from the water with my hand. As tired as he may seem, the touch of a human hand will galvanize him and send him flurrying off

again. This can be a critical moment, the point at which many a fish has been lost. The net, in fishing for landlocks, is essential.

Landlocks can be found in the unrestricted waters of hundreds of lakes in northern New York, New England, and eastern Canada. Some streams are good landlock waters, too, notably the Kennebec in Maine and the St. Croix, which forms the boundary between Maine and Canada.

Each region has its own ideas about which lures are most effective for landlocks, a fact that is readily observable in local tackle shops. In streamer flies it is said that any pattern is good if it "looks like a smelt." I know of at least a dozen patterns, each purporting to simulate a smelt with no two quite alike. The landlock fisherman, like a woman choosing a hat, sometimes seems to exhibit little rhyme or reason in selecting his flies for trolling. The trouble is, I am certain, that the angler cannot view the fly or lure through the eye of the fish. If the Grey Ghost looks like a smelt then so can a Nine-Three, Supervisor, Green King, or Sanborn. The rule for taking a landlock—if rules there are—is to "keep the fly in the water."

Excitement of landlocked
salmon fishing is in the high leaps
and furious flurries
at the landing net. Hooked fish
fights to the end,
whether taken on spoon (above)
or trolling fly (below).

PACIFIC
Salmon

Admittedly, there is some question whether the Pacific salmon belongs in a book on fresh-water angling. These bold, strong fish spend most of their lives in the ocean depths following a life cycle still largely unknown. Only at the terminal points of their existence are they creatures of fresh water; they are born in the rivers and streams of the Northwest, from Oregon to Alaska, and at the end of their span they return to them to die.

Yet in the period of their spawning run, as they invade fresh water from the sea, the Pacific salmon, grown to magnificence and full of fight, are game fish far too worthy to be ignored.

There are two fish, two seasons, and two fishing methods for the fisherman to consider. The king salmon —also known as the spring, Chinook, or tyee, depending on where you are fishing—is the largest Pacific species, a great fish that regularly runs to more than sixty pounds. The silver salmon, or coho, is much smaller—say, five to fifteen pounds—but a much more active and volatile fighter. The king appears in April and can be fished through the summer (except in some of the streams of Alaska's southern coast where the fish are protected). The silver comes after the first fall rains, about September 1, and can be fished until the weather turns cold. Both can be caught in the "salt-chuck," where a river enters the sea, on fairly light tackle, with a plug or a strip of herring for bait. Or both will strike readily at a bucktail or other artificial lure in fresh water.

The king salmon begin to gather in the estuaries in the spring. They—and the silver salmon, too—wear the

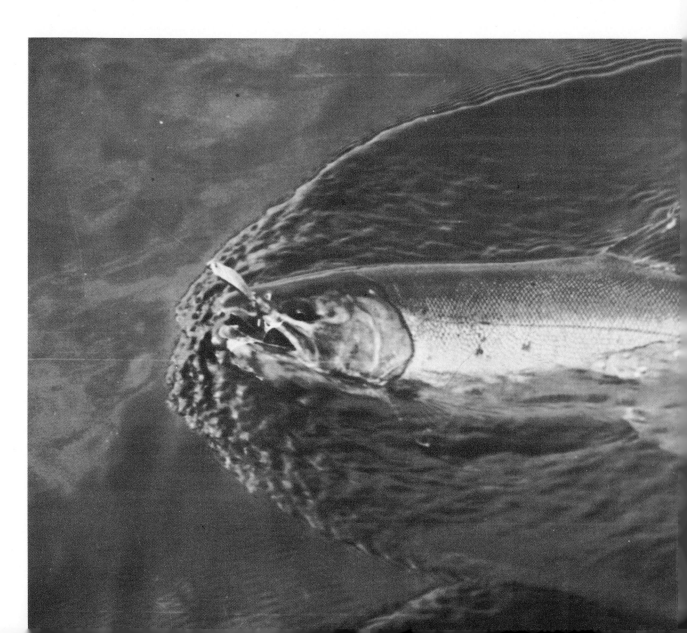

blue-green of the deep sea upon their backs; their sides shine with silver scales, and both sides and back are flecked with the black spots of the true salmon.

As the great kings move in toward shore, feeding bountifully on schools of herring, the fisherman may go "mooching" in a light skiff with a small outboard. The outboard will work against the tide rip, barely moving the skiff—just enough to give the herring strip bait a lifelike wiggle in the water. The kings feed best on these incoming tides and they do their dining fairly deep, from twenty to sixty feet down. But a two-ounce lead weight will carry bait and the light monofilament line to the proper level.

Sometimes a rapacious king will grab the bait without ceremony. At other times he lashes at it first with his broad, square tail to cripple the lively herring. You will feel only a faint tap on the thread line before he turns and seizes the bait with a rush. But once the hook takes hold he will "jig," shaking his head vig-

orously in movements that are quite clearly defined in your rod tip.

Then he's off on a powerful run, taking a hundred yards or more of line from the reel in a steady rip. No fisherman ever turns a king in his first run with sport tackle.

As the fish moves away it is well to keep pressure firmly on him, meanwhile making after him with the skiff and hoping he will tire of running while there still is line on the reel. At the end of his run he may breach, showing his broad side through the surface of the water, and with a lash of his tail submerge again for another run or a dive toward the bottom. A king seldom jumps clear when he is hooked and fighting. He is such a powerhouse that he depends on strength and speed to tear loose. He always makes his first bid for freedom under full power, but if you can stay with him to the end of the run you have a good chance of boating him.

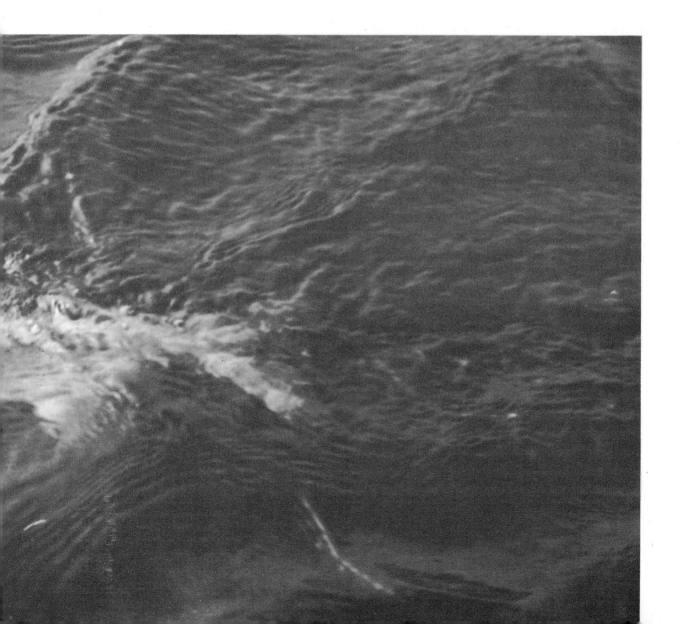

The largest king I ever hooked was taken near Ketchikan, Alaska. He was a fine fifty-two-pounder that my partner and I came upon while mooching in a tide rip that pours around the point of Grindell Island. Our plug-cut herring was about thirty feet down, at the end of an eight-pound monofilament line, rigged on heavy, fresh-water spinning tackle. The fish tapped the bait lightly at first, then seized it solidly. As I struck him, he chugged sharply, jerking his head a few times before he was off and away, down the edge of the tide rip and into the broad bay before us. He made off with about eighty yards of line before we could get started after him, and it was give and take for at least half an hour before we had him by the tail and securely into the boat.

This, of course, is salt-water fishing, although if you choose a stretch of coast line studded with wooded islands, the experience will have all the charm of fish-

ing an inland mountain lake. And here, in truth, is where most Pacific salmon are taken, but opportunities also abound once the salmon begin to move upstream. The sleek fish surge purposefully through the inland waterways of the Northwest, where deep, clear channels reflect the towering evergreens that line their banks, and snow-capped mountains rise in the distance. And finally, by July, they enter the cold mountain streams of their birth. Here, through the summer, you

can find kings by the thousands, lying fin to fin, each a streamlined, silver-plated form, strong, vital, and ready for action. Few angling experiences are more exciting than taking such a king on fly rod or stream spinning tackle.

I remember one spring when I was fishing the great rainbow and grayling country of the Katmai, in southwestern Alaska. I heard that the kings were coming back to Nak Nak River, near King Salmon, and I was

eager to tangle with one or two before ending my trip. Next morning I was casting over the Nak Nak where it meets the George River. I used the heaviest fly rod I had—a nine-and-a-half-footer—rigged with an Atlantic salmon reel, one hundred yards of line (fly line with backing), and a bushy bucktail fly. I could see the big kings finning their way in the current, about two feet below the surface, and I stole to within casting distance of one that appeared to be three feet long.

I dropped the big bucktail upstream, well above him, and watched it sink to the king's level, tightening the line a little just as the fly reached him, so I could swing it directly in front of his hooked nose. As it glided past him, the fish followed it for about a yard. Then he seized it with a grinding movement of his jaws. When the fly disappeared, I struck hard.

I felt as though I had tied onto a submerged log. But the fish seemed unconcerned. He drifted toward me slowly as I strained the flexible rod against him. Then, apparently seeing me for the first time, he went berserk. Up and out to the middle of the river he whipped, in a wild charge that straightened the rod out as if it were a piece of string. Quickly the drag on the fly reel took over; it sang mightily while the huge fish smashed out of the gliding current, turned, and rushed downstream. It was all I could do to follow him, stumbling over small, round polished stones as my line ran out.

Finally he stopped, ending the charge in a long, smooth glide and allowing me to keep a dozen yards of line on the spool. I reeled up line as I moved downstream toward him; then I came hard against him with the rod to stir him into action. Once more he lashed out above the surface, long and silver and blue, with a faint trace of red gleaming from his side. The tussle began anew—he maneuvering to free himself, and I to maintain what little control I had.

In time he tired, as did my rod arm, and grudgingly permitted me to lead him to the shallows along the foot of the run. There, lying on his side in the gravel-bottomed waters, he gasped from fatigue, causing one gill cover to lift just enough for me to slip my fingers in and raise him in one motion. He was a big fish, deep and long, with a broad tail and a cruel, wild head and a jaw hooked like a lobster claw. He was all I wanted to lift, probably well over thirty pounds. I never really knew. I turned him loose into the Nak Nak's waters to continue his run without further interruption.

The kings will have disappeared from these creeks by the time their smaller brothers, the silver salmon, arrive. Silvers run up in the fall, leaving salt water to seek their natal streams in early September. They provide fast light-tackle sport to the edge of winter.

The silver is a surface feeder. In the estuaries they chase needlefish, candlefish, and herring with great gusto, breaking on the surface as they chase the bait schools before them. Gulls and other shore birds wheel and cry above the tumult, darting and diving after the showers of minnows that erupt from the water in frantic efforts to escape the salmon.

It is here that a bright, long fly of bucktail or polar bear trolled from a fast-moving skiff along the edges of the feeding schools produces great top-water action.

Yet even better sport awaits the entry of fresh-run silvers into the small, wadeable streams on their way to the spawning grounds. Once in fresh water they take a fly readily. Bright, wet-fly patterns, in medium or small sizes, cast across the flow and drifted above the fish, just an inch or two under the surface, are temptation enough. The crafty fish will follow the fly for a moment or two, forming a V-ripple in the wake of the lure, before rising. When they finally take, they take hard, lashing at the fly and churning the water with a potent swirl.

In fighting form and habits, the silver bears about the same relationship to the king as the landlock does to the sea-run—his action is fierce, his maneuvers are spectacular. For, like his East Coast cousins, the Atlantic and landlocked salmons, the silver is a leaper, and about as proficient a leaper as any. The first prick of the steel makes him jump—a clean leap, high in the air, head pointed toward the sky, the burnished silver of his sides shining brightly in the fall sunlight. When he drops back, he drops back on his tail, and runs a bit before he leaps again. He may run as far as a hundred yards, hurdling periodically up and out of the water more than a dozen times. His jumps are the cleanest of all Pacific salmons, and for his size, the highest and longest.

His fight, however, like that of the sailfish, is a top-water frenzy in which he spends himself quickly. A ten-pounder will give about ten minutes of furious action —three or four long runs, a dozen or more flashing leaps, and a minute or two of flurrying near the boat or in the shallows before he sinks into the landing net.

So well created to cleave swift currents, their spirits ever resistant to the subjugation the fisherman promises, both silver and king are portraits of perfection in the giant family of fine finned creatures.

The
TROUT

BROOK
Trout

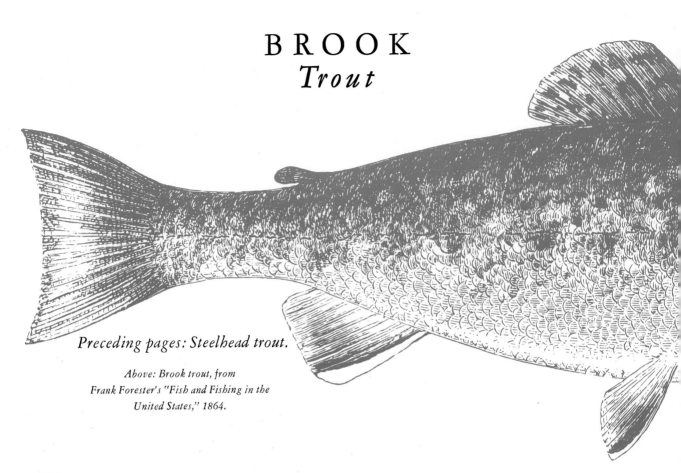

Preceding pages: Steelhead trout.

*Above: Brook trout, from
Frank Forester's "Fish and Fishing in the
United States," 1864.*

W i n t e r still gripped the stony bed of the mountain brook, subduing its chatter to a murmur. Thick, undulating, and unmarked stretches of white blended rocky bank and forest floor into an unbroken line. At every quiet pool, a framework of thin ice bridged the brook, leaving only a small dark opening here and there, where a tiny waterfall might run free and encourage the stream's movement. Sober gray limbs of nearby beech and maple trees spread weird tracings across the whiteness and over the pools. Further up, a wall of white pine lined the bank to form a murky cavern at a boulder-bound pocket of the stream.

The sunlight grew brighter now. Winter was waning. Its beams sparkled on the stalactites of ice framing the small cascades. These were the only bright spots over the hibernating landscape. Yet life stirred in the gloom of the ice-covered stream. Brook trout finned rhythmically near the polished stones of the stream's bed. Weeks would pass before warm winds from the south would bring a rise of water to break the blanket of winter and release the fish—to move as they pleased, to feed heavily on the insects of the stream, to begin anew the endless cycle of growth, renewal, and death.

In this quiet world of somnolence and semidarkness Fontis began life. At first he was an egg, the size of a small pea, faintly orange in color, one of several hundred which his mother, a silvery-blue henfish, had deposited in the coarse gravel under a shallow riffle. When the solid green canopy of foliage was swiftly changing to golds and reds, she had left the big river in the deep valley below, driving steadily up the tributary stream. Heavy with spawn, she fought successfully a dozen tiny waterfalls, a hundred swift glides of current. In each pocket and pool she rested her plump one-pound body to gain fresh strength for another assault on the water ahead. It took her seven days to move almost two miles from the home river, followed by two males, one of her own size, one slightly smaller. The males wore the bright red sides and belly coats of the spawning cock fish.

In the speckled shade of a gravel-bottomed riffle, she found a spot to her liking. Unaided by the males, who watched and waited downstream, she went to work on her bed. She pushed gravel up and out from

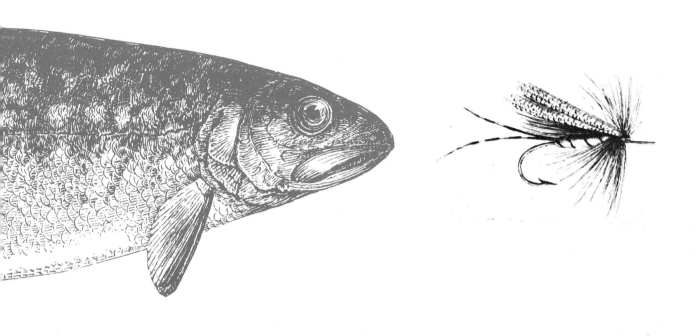

its natural level with her tail, paired fins, and body to form a shallow depression. Finally, she rested from her nest building, and began her share in the procreation of the salmonoids—twisting, weaving, over and into the depressed oval redd, until a short stream of gelatinous eggs spurted from her vent. When this was done, the larger male quickly rushed up to her, turned, and bumped her aside. As the eggs settled into the gravel, a milky stream squirted from his vent to follow and blanket the eggs. Some of the thousands of sperm would wiggle their way into some of the eggs, to complete the act of spawning.

Fontis, along with a few dozen of his brothers and sisters, now slept in the crevices of the gravel bed. Temperature, in time, would awaken them to life. From the eggs tiny wiggling forms eventually would emerge, each bearing a portion of the yolk sac—sustenance enough until the new fry could work up and out of the gravel to find food for themselves.

Fontis grew quickly as the warm sunshine of late spring took the chill from the water. Soon the last vestiges of the food sac disappeared, leaving him to fend for himself. He began to swim up toward the surface looking for food. There for a while he stationed his minute body—less than an inch long—near the bank and busily inspected every organism that the currents swept toward him. Unlike his cousins, the brown-trout fry, some of which shared his home riffle, Fontis ranged gaily from stream top to bottom with his brook-trout brethren. The young browns hugged bottom, not interested in surface food during the first few months of their lives.

By midsummer, Fontis became large enough to be visible to preying eyes. As his parr marks—dark splotches along his silvery sides—developed, he discovered that staying alive involved more than swimming about in the pulsing currents and looking for drifting food. He was particularly concerned one morning with a hatch of midges floating by, which, tiny as they were, would have been too much of a mouthful for him, although he was tempted to try one. Thus absorbed, he almost did not see the white flash of a kingfisher's belly, as it rattled and dove down from a dead stub, crashing into the water, pointed beak

*Lady angler (above) fights a brook trout on Manitoulin Island,
Ontario, which is noted for big square tails. Typical brook-trout streams
in New Hampshire (right) and Maine (far right).*

outthrust. Fontis fled under a flat rock on the stream bottom, as the bird broke from the surface carrying a wriggling trout toward his dead stub. Once perched, the kingfisher quickly turned the trout in his beak and swallowed it in a single gulp. Then, again he looked down from his perch to locate another victim. Fontis stayed under his rock until hunger drove him out for food, but this first lesson sent him scurrying for cover whenever a darting shadow passed over his feeding ground.

When the heavy rains of late summer swelled the mountain brook, Fontis moved downstream with the currents. The roil of water made him unsure of his position on the swift riffle and soon he took to lodging in a quiet pocket behind a rock, a dozen yards from his old home. Now almost two inches in length, he felt a little bolder about feeding on larger insects. He gulped dozens of tiny May-fly nymphs each day and picked small net-caddis from submerged rocks, where they clung in their little baskets, somewhat

precariously. Once, venturing across stream toward a dark hole under the bank, he was rushed by a big trout—all of ten inches long—and he barely escaped by boring into a crevice between two mossy stones, where the bigger fish could scarcely poke his head.

One summer day, Fontis had been alarmed by the sight of a water snake swimming over the pocket, carrying a flopping six-inch trout crosswise in its jaws. As the snake made for the security of the bank to swallow the fish at his leisure, Fontis ran out of the pocket in terror. He fled downstream, flipped over a small waterfall, and found another dark hole under another boulder for a hide-out. Here, where there was less current to fight and where the greater depth gave him a feeling of security, he made his new home for the oncoming winter.

Fontis did not grow much that winter. The temperature of his mountain brook dropped close to freezing; his body temperature dropped with that of the stream and slowed his metabolism. He did not feel the urge

to eat, nor did he feel the urge to forage about the pool bottom for nymphs or caddis. He took what came to his attention as the run of current carried it along.

With the coming of spring, the ice melted and Fontis could see the gray branches of the hardwoods swinging above the stream in the soft, warm breeze. He went about the business of digging hard-bodied May-fly nymphs from their hiding places in the gravel, often standing on his head as he groped for them. Stick caddis were somewhat easier to find since the penetrating rays of sunlight had warmed the stream bottom and they had started to move about, dragging their cleverly contrived houses with them. Fontis ate them —house and all.

The last patches of dirty snow were barely simmered into the leaf mold beneath the hemlocks when the first fly life of spring fluttered across the little pool where Fontis had made his home. These were the tiny, iron-gray May-fly duns which appear in mid-afternoon in early spring. Fontis had been watching

and feeding on the nymphs. His fins quivered in anticipation as the first of the nymphs, warmed by the sun's rays, broke toward the surface, shucked their leathery cases, and stood above water with wings erect toward the drying, warm sunshine. They rode and danced atop the current, sliding down the tiny waterfall that fed the pool, sweeping away to pirouette over a back eddy. Fontis stationed himself at the edge of the incoming flow, his one side caressed by the fast water, his other side soothed by the contra-current of the backwash. He dashed to the top as the tiny morsels began to appear over his window of vision, flipping and splashing the surface as he sucked in the tasty, fat-filled duns. His enthusiasm was often greater than his accuracy, for he made many false rises. Precision in taking a fly from the surface would come only after several days of feeding on the floaters. But now he did not care. The warm water invigorated him after the months of dullness and poor appetite. In an hour the hatch of tiny blue duns had sped from the stream

Trout anglers, from "The Complete Angler," Vol. 6, London.

and Fontis rested. The pouch of his stomach was crammed with insect delicacies.

The first rainstorms of spring brought a great rush of murky water down into the little pool. Fontis, along with the other brook trout of his size, moved further downstream, running the cascades, resting briefly in the pools, until they reached a point where the brook flattened out before disappearing into the great river. Here in a larger pool, broadened and eddied behind a huge boulder, Fontis made his final hold. He chose a spot between two moss-covered stones deep in the pool's bottom. He was almost six inches in length now, and he no longer feared attack from the bigger trout in the brook. The older, heavier fish in the river were something else again. He would not risk a foray there until the coming of winter.

While the dogwoods were filling the ridges with patches of white, Fontis was quickly maturing as a brook trout. His silvery sides filled out from good feeding as the later, larger hatches of May flies rode over his pool. When hatches did not appear—which happened some days—he grubbed busily on the bottom for stick or stone caddis and had already raised enough courage to engulf the large stone-fly nymphs that now and then worked up from the river. His parr markings had disappeared with his babyhood, rows of tiny red spots bloomed on his sides now, and the leading edges of his belly and anal fins were stark white. In the depths of the pool, shaded by the fresh green foliage, the bright colors on his body gleamed, as his background color darkened. In time, when he moved into the open water of the river, his background color would again turn to silver.

Fontis spent his second summer in the pool near the river. There was no lack of food, and the clear water tumbling down the wooded, rocky mountainside was always cool and charged with oxygen. Only in mid-August did the stream level drop perceptibly and the movement of insect life diminish. On one hot day, searching for better feeding grounds, he moved down into the river, threading his way between mossy rocks as he went. But the water of the big stream contained less oxygen than his brook and almost suffocated him at first. He swung quickly around to head up into the waters of his home brook. He struggled until it was nearly dark before he reached the comfort and security of his former lie, deep in the mossy pool bottom, where the dark shade of the hardwoods made for comfort.

Sunny days grew shorter; autumn's magic showed itself in the changing colors of the foliage. Deep greens blended into gold, then the brilliant reds of the oaks and maples broke through. And with this magic a change bloomed in Fontis. Still precocious perhaps, in his second year, his coat grew in brilliance with the foliage, and the first sex urge stirred within him. His rosy sides grew a deeper red, the vermiculations of his back became more distinct, the white edges of his lower fins became a truly dead white, and the fins a glowing pink. With his tiny milt sacs filled for the first time, he was ready to ascend to the headwaters of his domain to await the arrival of mates.

His urge was strengthened by watching the larger male trout, each in his gaudy spawning coat, pass through the pool. And when the first of the fat females passed by, in their less flamboyant garb of silvery blue, his excitement grew. On an October morning, when frost glistened on the boulders at the side of the stream, his impulse was triggered.

His first upstream obstacle would be the most strenuous of the journey—the little waterfall, about two feet high, at the head of his home pool. His initial attempt was a feeble leap, bringing him barely six inches above the surface, and he flopped ungracefully back into the roil of current. After a few minutes of rest, the next jump carried him well up the fall. His body buried in the descending flow, his tail flipped furiously. For a few seconds he hung there, then the drive of that broad tail carried him up and over the lip into the quieter glide above.

The upstream passage was easy thereafter. He moved steadily over the shallow riffles, sputtered up the cascades, encouraged always by the trailing scent of the gravid females ahead. Hours later he came to rest in a flat, shallow riffle already occupied by a nest-building henfish. And as he moved eagerly toward her side, fins fluttering expectantly, he was rushed by a

Brook trout are found in fast-water pockets in this small, rocky stream.

93

hook-jawed male twice his size. The blow drove him to the side of the run where he sought shelter under a flat rock. Fontis had to wait his turn.

His turn did not come for several days. The henfish, after releasing part of her egg load for the attentions of the big male, covered the nest with gravel and moved on upstream to build again. The cock fish followed, leaving the field to Fontis. More henfish stopped in the riffle as the days passed, but always larger males appeared to frustrate his ardor.

Dawn of his last day on the riffle found Fontis alone. The larger fish had gone, some of the spent males had already passed down to the river. About midmorning a young female, somewhat larger than Fontis, moved up from the pocket below. By then he knew the ritual well and, undisturbed, he spent his ardor in response to her nest building. As darkness came on he drifted down toward his home pool. Sunrise found him at the great river. There he rested over the sand-and-gravel bar washed out by the stream of his birth. He had completed the first full cycle in the life of a brook trout.

Once again, Fontis spent the winter uneventfully. He stayed in the deep run near the brook's mouth, lying near a rock, feeling the greater surge of current from the river. Earlier, winter ice had locked up the eddies along the river's shores, and he had fed well,

regained his strength, and had grown to a foot in length. The river abounded in food life—large stonefly nymphs, hellgrammites, nymphs of the dragonfly, and the swift little black-nosed dace, which were difficult to catch but invigorating to chase. By dead of winter, Fontis was again on his normally meager diet of cased caddis, which served him well enough until the spring thaw.

With April's showers came the first spring freshet. It raised the level of the feeder brook to match the full-flowing mass of the river, still at its peak from melting snows pouring down from high mountain headwaters above. The rise brought a new food supply and Fontis fed eagerly at the break of current, in the confluence of brook and river. The waters were still cold, and he had not yet begun to look for insects working near the surface—for there were none, other than a few of the tiny, midafternoon, blue duns that at this stage of his life were insignificant to him as food. His taste one particular morning leaned toward a bigger mouthful.

Vivid coloration of the male brook trout contrasts strongly with the more somber female in this Canadian pair.

Fly-fishing for trout, from "The Complete Angler," Vol. 6, London.

"Sunrise, Fishing in the Adirondacks," by Winslow Homer. Courtesy of Colonel Edgar W. Garbisch, New York.

He had already picked up a hellgrammite and pouched a few stone-fly nymphs as they eddied over the gravel bar. And he had given chase, although briefly and unsuccessfully, to a small school of minnows. Fontis was alert, then, for the flash of any small, food fish hovering over the tail end of the gravel bar. When the flash came swinging out of the river current toward his lie, he was ready. He met it swiftly, surely, in a side attack. The flash ended between his jaws as they snapped over a hard, unyielding object. Fontis felt his head jerked roughly to one side, felt restraint as he fought the odd pressure leading him from the familiar surge of river current. Regaining his headway with a thrash of his tail, he made for the heavy swell at mid-river to enlist the power of the stream. But the thrust of his wide tail was not enough. His dash ended in a tightening arc upstream, where he was forced to stop by the rush of the current and the added pressure of fine monofilament, stretched taut by a stiff spinning rod. Turning now, he dove across the gravel bar, driving into the mouth of the brook that had always given him security. It was not to be. He buried his head in the shelter of a mossy rock, turned toward the surface, rolled and twisted there for a moment, but finally flopped on his side. He was still writhing vigorously as he felt the meshes of the net swing beneath him. Fontis had met his fate, and the angler had had his sport—a brief encounter with a foot-long brook trout.

∾

The brook trout, in itself, is a thing of rare beauty. Shiny and smooth, with no visible scales, its colors are at once subtle and vivid. The age-old phrase among fishermen "bloom of trout" was born of the brook trout. For here are nature's colors: the pink of the wild rose, the yellow of the adder's tongue, the green of ferns, the white of dogwood, the blue of the sweet flag. His spawning red and rows of red spots match the cardinal's hue in brilliance.

He is now, and always has been, a fish of clear, clean, cool waters, a child of the wilderness, forever upholding the scientific name offered him a century and a half ago, *Salvelinus fontinalis*—which means, literally, a diminutive of a salmon "living in springs."

Our first anglers in inland waters fished for them for food and sport, and it is certain that these were the first fish to be taken on an artificial fly. In these early days, brook trout abounded in all spring-fed waters of the Northeast and as far south as Georgia.

His choice of waters—when given a choice naturally—is always pleasurable to fishermen. Shaded, brisk mountain brooks, small, deep-running meadow creeks, and little forest-locked wilderness ponds top his list of homes. In recent times, forced entry into less picturesque waters has been inflicted upon the fish, but, happily, his basic instincts will not permit him to tolerate slovenly surroundings for long. If there is an escape, he will run to purer headwaters, or turn about and head for the sea. If there is no escape, he dies. Along with the grayling, this is the most fastidious fish in fresh water. He is sensitive to hot and cold, too. Temperatures above seventy degrees enervate him; held in water above seventy-eight degrees, he dies.

The works of man have reduced the range and abundance of the brook trout considerably, but this does not mean the fish are scarce. Extensive restocking has carried it west into all the states of the northern belt, although once brook trout were not found west of the Mississippi. They now range throughout most of southern Canada and are, in fact, the most widely distributed of all the salmonoid species. Along the northeastern coasts they run to sea and return as "sea trout"—much larger than the average stream fish, sheathed in silver, deep bellied and heavy from lush feeding in the ocean.

The brook trout has always been accused of being a ravenous feeder. Of this he is surely guilty. In all types of water, he has a cosmopolitan appetite and is not dedicated, in adulthood, to a diet of insects. All small creatures living within, on, or around his stream or pond are acceptable to him. The stomach of one two-pounder, for example, gave up a few score tiny insect larvae, a couple of newts, a brace of small frogs, three black-nosed dace, a beer-bottle cap, and a mouse. In addition, this fish was taken on a Red Ibis bass fly to which was rigged an aluminum dog license!

In spite of the menu of miscellany favored by one rugged brook trout, the species as a whole feeds on insects in one form or another for about seventy-five per cent of its diet, most of which is taken under the

Five-pound brook trout come only from remote, wild waters in the north.

surface. Frederick Halford stated in 1897 that floating food is the trout's caviar, but "sunk or underwater food" is its beef. Halford was, of course, referring to the brown trout, but the rule also applies to our native speckled variety.

The average-sized eastern brook trout, aside from the golden variety of the High Sierras, is the smallest member of the trout family taken by fishermen. This eastern trout leads a short but happy life in ideal surroundings, seldom passes the age of five years, and can vary enormously in size at this maximum age. In some remote headwater streams and isolated north-country ponds—where fishing is light or nonexistent—many brook trout live and die before reaching a length of ten inches. Limited food supply in overcrowded waters stunts their growth. In the headwaters of West Canada Creek in New York's Adirondacks, for example, it is no problem to take fifty trout in a day on the fly. Many of them may be four- and five-year-old fish,

although not one will be over six inches in length. Back-country trout ponds in wilderness regions of Maine and Canada often hold no trout over a foot long for the same reasons.

Most stream fishermen, angling in brook-trout waters that are readily available, will pass their entire lives without encountering a brook trout in the two-pound class. This trout is such a gay, eager, and omnivorous feeder that he is almost certain to fall victim to bait, fly, or lure during his second or third year—and stream trout simply do not grow large in this short span of life.

But there are still many waters where big brook trout can be taken. The key word is "wilderness." The situation today is little different from that of a century ago, when a few wealthy anglers in search of three-pounders would trek into the Adirondack Mountains by train, in horse and buggy, or by guide boat. The waters they fished can now be reached easily

97

Brook trout taken from Basha's Kill, N. Y.

by car, and heavy tapping of these streams has depleted their stock. This generation's sportsmen must go deeper into the wilderness, far from highways, to areas where only a float plane offers ready access. The big brook trout are still with us—three-, four-, even seven-pounders can be hooked in the lakes of northern Maine, Quebec, Ontario, and other remote areas where the fish can live in cool, unpolluted water, feed well, and are tempted less often by the angler's lure. The pattern is not so much "know-how" as "know-where," for these fish respond to all legal angling techniques.

The pair of big brook trout shown on page 95 was taken forty-six miles from the nearest highway, at the end of a three-day, paddle-and-portage canoe trip. (A float plane could have shortened the three days to about one hour.)

The history of American fish culture begins with the brook trout—oddly enough, in Ohio in 1853. Here Dr. Theodatus Garlick and Professor Ackley undertook to strip male and female trout of milt and eggs; then hatched the eggs. Their experiment produced fingerling trout. During the Civil War years, Seth Green, generally considered the father of artificial fish propagation in America, carried on the experiments on a larger scale at Caledonia, New York. The post-Civil War period began a boom in trout production for the market, since the supply of wild fish was already on a serious downgrade.

The program of restoring wilderness ponds in recent years has been a good one. It has been marked with success in producing fish of two pounds or more, in waters that for many years were filled with stunted six-inchers and competing hordes of perch and rough fish. The operation involves poisoning of the pond with rotenone to kill all fish life. The following year, after the pond has been purged, advanced fingerling trout and the proper food life are stocked in the barren waters, and a new start is made. Many of these ponds are producing three-pound brook trout within three years of their restoration. These waters, however, are still quite remote, in the Adirondack Preserve, and will remain so for the foreseeable future—a good thing for both the trout and the fisherman.

And, as the airplane aids the fisherman in reaching big-trout waters in the back country, so does it aid in replenishing the supply of fish. Brook trout are carried in aerated tanks in the belly of the plane, and are dumped, without ceremony, into the pond as the plane swoops low over the water. Survival of the fish is, oddly enough, quite high after such rough handling.

The special regard in which the brook trout is held by American anglers is somewhat paradoxical. For one thing, he is not a true trout but, rather, one of the smaller members of the char family, which includes the lake trout, Dolly Varden, Arctic char, and others not so well known. True trout have readily visible scales. Chars have them too, but theirs are tiny and buried deep in the skin. Secondly, the brook trout is by no means a spectacular fighter. He is a savage striker, true enough, but once hooked, he rarely shows himself above water. He rushes in short, quick dashes as pressure is applied with the rod, bores deep when he can, and shows no reluctance whatever to foul leader or line around underwater snags, tree roots, or whatever may be handy. He gives fervent battle, but spends himself quickly. The rainbow outleaps him and the brown outlasts him.

Neither is he at his best in the element that gave him his name—the brook. In a small stream he is a gay blade, indeed, but he simply does not grow very large in a brook. He achieves his greatest size, weight, and power in a pond—with a few exceptions like the Nipigon and Albany Rivers in Ontario, which are somewhat out of the "brook" class. Brook trout of "squaretail" proportions are pond fish, two pounds or more, with enough age behind them to develop longer central rays of the caudal fin. Thus the "square" tail.

Yet the brook trout has much to recommend him. An old Spanish proverb offers a clue: "Through the mouth dies the fish." His ravenous appetite and willingness to rise to a fly on or near the surface or, in the next instant, pick up a worm rolling along the bottom, endears him to most fishermen. He is one of the easiest game fish to catch—at the right time and place.

On a canoe trip down the St. Croix River in New Brunswick, I witnessed a perfect example of this trout's complete disregard for the niceties of selectivity. During the late afternoon a great hatch of large May-fly duns fluttered over the smooth, swift currents of a long run. Brook trout were gulping them in a frenzy. Fish were rising all along the run, smaller fish near the middle, heavier trout pushing up bow waves near the tail. I selected one fish for a cast and dropped a wet Cahill ahead of the trout's lie. At once the trout came, in a heavy, surging rise, sucking in the fly solidly as it swung just under the surface. I struck hard, too hard, leaving the fly in the fish, apparently disturbing him not at all. My partner, not impressed with the gentle art of fly-fishing, was rigged with a strip of trout belly on a bait hook—after big game. As the fish continued to suck in surface flies, I suggested that he might come to the strip bait. Making a short cast from the bow of the canoe, my friend worked the wiggling morsel over the same spot my fly had reached. Again the trout came solidly, felt the hook, and rushed downstream. We netted a fat two-pound, male brook trout, extracted from his long upper jaw the long-shanked bait hook and, next, from his hooked lower jaw, my #8 Cahill.

Fontinalis is an image. You can take him from a stream crossed by a superhighway where he has been dumped "for the rod," knowing full well that he is not long out of the hatchery. His basic form is still the same, albeit his fins may be frayed a bit. His colors will be dim and his belly gray and pudgy. But there will still be the silver shine of a waterfall along his sides, faint traces of mossy brook-bed boulders in the twisting wormlike markings over his narrow shoulders. For this is *Salvelinus fontinalis,* and he is of noble lineage.

R A I N B O W
Trout

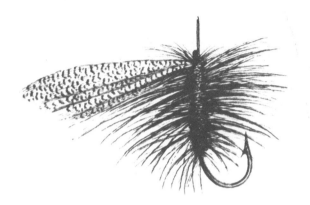

A fisherman's first view of a rainbow trout is likely to be fleeting, but it will remain forever etched in his memory. The fish appears suddenly, its body full bowed over the white water of rapids, or the smooth slickness of a deep run. The arched, twisting form shines pink and silvery in the sun. A spray of sparkling water droplets surrounds him as he breaks the surface, reflecting glints of opal and mother-of-pearl as, momentarily, he becomes air-borne. The rainbow, like his cousin Salar, is a leaper. He takes to the air when the hook first pricks him.

Long ago some unknown, but singularly astute angler-naturalist gave the rainbow his name. None could be better. For his frantic above-water gyrations inevitably produce the full arc of a rainbow—and the colors are all there. Only when he runs to sea is the bright rose-pink of his side stripes subdued as it slowly turns to silver.

Of the true trouts—and oddly enough, all of these were originally western species in America—the rainbow is the only native American to achieve world importance. In the beginning, he was at home exclusively in the coastal streams flowing into the Pacific, from California to Alaska's Bristol Bay. (When first transplanted to eastern waters in the 1880's, he was called the California trout.) But the beauty, fighting qualities, and hardiness of this trout were not to be restricted to Pacific Coast waters for long. During the early days of fish propagation, rainbows were introduced to the

A fighting rainbow
is engaged by
Roderick Haig-Brown,
famous Northwest angler (left).
Fish weighed six pounds,
was caught on a fly
in a coastal river, original
home of all rainbows.

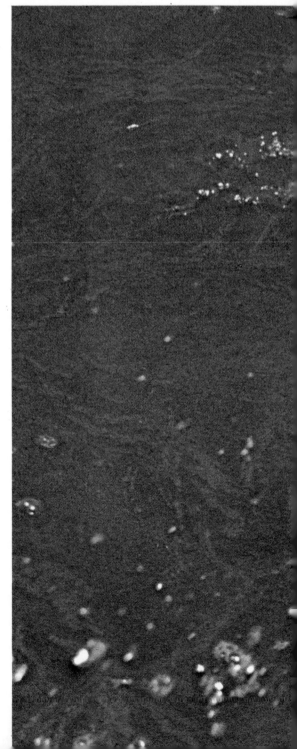

No waters are too fast for rainbows, even big streams of the high Rockies.

rivers of the Ozarks, the Alleghenies, New England, and Michigan. They are now found almost everywhere in the United States and, by more recent transplants, in such far-off places as Africa, Chile, India, Australia, and New Zealand. The sad truth is that rainbows have done better in some foreign waters than in our own American lakes and streams. Chilean and New Zealand rainbows, for example, are among the world's largest.

Like the area of his origin, the rainbow has a lusty, brawling character. If rainbows are planted in feeder streams, along with brook trout, it will not be long before the brook trout are free of competition. The rainbow is constantly on the move toward bigger waters, and eventually to the sea. This migratory tendency is a problem that has forever beset fish-culturists. To keep him in hand you must offer him a large body of water for a home base or dam the streams to hold him.

Rainbows grow fast and they grow big. Further, they enjoy a longer life span than brook trout. A four-year-old fish from New York's Finger Lakes, for example, may be more than twenty inches long and weigh up to eight pounds. These fish will continue to grow until their age limit of eight years has been reached, and often become prize fish of twelve pounds plus. Big lake rainbows of the Pacific Northwest (Kamloops) frequently reach thirty pounds or more. Obviously, food and water conditions must be ideal to produce trout of this size, but they surely respond when the situation is right.

The stream rainbow is the angler's choice as an adversary. He is always at home in fast water; the spirit of the stream lives in his muscular body. When he comes to the flash of a spinner or spoon, it is with a savage rush, an underwater gleam of red-silver that winks briefly as the rod tip curves down. To a drifting, sunken fly his rise may be less savage, but just as sure in the attack. The gleam of his bright body may be still brighter since his side turns closer to the sky. A floating fly he meets head on with a great push of water, and a big trout will often leave a bucket-sized hole in the surface where before the fly rested.

Not only are the rainbow's habitats varied, but his tastes are catholic. In a stream matching his size—which may mean a fish as large as three pounds—he is an insect feeder. When his bulk is not too great, this diet satisfies him. But as is true of all trout, the rainbow

102

is ever alert for tiny tidbits which vary his diet and permit him to be fooled by the angler's artificials.

As the rainbow moves to bigger waters, his appetite becomes more demanding. Stream minnows tempt him. In the East—Esopus Creek in the Catskills, for example—he preys upon the black-nosed dace. In the West, the sculpin or bullhead of the rivers is his mainstay. The big rainbow is usually sought with the bucktail or streamer by fly casters, or with the natural minnow by less fastidious anglers. A red-and-white-striped wobbling spoon, or any flashy spinner or wobbler, has victimized thousands of big rainbows in their river habitats. In the murky waters of the Colorado and Gunnison Rivers, or the Yellowstone of Montana, more big rainbows are taken on bright hardware than on any other type of lure.

Lake-bound rainbows convert quickly from immature insect feeders to minnow eaters. A young fish spawned in a feeder stream of a large lake begins the normal trout life feeding on flies. During his second year, he abandons the stream for his parental home in the lake, where he feeds on the more filling food fish native to those waters, and so grows quickly. Usually this diet is made up of ciscoes, sawbellies, kokanee, smelt, or whatever. From this stage on, this rainbow becomes an all but unattainable target for the fly caster.

When he is a mature fish, the rainbow runs up the spawning streams to gorge on fish eggs—very likely the spawn of his brethren. The rainbow's penchant for eating the spawn of his fellows is so great that laws have been enacted to prohibit the use of rainbow eggs as bait. Primarily, these laws seek to deter scavengers, lacking the spirit of conservation, from entering spawning streams to strip female trout of their eggs and sell them to hopeful fishermen. As a substitute for the real thing, the fisherman can bait his tiny, short-shanked hook with tapioca dyed to a salmon-pink, or with a glob of carbolated Vaseline, first chilled in the cold stream, then shaped with the lips to simulate a salmon egg.

In Alaskan waters, great runs of big rainbows follow the spawning salmon to the redds, hoping to gorge on the eggs that fail to reach the security of the gravel bottom. At the height of the sockeye run in the Bristol Bay watershed, the headwaters teem with spawning salmon, brilliant red in color, grotesque in shape, and all engaged in the fight to perpetuate their kind. The shallow riffles are literally covered with weaving red forms rushing the currents, resting in the pools, constantly moving upstream in search of the proper gravel bed for nest building. When a good bottom has been found, the female begins to prepare the nest, while the humpbacked, pincer-jawed males await the completion of her task. Not far behind the engrossed salmon, a rear echelon of rainbow trout fin the waters patiently, waiting for the discharge of eggs. While many eggs drop to safety in the scooped-out nest, a fair number drift downstream to the poised trout.

Fishing for these big rainbows becomes a matter of selection. Although the sockeyes—"Russian trout" to the Katmai native—are by no means desirable game during their spawning period, it is not easy to avoid hooking one on a random cast. And, even if your fly or lure manages to weave through the forest of dorsal fins and tails over the redds, the sockeye will resent the presence of a foreign object near his nest and may strike at the offering. Taking the salmon is strictly taboo from the point of view of a sportsman. In addition, a foulhooked sockeye, weighing six pounds or

Pausing to lunch, from "The Complete Angler," Vol. 4, London.

more, will rob you of valuable fishing time before you can follow him fifty yards or so downstream, beach him, free your lure or fly from his bear-trap jaws, and release him in the river to resume his life's work.

In these fast-flowing, crystal-clear waters rushing over gravel bottoms sparkling with mica, fishing for rainbows takes on some of the qualities of the hunt. The fish must be located, then stalked. The rainbow's form, lying behind the bright-red spawning fish, appears as a dark shadow over the stream bottom. You carefully study the currents ahead of the fish, noting the water's depth and speed. You make a judgment in the cast to pass the fly just above the trout's nose and carefully out of reach of the salmon. If your fly is well chosen, meaning a pattern with a fat, orange-red body that could be a string of salmon eggs, the rainbow should tilt upward slightly and a long line of white should appear as he opens his jaws to suck in the fly. A quick lift of your rod to set the hook will, without question, be met with an abrupt explosion as the fish boils out of the clear, swift water in protest.

In Alaskan waters where the rainbows are at a peak of vigor and beauty, the response to the sting of steel is immediate and spectacular. Often, if a long cast across a wide stream creates a deep down-current belly in the line, the rainbow will be over the surface, with the lure jingling, before you feel the thrust of his strike.

I remember casting for big rainbows early one spring at the outlet of Nonphyanek Lake in the Katmai. Here, in late May, the waters are high but clear, and the river swells as it breaks from the lake, flowing swiftly and smoothly, quickening its pace toward the rapids below. The width of the stream where I stood was at least two hundred feet, and the trout lay deep in its middle, where the water looked black over the gravel and small, round stones on the bottom. Since it was far too early in the season for fly-fishing, I was leisurely tossing a small gold wobbler across the center of a heavy flow slightly upstream and letting it sink well down before tightening the line in retrieve. The spoon worked its provocative wiggle directly crosscurrent from my location, and the thin monofilament was bowed well downstream, ahead of the working lure. My first few casts did not allow the wobbler to make the right depth. I was testing the speed of the current, checking the time lag before turning the spinning-reel handle,

giving a second or two more on each succeeding cast. Absorbed, then, for a few minutes in the mechanics of the problem, I was not prepared for the big fish breaking clear from the center of the river, directly in front of me, some twenty-five yards away. He came clear out, three or four feet into the air, all pink, silver, and green, then dropped back with a great show of spray. Until he disappeared beneath the slick I felt nothing—and the thought flashed by that he had rushed the lure and missed. But as the thought faded I felt him come hard against the rod tip. Now as the trout felt the hook sink in well, he rushed out into the air again. One, two, three more jumps—then back out of sight to shoot down the swift flume of the current, into the white water below.

He made fifty yards down river before the drag checked him. He leaped frantically at least another half-dozen times, fought the churning current and the reel drag in mid-river, and then, tiring, swept out toward the bank below me. I followed him for almost a hundred yards before I could pressure him into shallow water. Here he struggled valiantly to stay upright. But he was tired. He rolled, turning his broad rose stripe toward the Alaskan sky, and at last permitted me to free the small treble hook from his lower jaw.

I watched him swim away in the quick water, slowly as he gained headway, then with a tremendous burst of tail action that sprayed me from the hat brim down with the chill waters of Nonphyanek. I wiped my glasses, went back upstream to the dark, swift channel, and caught another six or seven rainbows. These were apparently from the same hatch, for they were all of a size—perhaps five pounds or a bit more.

Curiously enough, each fish gave the same performance in taking the lure. First came the clean, fast break from the river, the spray and splash as he dropped back, and the sharp tug at the rod tip as the hook bit. Then it was away, down into the rapids, leaping, shooting across stream. There was no pause in the fight to escape until exhaustion put each gladiator on his side in the shallows, awaiting the end. In each case, happily, I could write no end. These rainbows all were returned to the river.

The rainbow in hand, fresh from the stream, is a creature of great beauty. You note first, if you are already familiar with brook and brown trouts, his smaller, rounded head. His back and upper sides are sprinkled with black spots—a lot of them—which run in rows across the length of his broad tail. Dark spots on a lighter background are the mark of the true trout as

against one of the char family, which show *light* spots on a *dark* background. If the rainbow is a truly wild fish, his belly will gleam dead white, his back a vibrant green. Between will lie the broad pink band of his sides and, if you look closely, faint tinges of blue and purple can be seen on gill covers and, sometimes, the upper edge of his stripe. His form is clean and streamlined, fashioned to cleave fast water and to hold in the swiftest currents with a minimum of effort. I am quite fond of rainbows.

The rainbow adds much to a fly-fisher's life. He dotes upon insects until he reaches lunker size—and these larger fish are seldom the ones a fly caster expects to meet. He rises to the fly with a gay abandon—a swirl and attack seldom matched by other trouts. And his response has changed little over the years. He is continually attracted by colorful fly patterns, particularly those with colors that match his own. A half century ago, Dr. Henshall wrote: "No trout surpasses the rainbow in rising to the artificial fly, and almost any trout fly will capture it, though the Silver Doctor, Coachman, and the different hackles, seem to be more favored than others."

In the East, the fly angler lures his rainbows with the somber "natural" patterns. In the West, he offers a

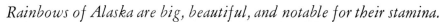

Rainbows of Alaska are big, beautiful, and notable for their stamina.

A pair of early spring rainbows from Alaska's Nak Nak River.

host of gaudy flies. In the high mountain lakes and streams, the scale of brilliance in fly patterns increases with the elevation: the higher the waters, the brighter the flies. This, of course, is a reflection of the sophistication of the trout. The high mountain rainbows see fewer fishermen and fewer lures, and they are as easily excited by a fly that looks as though it might be good to eat as by one which closely imitates a natural food. Rainbows have taken flies for me that were dead black, dead white, and every possible variation in between.

As to sizes in flies, I have tangled with big rainbows in western irrigation ponds, where the fish fed mainly on fresh-water shrimp, and found them rising best to a #16 hard-backed nymph. In the brawling Nak Nak River, feeding Alaska's Bristol Bay, rainbows of similar weight were more interested in a #2 Alaska Mary Ann, a large wet fly, almost all white and tied with polar-bear hair wing.

Probably the rainbow, more than any other trout, responds best to the fly-caster's efforts. There is no doubt at all that he satisfies the dry-fly fisherman's hope of taking a five-pound trout on the floater more readily than either the native brook trout or the brown. The fish simply retains the urge to take surface insects longer than most other trouts.

Rainbows fill the gap left by other trouts: the brook trout in the East, the cutthroat in the West. They can withstand higher water temperatures than other native trouts, and would probably have replaced the eastern brook trout long ago if it were not for the rainbow's compelling desire to run down to the sea.

For considerably more than a quarter century, I have fished the Neversink River in the New York Catskills. Before my day, much before, the upper reaches of this stream were well stocked with legal-sized rainbows every year. And yet, while I have taken thousands of brook and brown trout from these waters, the rainbows I have encountered can be numbered on two hands. The water is fast, cool, and well aerated, and the stream is surely large enough to make a rainbow happy, but this species seems to head for the Delaware almost as soon as it is big enough to travel.

The "father of American dry-fly fishing," Theodore Gordon, was also confounded by the fleeting nature of the rainbow. Recounting his experiences fishing another of these Catskill waters, in the *Fishing Gazette,* in 1907, Gordon wrote regretfully: "Formerly there was a grand stock of the rainbow trout in this stream, the Esopus, but since the advent of the brown trout they have decreased greatly in size.... Rainbows have often done well for two years and then disappeared. They try to go to sea, probably."

In the same year, Gordon cheerily described his bout with some rainbows: "Last week I killed three species of trout in one stream, *fontinalis, fario,* and *irideus* (rainbow); this was a pleasant surprise, particularly the taking of the rainbow trout. What gay fellows they are! They leap and fight until completely exhausted."

Two years later, he took the prevaricating angler to task: "The ancient habit of lying about fish of all kinds is a wretched nuisance. . . . I read a story about the Esopus recently, which gave an account of wonderful sport had in that stream in April. Brown trout were killed up to 6½ lb. and the rainbows *averaged* 2½ lb. [Actually] the rainbows do not run [that] large, and have averaged much smaller since the *fario* (brown) were introduced. They never *averaged* 2 lb."

Fishermen who cast in the Esopus today will not be disappointed as Gordon was. For despite their seeming rarity, rainbows are at home there. They are now prevented from running down to the sea by the Ashokan Reservoir and its fishproof dam. Landlocking these fish is apparently the only reliable means of controlling them for the fishermen of eastern waters.

Each spring, these eastern streams are replenished by the annual spawning run—a well-heralded and exciting event. The run-up fish are always large, for a lake rainbow seldom spawns until its fourth year. And the smaller, immature trout stay to populate the stream throughout the fishing season, offering good fly-fishing for eastern anglers before migrating to some larger body of water, be it reservoir or lake. In some ways, this is part of the age-old pattern of migration inherited from the rainbow of the West Coast, the difference between the eastern and western migrations being the difference between a large body of fresh water and the open sea.

Although rainbows are, and have always been, spring spawners, selective breeding and environmental evolution is gradually developing a new strain in the eastern variety. The new breed will spawn in autumn, during the same season as brook and brown trouts. This will not provide large rainbows for this season's angler, but the protection of "closed-season" conservation laws will give the species time to recreate itself to the ultimate benefit of future fishermen.

STEELHEAD

Trout, from
"The Complete Angler,"
Vol. 6, London.

Everything you can say about the rainbow doubles when the talk is of steelhead. This wild, mystical fish, starting life as a rainbow trout in the headwaters of the coastal rivers from California to Alaska, gains strength and beauty in the depth of ocean currents. Fresh from the sea, he is a spirit incarnate of wild waves and rushing rivers, for he has experienced both in his few years of life. The steelie—*Salmo gairdnerii*—is king of the trout family in America.

A steelhead remains a steelhead only in the rivers of his natural birth. When transplanted to other waters, he reverts quickly to his rainbow ancestry. Evidence of this may be seen in every steelhead, from the many black spots on his body to the pink bands on his sides. Yet, while the lovely coloration is there, the steelhead has a rapacious look, lacking in smaller members of the family. The sea gives him a wild, savage aspect— the head of a hawk, the jaws of a wolf, and the glinting, fire-filled eyes of a mountain lion. With your hook fixed to a steelhead you feel the fierceness of these characteristics in his driving runs, his passionate, high jumps to free himself, his rolling and twisting over the leader as his vibrant energy subsides. A battle with a steelhead is a memorable, soul-filling, and often frightening phenomenon. No previous experience with fish can prepare you completely for that first encounter with a fresh-run steelhead.

107

A veteran of vigorous years in the sea is this eighteen-pound, fresh-run summer steelhead (left) from the Sustut River in British Columbia. Another big steelie (right) splashes the angler in surprising final bid to escape.

The big, brawny fish come into northwestern rivers during late autumn, ripe with eggs or with filled milt sacs, ready to spawn. Usually, a heavy spate of river water starts them on the way and, when the word goes out that the steelies are arriving, fishermen descend to the rivers with their long bait rods and "strawberries" of egg clusters, tied in tiny red bags of veiling or cheesecloth. For, unlike the fasting salmon entering fresh water to spawn, steelhead are feeders. Fish eggs tempt them most, although some bait fishermen use worms or crayfish tails. Others fish deep with flashy spoons or spinners, as all baits and lures for winter steelhead must be fished.

The steelhead travels continually from the time he arrives in fresh river water. The trick in taking him with bait or lure is to know his path of migration. He sticks to the deep channels in open water, disdains hiding places among boulders or log jams. In this re-

spect, he is similar to the Atlantic salmon. A good steel-header knows how to "read water" and can predict, by a studied inspection of the run, just where the fish probably will be found.

These "winter" fish are always heavy with spawn. A few are taken on flies by the hardier anglers, but these are not the real trophies for fly casters. As a rule, the time of the winter run finds the streams high and muddy, the fish running along the bottom. To take them, whatever bait or lure is used must be fished just off bottom, on a slow drift.

But "summer" fish are much different. These are trout at the absolute peak of life and energy, with spawn just developing. They feed briskly, rise with a purposeful attack to a fly, and fight like demons. Summer fish begin to run the rivers in May, and at that time are nearly a year away from their breeding period. True, they are not as large as winter fish; they generally

109

Contemplative angler casts, hooks a leaping, silvery steelhead, lands him without ceremony.

*Every steelhead struggles
to the end. Buzz Fiorini (below),
now has his fish,
although many steelhead are lost
in the final stage
of the encounter, either by
tearing out the fly
or breaking the leader.*

average between six and ten pounds, but they make up for the difference in weight with spirited fighting ability. These are the fly-fisherman's dream—big enough to test tackle to the limit, yet attainable with fairly light rods and small flies.

The summer fish, fresh from the sea, are clad in the same silvery sheath as the steelhead that come later, during the winter run. But they soon develop the pink stripe along the lateral line, with a touch of red on the gill covers, and this rainbow bloom remains with them for much of the year. Winter-run fish, especially the cock fish, darken quickly upon arrival in the river.

The steelhead shown on page 108 is without much doubt a prime example of the species—summer-run fish in brightest color. He was taken in the Sustut River of British Columbia in August, by an angler flown in by Buzz Fiorini of Seattle, Washington. In this wild spot, the fish are relatively undisturbed and tend to run big—from fifteen to twenty-five pounds. Many of them are taken on the fly rod, as well as with spinning tackle. It is unlikely that bigger summer-run steelhead can be found anywhere in the world.

Steelheading is the big-game fishing of fresh water. The fish are not easy to find except at the very peak of their runs, and sometimes are extremely stubborn about rising to bait, lure, or fly. In waters where the steelhead are plentiful, taking even one fish a day is successful angling. Two fish make red-letter days. The great strength and vigor of a steelhead makes him difficult to keep on a hook. He leaps with terrifying speed and energy, melts a hundred yards of line from your reel in a downstream rush, then if he is not yet "unbuttoned," he goes into that peculiar, twisting, gyrating dance that has better than an even chance of tearing out the hook.

My first steelhead caught me unprepared and undergunned. I was working a small Alaskan creek filled with cutthroat trout running up to three pounds. They were taking a tiny gold Wob-L-Rite without any hesitation, and I was co-operating by using my lightest six-foot spinning rod, Micron reel, and three-pound test monofilament; I was releasing all the fish anyway. The steelhead, a fresh-run July fish, came to my lure in a deep, smoothly gliding pool.

The little wobbler worked its way downstream, flashing through the middle of the pool. It disappeared from time to time as it passed through the mottled sunlight and shadow on the water. And then the lure stopped dead, the gossamer line came taut, and I felt the solid throbbing of the big body working in the current. But only for a flash of time, until the fish felt the nip of the tiny needlelike point. Then he exploded from the center of the pool in a great wash of spray. He shook furiously above the boiling surface for a moment, and dropped back into the pool. He made a quick run toward the tail, where shallows broke through big boulders. These stopped him—for I could not—and he swept back into the depths of the hole to his lie. Again he came clear, tossing his silver and pink side to the sunlight, then rushed this time into the quick water pouring in at the head of the pool.

Ten minutes or more passed before he came gasping, on his side, over the gravel shallows. He twisted himself upright; his blue-gray back emerged from the water. I lifted him gently by the gill cover, hung him on the pocket scales, and watched him draw the pointer down to fourteen pounds. I carried him out to deep water, held him in the slowly moving current until his gill action became firm and regular, then watched him swim slowly into the darkness of the mossy rocks on the bottom. And within a half hour I repeated the pleasurable episode with his mate, a svelte henfish weighing only two pounds less.

These are the steelhead, the great trout that carry a store of energy from the sea to challenge the angler, whether he takes them in the warm rays of summer, as the glory of autumn departs the hills, or even when the first snows blanket the riverbanks.

BROWN
Trout

In the early days of the Depression a ponderous Buick sedan slewed over the deeply rutted back roads of the northern Adirondacks. Two fishermen were searching for waters mild enough for fly-fishing. They had driven three hundred miles to the big Salmon River only to find it swollen by the rains of late May, its great stream-bottom boulders smothered by muddy waters. There would be no fly-fishing here. The topographical map came out of the glove compartment. Perhaps one of the big river's tributaries would have fishable water.

The map showed a thin, wiggling blue line joining the Salmon a few miles south of the Canadian border. The Buick headed north, out of the big timber, and into a narrow valley. Eventually it rattled over the rough-plank flooring of an ancient bridge that crossed a clear stream about fifty feet wide. The anglers halted and walked back to inspect their find. Beyond the bridge the waters narrowed and chuted through mossy stones into a deep, swirling pool. Farther on, the stream vanished around a bend, but its course through peaceful farm lands was marked by the willows and alders that lined its banks.

The water looked trouty and the fishermen were disposed to give it a try—if they could make sure the "No Trespassing" signs tacked to the sugar maples along the road did not apply to them. The fishermen climbed back into the Buick and headed down the road, toward the weather-beaten farm buildings visible in the distance. They turned into the farmyard as a lanky, bent figure in floppy bib overalls was urging a herd of cows into the barn. He ignored his visitors

*Angler-entomologist
Ernie Schwiebert selects,
then casts
a high-floating dry fly
to tempt a rising
brown trout in one of the
limestone
streams of Pennsylvania's
Poconos.*

The late Harry Wall,
veteran fresh-water angler, selects
a taking nymph.

until the last cow was in her stall, then turned to appraise the Buick. The fishermen got out of the car and approached him.

"Fishin', hey," he said, noticing their thigh-length wading boots. "Ketchin' any?"

"Well," said the shorter fisherman, "we haven't yet. We were wondering about trying that creek about a mile back, if it isn't restricted."

The farmer considered this for a moment. "Well," he said, "I own this here valley and about three miles of that creek. You can fish it if y'want. I only post for them damned hunters. But there ain't no speckle trout in her any more. When I was a kid you could ketch a dozen or so there in a couple o' hours, but that's a fur time ago."

"That sure looks like good trout water," said the taller fisherman. "It should have plenty of fish in it."

"Oh, there's fish in her, all right. They put some of those durned bray-own trout in her a while back. Guess there's some still in there, but you can't ketch 'em, 'cept once in a while after a shower. No good to eat any-

ways, so I don't bother 'em none. You can try if you want—but you won't git no speckles."

The fishermen were not discouraged. Brown trout of the Salmon River area were worth working for. Back to the car. Back to the bridge. And then to business—the shorter fisherman upstream, the other down.

The creek was rich with insect life, as the coming of dusk brought out clouds of duns and caddis. Trout of a pound weight and more were feeding in the long shadows that already stretched over the pools and runs. They rose to the floating fly of the upstream angler and took the wet fly solidly for his companion downstream. In the two hours of daylight left to them, the fishermen took enough browns to fill both creels—good fish with shining sides of golden-yellow and the rich vermilion spotting which marks the brown trout. And it can be said that the half-dozen fish kept for breakfast the next day were pretty fair eating. I can vouch for it, since I was the shorter fisherman.

The farmer's attitude toward the brown trout did not surprise us. My fishing partners and I have been exposed to it many times, but usually in the "back country" where people still deplore the loss of their cherished "speckle [brook] trout." For many years, the brown was resented as an invader in these regions —which, as a matter of fact, he was—and was scornfully referred to as a "German" trout—which, in truth, he also was. More serious were the accusations that the brown was a poor fighter, a nonjumper, a night forager, a small-fish eater (always small trout), a worm lover, and poor fare on the table. Most of this was slander, but even a sportsman of the stature of Louis Rhead complained of the cannibalism of the big browns in the early 1900's: "An unpardonable mistake has been made in planting them in small streams where they feed on and destroy the native *fontinalis* [brook trout]."

Theodore Gordon, writing for the British *Fishing Gazette* in 1900, took a more generous view of the fish: "I wish you could see how successful the introduction of *Salmo fario* (brown trout) has been in this country. It is rapidly increasing in America, and in many waters grows to large size. I have taken them up to 3 lb. with the fly, and specimens have been caught up to 8 lb. or 9 lb. They can endure a higher temperature than *fontinalis* . . . and seem to displace him."

Indeed, the brown was and is a fine fish, and has come to be appreciated by most anglers for his cunning and elusiveness, as well as for his fight.

Whether his sophistication was gained through long experience with the sportsman's wiles, or whether it was simply a gift of nature is not known, but of the fish's craftiness there can be no doubt. Izaak Walton had his troubles with brown trout, as we all do, but he admired the fish nonetheless: "The trout is a fish highly valued both in this and foreign nations. He may be justly said, as the old poet said of wine, and we English say of venison, to be a generous fish: a fish that is so like the buck that he also has his seasons; for it is observed, that he comes in and goes out of season with the stag and buck. Gesner says his name is of a German offspring, and he says he is a fish that feeds cleanly and purely, in the swiftest streams, and on the hardest gravel; and that he may justly contend with all fresh-water fish. . . ."

Certainly the brown trout has enduring qualities which seem to set him apart from all other species of trout. For one thing, he is extremely adaptable. He can survive in the slow-moving, murky river, the sparkling, chill mountain brook, or the roaring, tumbling, high-country stream. He can tolerate much higher water temperatures than the brook trout, as Gordon noted, and does not require the purest waters for his survival. His diet varies widely—he will eat almost any natural food he is able to swallow. As long as the food supply is good and he has his share of choice hiding places in the stream, the brown is at home.

Undoubtedly, these very qualities made his emigration to American waters so successful. For browns have been thriving in our streams now for almost a century. Exactly when the first members of the species arrived is not certain. In 1885, Edward Ringwood Hewitt wrote of taking two large trout—one of three pounds, the other a half pound heavier—from the Neversink, which were identified as brown trout planted in the river in 1879 by Professor von Behr of Germany.

Despite this reference, however, some authorities still maintain that brown-trout eggs for hatching and

Starkly distinct pattern of brown spots marks the wild brown trout.

117

Brown trout in quiet pool must be stalked carefully and the fly delivered with a soft touch to avoid frightening the fish. Below: Brown usually makes deliberate, sure rise.

Trout fishing, from "Fishing in American Waters."

stocking never reached these shores until 1883. According to some members of the New York State Conservation Department, Fred Mather, Superintendent of Cold Spring Harbor hatchery, returned from a visit to Germany that year and either brought the trout eggs with him or had them shipped to his Long Island hatchery. Other members resist that explanation entirely, however. They claim that Green—long a rival of Mather's—imported the eggs first and raised browns in his hatcheries at Caledonia, New York. Whatever the time or manner of their importation, the browns quickly became part of East Coast stream life.

A true trout, the brown is more closely related biologically to the West Coast rainbow and to the Atlantic salmon, than to the brook or lake trouts, but his life pattern follows that of the brooks.

In late winter, following the fall spawning, the young brown emerges from his gravel-bottom birthplace for the first time. Even as a small fry his innate shyness inclines him to feed on or near the stream bottom, and to seek dark, sheltered hiding places in the stream. This behavior will be habitual during his life.

Yet, when surface insects are plentiful, browns will

feed near the top—in fact, among the surface-feeding game fish they are rated highest. But these surface-feeding parties consist mostly of young browns. Only a heavy, sustained hatch of succulent May flies will bring three- or four-year-old browns topside to dine. Ever cautious, the brown exposes himself less and less, as he matures, to the eyes of the angler. By the time he has reached maturity, his size and weight require more filling fare from the stream. Now, as Louis Rhead said, he becomes a cannibal, gorging himself at every opportunity on minnows and small trout. He also will choose, early in his life cycle, a hidden lie—under a rock ledge, a log jam, or a tree root—where he will hold forth until overtaken by old age, if not by some persistent angler. Only flood waters, which occasionally change the conformation of a stream, can force a brown to move from his hold. Should a brown be taken from one of these choice lies, another will move in to take his place.

With the coming of warm weather and rising water temperatures, browns frequently migrate upstream in search of cooler water. If the angler chooses to fish them during these warmer periods, he must do so at

Brown trout do well in shaded, rocky streams. The fisherman casts his floating fly upstream in the conventional manner, hoping to raise a fish at the break of the current into deep water (left). On wide, open river (top right) author fishes sunken fly across stream at the edge of fast-current flow in deep pocket. Bottom right: He fishes wet fly over fast water at the head of a deep pocket —a good station for feeding trout when nymphs are hatching.

night. For in the low water of summer, big browns are consistent nocturnal feeders. To tempt them a big streamer or popper bass bug should be used.

Yet there are few rigid rules about catching browns because of their varying appetite and food choices. Years ago, on a warm morning in late May, when the toads were trilling love songs along the wooded banks, I coaxed a big brown from his rock-ledge hideaway with a heavily weighted, dark bucktail fly. I often had fished the same deep hole in the Neversink's headwaters and had been successful in taking trout, both native and brown, many of them a foot long, from the small waters above and below it. But never before had I been able to raise a fish to a fly, no matter how carefully I worked, in that shaded pool.

I always suspected that a big brown trout dominated it and had successfully scared the lesser fish away. I had seen this happen before. A big brown would take over a pool, or hide in a muskrat hole, or lie under the flashboards of a mill dam, appearing only after dark to cruise the shallows, chasing minnows and splashing through the warm summer night.

At first, that day on the Neversink, I fished the fly carefully along the deep water of the ledge, but the flow of current did not permit it to sink well enough. I felt the fly must fish deeper to attract the attention of any trout that might be there. I nipped a quarter-ounce clincher sinker next to the eye of the fly and swung the awkward lure over the ledge, where it

plunked solidly and sank quickly into the quiet pool.

As the fly moved through the deep water, I pumped the rod tip to give it pulsing motion. Out of sight, it drifted along the ledge and toward the shallow end of the hole. As it turned against the strain of the line, a long, golden side flashed from the bottom. I saw the fish turn but felt no touch. He had either missed or refused the fly.

I sat on the bank and waited him out—standard procedure when a fish misses a fly. It is supposed to restore his confidence, allay his fears, and strengthen his appetite, and it may well do all of these things. At any rate, it is an aid to the angler who must overcome that shyness which makes the brown suspect all objects or actions not in tune with nature. Strange shadows over his waters frighten him, a waving rod frightens him, and a sight of the fisherman frightens him. A dragging dry fly, wet fly, or nymph pulled against the current may not frighten him, but it will probably put him on the alert, and a suspicious brown will not take unless the angler gives him enough time to forget his fears.

The waiting often is hard to endure. I smoked a bit, watched two male toads wooing a much larger female in the shallows by the tail of the pool, and thought a good deal about changing to a different fly. In the end, I decided not to; the fly I was using had already raised the fish once.

I moved up toward the head of the pool, lengthened the line, and dropped the big fly a little further up-

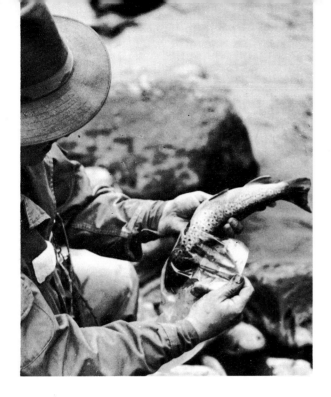

stream to get a bit more depth. Again it worked carefully along the ledge and through the deep water before stopping suddenly as a strong pull jerked the rod tip toward the water. The leader whisked up through the fast center current and the big trout dug back toward his lair under the ledge. Once there he tried to rub free of the hook, but I forced him out and downstream. We struggled for several minutes, and when his strength had given out I beached him on the shallow gravel at the lip of the pool. He was two feet long—too long for my folding net—but he weighed only a little over three pounds.

Apparently, his private hole and the once-a-year visit of the toads did not offer enough food to keep him in shape. For closer examination proved him to be an omnivorous fellow. Working the #2 hook from his long, beaked lower jaw, I could see a pair of toad's legs protruding from his gullet. Once the hook was free, I killed the fish with a sharp blow of the priest and performed the suitable surgery to check his diet. The freshly taken toad was only one morsel among many. With it were another partially digested toad, a six-inch salamander, a large pair of crayfish claws, and five hellgrammites—two of them still alive.

The old rule of "big fish, big bait," I feel, still applies to browns. My opinion on this has changed very little since I wrote one of my first books on taking big stream trout some years ago. If you are seeking browns of over two pounds, the best chances of suc-

Far left: Author spin casts
with weighted bucktail fly in the Neversink.
Brown trout, taken from this
pool, is slipped into protective plastic bag.
Above right:
A big Montana brown.

cess lie with the big wet flies and minnow imitations—or with various natural baits.

Curiously enough, the size of the brown trout an angler can expect to take relates directly to the fishing method he uses. A dry-fly fisherman can expect to catch fish up to fourteen inches long, but not much more, no matter how large or small the stream he fishes. Fishing with a wet fly or nymph may increase the range to twenty inches. With big streamers and bucktails, browns two feet long can be taken. Natural baits—minnows of many types, frogs, crayfish, and so forth—and a great variety of spoons and spinners (most of which suggest minnows) will serve to take the largest fish in any stream.

But big brown trout seldom concern the fly angler. He is after the sporty free risers of a pound weight or a bit more, which will take the fly with zest in full view. This performance makes the small brown trout

123

a most desirable opponent—and a co-operative one, when the cast is properly made, when the leader does not frighten him, and when the fly tempts him. Not too many uncertainties to meet and overcome when the reward is a fine brown trout.

Sometimes these uncertainties seem accentuated because of the acuity of the brown's eyesight. He is extremely sensitive to the glaring inconsistencies between nature and the inventions of the flytier. The centuries-old theory of "matching the hatch" is sustained by the brown's discerning eye. He is rarely disposed to try unfamiliar food and, unlike other trouts, hardly ever strikes a new "attractor." When the hatch of a specific fly is on the surface, this is the brown's menu. He will ignore all other alternatives. Consistent success in taking the brown is founded on offering him bait, fly, or lure which closely resembles a food on which he is feeding or on which he has fed in the past.

The caution and skill needed to put a brown trout in your creel involves not only the design of the fly, but the choice of terminal tackle. Dry flies should be tied with the stiffest hackles and on the lightest hooks, so they will float high and gently on the surface, as do the natural insects. An extremely fine section of leader material next to the fly will help in this respect. The fly, of course, should drift along the surface as if it were a free agent, unhampered by the pull and drift of line and leader. Such imitation usually takes a bit of doing—a careful observation of varying stream currents and a studied placement of the line and leader to give the fly a fair float before the insidious effects of drag set in.

Each year millions of trout are dumped into our heavily fished streams (regardless of the suitability of the water) to meet the demand for trout for the rod. Many of these stocked fish are hungry, inexperienced, and uninhibited. Quickly and easily, they fall victim to the early season trouter with his natural baits and flashing lures. First to go are the brook trout, then the rainbows and a good share of the browns. But the browns that survive grow more perspicacious each day. By the time the midseason fly caster appears, the fish will be confirmed natural feeders, able to forage for themselves and with the brown's strong instinct for self-preservation already in evidence. From this point on, they will be difficult to catch.

Late afternoon sunlight over a quiet pool finds trout ready to begin the evening rise. Small brown (below) is released by angler to grow larger and wiser.

A few years ago in Montana, I saw a most convincing demonstration of brown-trout survival. The stream was the Shields River, a lovely, gently flowing creek that winds down a wide valley lined with tall cottonwoods. The stream is heavily fished—by Montana standards—and is well stocked each year with cutthroats and rainbow trout. Browns had been introduced into the river some years earlier, but the outcries of local anglers had halted the program.

Now it was supposedly a "fished-out" stream worth visiting only for a few weeks after each season's stocking. Three other fishing writers and I were on hand to try our luck—for presumably we knew how to catch trout. Afterwards a section of the stream was to be closed off and the fish "shocked" to bring them to the surface for a count.

After two hours of careful fly-fishing over deep pools and fine, deep runs the four of us had caught just two trout: a cutthroat and a rainbow, each about a foot long. Then the Montana Fish Commission crew went to work, closing off about one hundred yards of stream with seines and utilizing an electrical device for the stream check. In less than one hour, one hundred and fifty-one pounds of fish had been netted and placed in live-boxes in the creek. Some of them were suckers and Rocky Mountain whitefish; there were also a few small cutthroats and rainbows. But at least half the total weight of fish recovered was made up of browns, many of them three- to four-pounders and all of them driven from hide-outs under fallen logs and gnarled cottonwood roots. They were heavy, well-fed fish with the look of good living upon them. Who knows how long they had lived securely in that stream, as only browns know how to do, immune to the temptations of the angler?

124

CUTTHROAT
Trout

Strangely enough, my first experience with cutthroat trout came in the cool, fast-running waters of the Catskills—an exotic spot for the cutthroat, some three thousand miles from his native haunts. How the fish came to be in those waters was a mystery to me. For all I know, he was the first cutthroat ever taken there, and he may well have been the last.

It happened more than twenty-five years ago, as I was working the stream, contentedly taking an occasional brown trout on wet flies. The water was cold as was the early morning air in the mountains, and the fish had barely begun to stir after a long, frosty night. Time seemed to ooze by before a hot sun, high over-head, finally brought a hatch of March Browns on the water and stimulated the trout into action. I watched as a trout steadily consumed nymphs at the foot of the smooth, deep run, his dorsal fin breaking the surface every moment or two. I moved along the shore-line boulders to put a #8 Lead-Wing Coachman over the feeding fish. He went for it with enthusiasm.

Once the hook was firmly set, I led the fish quickly into the quieter water along the edge of the run, where he flopped a time or two on the surface. On each turn above water, I noticed that a bright bit of red showed under his throat and I wondered how I could have hooked him deeply enough to make his gills bleed. Not until I had the fourteen-inch fish in the net did I realize that the red was only a skin coloration. I was looking at a trout totally unfamiliar to me.

He was a slender fish, more so than the brooks or browns of that stream, and his back was flecked with

black spots instead of the usual brown ones. His sides were the golden-yellow of the brown trout, but his head was smaller. The pair of fin-shaped, vividly painted red patches on his throat, just below his gill covers, were the clue to his identity, of course. And I soon recognized my fish as a cutthroat.

Several months passed before I had any inkling where the cutthroat might have come from. The owner of a private hatchery, miles upstream, had imported a few cutthroat eggs from California sometime before, and had attempted to hatch them in one of his estate ponds. When queried, the hatchery manager assured me that none of the experimental hatch had survived to maturity and that none had escaped down the hatchery brook into the big river. But I'm sure that at least one fish *must* have gotten away.

The cutthroat is native to the West exclusively. There, in high mountain lakes and wooded waters,

the big fish can be seen cruising near shore lines and feeding on nymphs along the edges of weed beds. They are not large as trouts go and they are neither particularly wary nor choosy about taking the fly.

One July morning I met with the assistant commissioner of Yellowstone Park to fly cast along the southern shore of the South Arm of Yellowstone Lake. Out from the shore line, perhaps forty feet or more, well behind a solid patch of pipestem reeds, we could see the trout rising. These were heavy cutthroats making little bow waves as they moved in twos and threes over the clear bottom. Every few yards they rose smoothly toward the surface to snatch a nymph.

Since we were wading close to shore, we needed a fairly long cast to put flies over the fish. I chose a pair of wet flies to do the job: a Gray Woolly-Worm and a hair-wing Royal Coachman attached to the dropper. The Royal was to serve as a marker for the cast, so that I could work the Woolly-Worm properly, ahead of the moving trout. With the aid of about sixty feet of line, I managed to drop the flies a few feet ahead of a trio of fair-sized trout traveling parallel to shore, a few inches beneath the surface. I twitched the rod only once and the flies sank quickly. I never made a second twitch. In the momentary pause, I had hooked fast to a pair of trout! After leading them through a channel in the reeds, I was lucky enough to land both. Fortunately, neither was powerful enough to break the leader at the dropper, although it must be said that they worked at it.

Within the next few casts I lost the Royal and a heavy trout with it. I fished, then, with a single fly and raised fish almost at will. Before noon my partner and I had landed about fifty cutthroats, all over a pound, many more than three pounds. The few we saved for lunch were brilliantly colored—inside and out—with sides of deep yellow from gill to tail, and orange-red flesh of a mouth-watering clarity showing in the fillets.

Floating the Beartrap in Montana.
One of the great western streams for native
cutthroat trout, it also
offers good fishing for big rainbows.

127

Cutthroat (above)
exhibits black spots and
red throat slash
which mark the species.
Fly caster (left) works
over western canyon river
for cutthroat,
while photographer
George Silk (right) also
tries his hand.

The cutthroat seems to have been first noted by the Lewis and Clark expedition in the first decade of the nineteenth century and was given the name, *Salmo clarkii*. Afterward, he was popularly called black-spotted trout, as well as cutthroat, although Dr. Henshall strongly objected to both titles. He was repelled by the name cutthroat and felt black-spotted trout did not properly distinguish this new species from the rainbow and the steelhead, which also bore black spots. He always referred to the fish as the "red-throat trout."

Since the days of his discovery, the cutthroat has suffered greatly from the onslaught of mankind. A burgeoning civilization has polluted his streams, denuded his remote woodland habitats, and lined them with new highways. In addition, new species have been introduced into many of the cutthroat's streams to compete for the same food. For a time, it seemed the cutthroat would become extinct.

Cutthroats have never been easy to raise in hatcheries. Early attempts proved so unsuccessful that for many years rainbows were used to restock depleted cutthroat waters. Recently, however, scientists discovered that by crossing the "sea-run" and "native" inland varieties of cut, the replacement situation could be somewhat improved.

The cutthroat is a true trout, endowed with all the wonderful and exciting characteristics a trout can have. Yet he is remarkably similar to the brook trout, which is a char. Both are at home in streams and lakes of any size. Both are omnivorous and indiscriminate feeders, enticed by every hatch of insects that lights upon their waters. In the wilderness, a gaily colored artificial will sometimes tempt them as quickly as the natural.

Big cuts, like big brook trout, are generally found by plumbing the waters of remote mountain lakes; their smaller, more sprightly brethren dwell in the stream. Unlike the mature "stream" brook trout, however, the cuts do not seek deep, gently flowing rivers where they can hide in dark pools and beneath overhanging banks. Instead, they enjoy fighting the stiff current of a tumbling mountain stream and reveling in sunlit rivers.

The cutthroat is perfectly at home in the Rockies, high up in the tall timber country, where elk, goat, and mule deer abound, and the waters are fast and icy. In fact, some of my best cutthroat fishing has been done in that area. In the fall, Rocky Mountain streams are low and clear, and it is possible to stand on the bank and see trout finning quietly over gravel-and-limestone bottoms of little backwater pools. If you stalk them properly, it is no trick to drop a fly over a trout's window, watch him start from his lie with a quick flirt of his tail, and see him come to take the lure.

I recall one incident on the South Fork of the Flathead River, where five trout were visible near the bottom of a sunlit pool. I moved cautiously along the bank to within easy casting distance. From my hiding place behind a log, I flipped an Abu-Reflex spinner and watched its splash alert the fish—their fins beat a faster tempo and the smaller fish rose up slightly from the bottom. As the spinner flashed its way down current,

Pool below falls in mountain stream.

passing the little school, the lead trout turned, followed it out slowly, then took it with a quick thrust. I struck, checked his dash toward his position in echelon, and led him down to the tail of the pool, where I released him into the fast water below. I was not about to frighten the big trout if I could avoid it.

On the next cast, I dropped the little spinner alongside the big cut's head. But before he could move, a second small trout had it. Again I led the fish away for releasing, and despite the commotion the big cut held to his lie. Again I dropped the lure over his head.

This time he seized it—so promptly and so savagely that my reflex to set the hook was too much for the two-pound test line. I left the lure with the fish. In the clear water, I watched him return to his lie, the spinner flashing in the current, his lower jaw pulsing in rhythm with his gill action.

On the next cast, I dropped a peanut-sized wobbler over him and discovered he was not a fastidious feeder. He gulped it quickly. Surprised by the prick of the lure, he struggled furiously to get under the log and foul the line, but the strain of the rod was too much for him. At the tail of the pool, I lifted him from the ice-cold water. He was a fine two-pounder—and I recovered both lures.

Despite the fact that the cutthroat has never been considered a notable fighter, he can leap as well as any rainbow of matching size, and he will give a fairly good show of top-water flurrying when hooked. The bigger specimens found in large inland waters are, of course, formidable opponents for the angler, but the cutthroat is at his best in the rivers that run to the sea.

Sea-run cutthroats are not truly migratory fish, like the steelhead or the salmon. Generally they take to the sea in search of better feeding grounds, rather than to fulfill any instinctive urge. In many coastal streams food supplies have fallen off, while the number of fish that must share them has increased.

Once in the sea, cutthroats are transformed into a special breed. They grow to fairly large size, many of them weighing between two and four pounds when they return from the salt water. By this time, too, the rich yellow coloration of the inland fish has given way to silver, and frequently even the red slashes at the throat have so faded as to be almost indiscernible.

Sea-runs return to the streams of their origin when it pleases them—and this can be anytime during the spring or summer fishing seasons. The biggest trophies come in the fall. In the Columbia River area these are known as "harvest fish"; for by the time they appear, the angler can make a good harvest of cutthroats, steelheads, silver salmon, or Jack Chinooks in the same river, on the same day, and sometimes even on the same fly—if it is a hair wing or a long bucktail pattern.

Cutthroats rise readily to flies from the time they approach the tidal beaches until they are far up river. They are not choosy as to design: streamer flies are effective; dry flies probably give the best sport when the fish are lying in holding pools. Whatever your lure or fishing method, the cutthroat will help you out, for like the brookie, he is both gullible and eager.

s a likely spot to cast for cutthroat.

*Quiet, smooth glides
in Yellowstone River are also
habitat of the cutthroat.
Wet-fly fishing here is fine.*

GRAYLING

*Grayling, from
"The Complete Angler,"
Vol. 6, London.*

A dark fly drifted down the riffle, bobbing in the bright sunlight. Near it a boil of water thrust through the serrated surface. Behind it a dorsal fin appeared, glistened momentarily in the sun, and slipped from view. Across the riffle, in quiet water, the inverted image of snow-capped mountains undulated gently.

Many more flies now rode the riffle. It came alive with rises, splashes of spray, tiny dimples—all the action of water broken by the movement of feeding fish. Amid the turbulence, slender, amber-colored bodies could be seen, surfacing, then diving quickly, smoothly, rhythmically.

The stream was the Battle River of the Katmai, in Alaska. The fish were grayling.

I could not sit for long on the bank in the shade of the alders with a dozen fish gorging within easy reach of the rod. I watched just long enough to locate the feeding station of the biggest fish—at least he exposed the longest dorsal fin as he rose—and then unhooked the Badger Bivisible from the fly ring.

I waded out to the foot of the riffle, well below the fish, far enough from the alders to clear the backcast. My fish was rising steadily, sucking in surface flies with precision. Few escaped him and these only because he was occupied with others. I switched out a sidearm cast, looping a few false casts over the fish as I stripped enough line to reach him.

He rose beautifully as the fly came to him. As his flag dipped from sight, I lifted the rod gently. Startled and stung, he came out in a clean, full arc, a yard high over the riffle, for my first full view of him. His rose-tipped back fin was sprinkled with circular markings, like so many tiny eyes. The tail, anal, and pelvic fins were a faint cobalt blue. These colors contrasted subtly with the light amber of his sides and the dark-purple stripes of his forward fins. Altogether he was a mag-

nificent specimen of one of the world's handsome fish.

Headlong, he re-entered the stream. He executed short dashes over the sparkling bottom, leaped again and again into the air, and dove back with grace and style. It was a short battle, but he fought all the way. He came in at last at the tail of the riffle, in quiet water. His dorsal cut through the surface, his pectorals flared, his fin stripes and colors flickered and blended with the shadows dancing on the current. He was about twenty inches long, big as grayling go. I gripped him over the gill covers, removed the hook from his small mouth, and let him go.

The grayling is a gentleman adversary. He was born with a set of well-defined fighting rules, and he sticks to them in every battle with a fisherman. His rise to the fly is sure, without deceit. He seizes it with conviction, almost with eagerness. It is nearly impossible to pull the hook from him.

The prick of the point goads him into the air. It is not the explosive thrust of a musky, a steelhead, or a smallmouth, nor does he make a great, abandoned splash like these fish upon re-entry. His leap is a pretty thing to see and impossible to forget; his plunge back in is a smooth completion of his flight. The total action ties surprise to dignity, grace to speed, strength to purpose. If a human quality can be ascribed to a fish, the grayling has true *savoir faire*.

Like the salmon, he fights in the open and does not try to foul the line or leader on snags or rocks. His fight is short, to be sure. He spends his power quickly in his many leaps and short, swift runs. Yet he always seems to save one last clean leap for the moment before he accepts defeat.

Unfortunately for most American anglers, grayling are almost unattainable. A few streams in Montana, mostly within the limits of Glacier National Park, hold

Float plane (above) offers only
transportation to the best grayling
fishing. Fish (top right)
lives only in clear, cold water over rocky
bottoms. Alaska grayling
(right) are large; those held by the
author average two pounds.

Spawning grounds of the sockeye
at the outlet of Battle Lake in the Katmai
attract many grayling, who follow
the salmon upstream to feed on the spawn.
Grayling (below and right) are
beautiful both in form and action.

all the grayling in the forty-eight states. Otherwise the fisherman must go north into the watershed of the Arctic Ocean—the northern regions of Western Canada and the Yukon—or to Alaska, which undoubtedly provides grayling most generously.

Grayling always has been a cold-water species, found only in northern latitudes on this continent. European anglers, among them Walton and Cotton, have been familiar with the grayling for centuries, but the fish was not known in North America—except to the Indian and Eskimo—until 1819, when Sir John Richardson, conducting the Franklin Expedition to the North Pole, found it in Arctic waters. Actually, grayling also inhabited Montana and Michigan, but early trappers and explorers did not identify them as such. They called them "whitefish" or "Michigan trout."

Frank Forester, writing in 1849, suggested that grayling were not to be found south of Canada, nor below the sixty-second parallel of latitude. This, of course, was incorrect, although it was not until 1865 that the Michigan grayling was identified. Montana grayling were mentioned by Lewis and Clark as coming from the Jefferson River, but this subspecies was not classified until 1872. Actually, there never was any generic difference between the grayling of the States and those of the Arctic, except perhaps for the larger size of the latter.

The grayling's scientific name—*Thymallus signifer*—proclaims certain physical attributes. The Greeks, who, it is said, first named him, thought he smelled of thyme. Hence, *Thymallus*. It may be so. I have caught hundreds and never have been able to note the odor. The *signifer,* appended by Richardson, means "standard bearer." This is the grayling's distinction: a long, wide dorsal fin carried by no other fresh-water fish.

Richardson was much impressed by the grayling's gameness: "This beautiful fish inhabits strong rapids,

. . . it bites eagerly at the artificial fly and, deriving great power from its large dorsal fin, affords much sport to the angler. The grayling generally springs entirely out of the water when first struck by the hook, and tugs strongly at the line, requiring as much dexterity to land it safely as it would to secure a trout of six [sic] times the size."

He was dead right on the spirited fight of the grayling and on its willingness to take a fly. How much of an assist the fish derives from the power of its dorsal is questionable, for the fin waves freely and limply at all times. In my observation, the fish has no power to erect it. But, apparently lost in admiration of the grayling's beauty, Richardson credited it with much more power than it has. I have yet to see a grayling that could match the stamina of either a rainbow or an eastern brook trout of equal weight. Grayling are such unwary fish, however, that after being hooked and released they may resume feeding and be hooked again.

The uninhibited freedom of the grayling in rising to the fly—or, for that matter, any other small lure fished shallow or deep—adds much to the angler's pleasure. I recall my first Alaskan trip years ago, when the camp operator instructed me on the proper approach to grayling.

"Well," I was told, "if you want to fish for 'em with flies, you had better have some Black Gnats. That's what they want." I had no Black Gnats. Neither did I have any misgivings about it. I fished for them with Lead-Wing Coachman wets and Hendrikson drys, and raised fish wherever they lived. They loved the trout flies I used back home on the Neversink just as well.

The angler with a big-fish complex will not be happy with grayling. It is not often that you encounter one much over two pounds. This is immaterial. You will fish for grayling with your lightest, most sensitive tackle to match the delicacy of his effort. He will fight well whether you are geared light or not. It simply is not cricket to challenge him with a bait-casting or a salmon rod.

And when you feel his firm, unyielding body in your hand, you may well be ready to adopt the philosophy of "Uncle Thad" Norris, who once said: "When I look into a grayling's eye I am sorry I killed it: but that feeling never prevents me from making another cast just to see if another will rise."

LAKE TROUT
& *Dolly Varden*

The lake trout—known variously as togue in New England, gray trout in some areas of Canada, and Mackinaw in the Great Lakes region and Alaska—has two paradoxical distinctions for anglers. He is the world's largest trout and his family's poorest fighter.

He was also one of the first fish encountered by the early explorers of the continent. French missionaries caught him in the drainage system of the Great Lakes and thereby became the forerunners of generations of anglers who have fished enthusiastically for this large—and palatable—trout from upper New England to Alaska's Aleutian peninsula.

The lake trout averages about six or eight pounds, but fifty-pounders are certainly not unusual, and he has been known to scale as much as one hundred and twenty-two pounds.

For a fish in this weight range he puts up an embarrassingly feeble defense. Yet it is only fair to say

Taken from cold mountain waters, the lake trout has vivid colors, but lacks red spots of other char.

that the problem is probably less a faint heart than it is the weight of terminal tackle used to catch him in deep water. It is roughly equivalent to putting a three-hundred-pound jockey on a race horse. For there are moments in early spring and during the late fall spawning season when the laker will rise from his basement haunts and battle with the angler, in much the manner of a heavy landlocked salmon. In New England, for instance, the ice-out fishermen have this kind of sport using a trolled streamer fly, fished atop the water with a fly rod.

I once hooked a heavy laker in Schroon Lake in the Adirondacks when the flows of melting ice were giving way to early spring. The fish struck powerfully at a Green King streamer that already had landed two salmon, and although he did not show himself, he fought well. He bored deep, made several long rushes from side to side and, all in all, put on a valiant performance. At the time, I was mildly surprised to find I was netting a six-pound lake trout rather than the five-pound salmon I expected.

For most of the year, however, lake trout are hidden in the deepest areas of large lakes, where the water is cool and still. The laker seeks depths of up to two hundred feet to assure himself forty-degree temperatures—or lower—during even the hottest summer days. He will seldom live in lakes less than one hundred feet deep, and even in autumn, when spawning begins, he rarely comes into water less than ten feet deep. He is not only a deep-water dweller, but a bottom feeder—the deepest feeder there is in fresh water. So you cannot expect to see a laker until you have hooked him, drawn him from the depths, and played him to the net.

At these depths, the choices of angling method are limited. The lake trout usually is caught either by still-fishing or trolling.

The former, sometimes called "buoy fishing" because of the marker used to locate the baited area, is the older and more primitive of the two. It was used by the Indians long before the arrival of the white man. They first baited a hole with chopped suckers or minnows and then fished it with a live minnow or a chunk of chum for bait. In some parts of the Adirondacks and New England, fishermen still outwit lake trout this way.

About a hundred years ago, however, a lake-trout

139

Above: Casting from bank,
"The Complete Angler," Vol. 4, London.
Below: Title page of
"The Angler's Own Book," London, 1867.

PRICE TWOPENCE
THE
ANGLER'S
OWN BOOK

GIVES A THOROUGH KNOWLEDGE OF THE ART

AND TELLS OF EVERY HAUNT OF THE FISH

LONDON: J. NEAL, 61, ST. JOHN'S SQ.

fisherman, cleverer than his predecessors, discovered that trolling permitted him to search a greater expanse of lake bottom for the deep-lying fish.

Slow trolling was then, and still is, the most successful way to take lake trout—or any other fish you must coax to a lure one hundred feet below the water's surface. Little light enters such deep water. The fish must have time to see the lure and to decide whether or not to take it.

The deep-troller's rig includes wire lines, trolling triangles, and plenty of lead weights. To these, the angler must add a big live minnow, a heavy wobbling spoon, or a string of "cowbells"—a series of spinners ahead of the bait.

Undoubtedly, it is all this hardware that puts the onus on the laker as a fighter. A fish, however stout-hearted, has little chance to perform with a pound or two of lead hanging to his hooked jaw. It's also likely that the swelling of the laker's swim bladder under the variation in pressure caused by dragging him suddenly to the surface from a depth of one hundred feet or more slows his reactions and may even stun him.

A laker struck in deep water seldom offers any resistance until he nears the boat. Then, in desperation, he will flurry a bit, or roll and twist around the wire, triangles, and sinkers until the fisherman or his guide ends the activity with a big landing net or billy club.

To be sure, it's not much of a battle, but the lake-trout fisherman finds his pleasure and reward in probing the depths of unknown waters and studying the mysteries of a lake bottom with either a lead-weighted lure or plumb line. Obviously, an accurate knowledge of the water's varying depths and the contour of its bottom is absolutely necessary for taking this fish. The late Fred Streever, known nationally as a lake-trout angler and "houn-dawg" man, spent forty years sounding the bottom of Lake George with heavy, lead drails on a graduated line. His charts of that lake and his ability to locate a spot of specific depth by triangulating fixed points on opposite shores were nothing less than phenomenal. The dedication he gave to these studies easily made him the most consistently successful angler on the lake.

Fishing with Fred was an education. He often trolled so slowly that—in his own phrase—he had to "spit in the worter" to make sure the boat was moving. Now

Fishermen who fly to remote trout lakes build rafts for deep trolling.

and then from his station at the cruiser's wheel, he would yell a few pointers to the less knowledgeable lake-trout fishermen aboard—which was everyone. First, as the boat got under way, he would advise us to release the wire until the sinker touched bottom. Then, when we came to a shallow area, he would shout: "Give her a dozen turns on the reel, boy." Or, if the depth increased, he would know exactly how many turns on the reel would be needed to reach the proper level. He was seldom wrong. With him, the lures fished well—and we always caught trout.

In the Far Northwest, where the lake trout is assured of cool waters throughout the summer, he is more likely to come nearer the surface to feed. Many Alaskan lakes, especially those in the Katmai area, teem with these fish, feeding furiously on the small salmon fry which lie in the estuaries of tributary streams and along the passageways between the lakes. Under these conditions, only light spinning tackle rigged with a small wobbler is needed to take all the "Mackinaws" you can tolerate—in about an hour's fishing from shore. There a fish hooked and lost matters little, for another will grab the spoon before you can retrieve it. Some-

times, I think the only sport in these waters rests in the fisherman's attempt to bring his lure back for another cast *without* taking a fish.

Standing with a companion at the outlet of Grosvenor Lake, directly in front of a Northern Consolidated Airlines fishing camp, I watched in amazement as the water boiled with feeding trout. Only minutes before, we had landed a four-seater Cessna float plane on the lake and taxied directly over the feeding fish before beaching. Apparently, we hadn't put them down for more than thirty seconds. Casting out gold Side-Winder wobblers, we landed and released forty-nine lakers with fifty casts. My partner once got his lure back without taking a fish, but I never made it.

Alaskan lakers are not large as lake trout go. They range between three and eight pounds. But they are beautifully colored fish, with ochre sides and deep pink fins. The wormlike markings which cover their backs are vivid, clearly indicating the laker's place in the char family and his close kinship to the eastern brook trout. He is a bit more slender than the brook, however, and has a deeply forked tail. The brook's bright red spots are absent from the laker's body and the dead-white

141

edges from his pectoral fins. In addition, the lake trout's teeth are far more prominent and effective than those of his smaller relative.

Since the lake trout is first, last, and always a minnow feeder, he needs these teeth to grasp his prey. The size, number, and sharpness of his teeth offer some clue to his feeding habits and suggest why the angler will rarely take lake trout on any fly but the streamer or bucktail—both of which simulate minnows.

The lake trout's western cousin is the Dolly Varden—and a more unlikely name for a fish is hard to imagine. The Dolly was discovered in the early 1840's, about the time Charles Dickens' novel *Barnaby Rudge* be-

came popular. Dickens' vivid description of his heroine's lavender-spotted dress so well matched the coat of this trout that he was made Dolly's namesake, and has remained so.

His form and habits are characteristic of other members of the trout family, but in particular of the lake and the eastern brook trouts—both close relatives of the Dolly. Like the lakers, Dolly seeks deep waters where he can feed on minnows far below the surface, with an appetite as omnivorous as the brook trout's. But unlike the lake trout, he is at home in the deep pools of swift-moving rivers and streams, as well as in the quiet waters of a northern lake.

Generally, the Dolly lives inland—north of the forty-second parallel and west of the Rockies—where he is usually taken by trolling. Yet he is also found in

Far left: Dolly Vardens, along with cutthroats, are usually found in big-game country of the Northwest. River Dolly (below) looks much like a lake trout.

Left: Fly-fishing from "The Angler's Guide," 1815.

the coastal waters where, when the time is appropriate, he runs to the sea, like the cutthroat. He returns to fresh water only to spawn and to take flies, metal lures, and bait without discrimination.

I have caught Dolly Vardens in Montana, where they are known as bull trout, in the South Fork of the Flathead River, where ten-pounders are fairly common, and in the headwaters of remote streams in the Alberta Rockies, where they were the only trout to be found. Each time it has been a new and exciting experience.

Perhaps some of this excitement is due to the beauty of the fish—for he is every bit as handsome as the brook trout. There are shades of violet on his sides and fins, which are often tipped with orange, and a rich sprinkling of red spots on his body as befits the true char he is. In Alaskan waters, he runs to golden-yellow in color. His form is similar to the brook trout's, but slenderer, and his head is smaller.

Unfortunately, he is not an outstanding fighter and he suffers a good deal from comparison with other members of the trout family. This is especially true on the West Coast, where rainbow, steelhead, and cutthroat may be taken from the same waters. In addition, the Dolly for years had an unsavory reputation along coastal waters for feeding on salmon spawn. Once, at the insistence of the salmon canners, there was even a bounty maintained on the fish. Dolly Vardens were destroyed by the hundreds of thousands for a few cents on each tail. It was an ignominious fate for such a fine game fish. Now, while the bounty has been removed, the stigma remains, and only a few anglers venture to have sport with this interesting and handsome fish.

GOLDEN
Trout

The golden trout is the most remote, inaccessible, and exclusive of American game fish. He lives only with his own kind, only in isolated lakes at high elevations, and only in California and the Rocky Mountains.

His origin and evolution are not definitely known, although his ancestors are believed to have been rainbows and his starting point the Kern River, which rises from Mount Whitney in the Sierra Nevada range of southeastern California. In any event, goldens were first discovered in High Sierra lakes at elevations of ten thousand feet or more.

One theory holds that the golden is the product of centuries of evolution in this specialized mountain environment, with its crystal-clear waters and bright, volcanic sand bottoms. And with steep cascades and high falls at most lake outlets to serve as an effective natural barrier against any run-up of rainbows or cutthroats from the streams below. For without his splendid isolation, it is doubtful that the golden trout would survive. Whenever he has been introduced into waters inhabited by rainbows, he breeds with them, and the offspring lose the brilliant individuality of golden-trout coloration.

The golden is indeed well named. He exceeds every other trout in flamboyance. A dark-spotted back of lovely olive green extends to a broad, horizontal band of red at the sides, and the lower sides and belly shine with pure yellow-gold. The red band is broken by a series of bluish patches, like the parr markings of a brook trout or salmon. His belly fins are brilliant red, sometimes tipped with white, and the same red is displayed on his gill covers. There is no mistaking him.

The golden is almost invariably a small fish. Most of them never reach a length of even one foot. The growing season at high altitudes is short and the insect supply is likely to be relatively skimpy. In larger lakes at somewhat lower elevations, however, transplanted fish have run as high as eight pounds, and the current record is eleven, for a fish caught in Wyoming.

Transplanting and restocking are arduous tasks. For, to maintain the golden's uniqueness, the programs are conducted only in high country and in lakes where other species are not found naturally. Fry are carried in on mule back over winding trails. Stops are made at every cold mountain brook to change the water in the carriers and accustom the fish to new conditions. Unhappily, few fry survive, and tribute must be paid to the dedicated men who undergo considerable hardships to assure the future of this magnificent fish.

Since the golden is no great shakes for size, it is the extraordinary beauty of the fish, matching the country he lives in, that attracts anglers from many miles away to catch him. I promise you will not find goldens within reach of a highway. If you want this rare gem of a trout, you back-pack or ride a horse into the wild, big-game country. Here you will find elk summering above the timber line, away from the flies, and the white Rocky Mountain goat standing in silhouette against a cliff face far above the trail, watching your pack string thread through the valley and up into tall timber. And beyond. For many of the golden-trout lakes nestle like jewels in the bright sun in the hanging valleys far above the growth of big trees.

144

Golden-trout lakes
lie like jewels
in high mountain country (left).
The horse is required
transportation and can assist
the fisherman.

Adult golden trout have the parr
markings of immature salmon and are usually small,
since mountaintop lakes offer limited food.

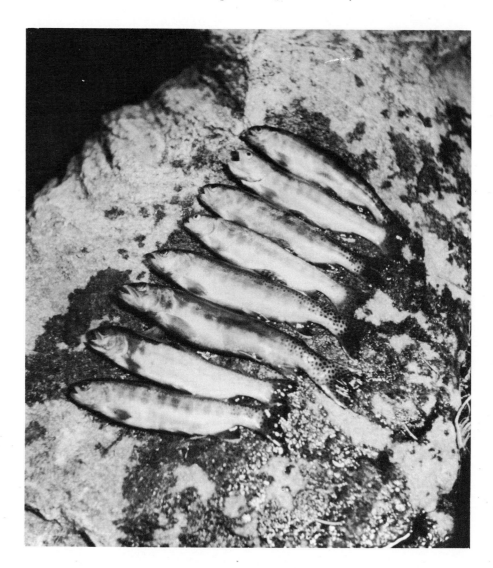

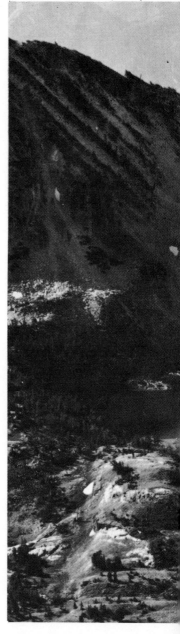

I caught my first goldens in a tiny lake in the Gallatin range, just north of Yellowstone Park. It was a seven-hour ride from the nearest ranch to the first golden-trout lake, some nine thousand feet above sea level. It was late enough in the summer to hear the first bugling of the bull elk. The call came first from a high, pine-studded ridge, low-pitched and flutelike in the beginning, then rising quickly to a shrill whistle, held for as long as the bull's big lungs could sustain it. When the sound had died away, faintly, from another ridge across the valley, the answering call came.

It may well have been as lusty as the first bull's challenge, but the distance it traveled made it sound thin and piping to my ears.

It was not difficult to take the fish. In the summer—which is the only time of year you can reach them, generally—the fish are hungry enough to rise readily to small flies, fished wet or dry.

The horse-riding angler has much the best of it in fishing the tiny lakes. The horse not only bears the brunt of the rugged climb into steep country at high altitude, where it usually takes two breaths to gain

one lungful of oxygen, but he will take you out to the rising fish. Fly casting from the saddle is a novel experience, and if you do hook a sizeable trout that resists lifting from the water at rod's length, your mount will tow him into the shallows!

A fisherman's stature—in his own mind, at least—grows a bit after he packs into the tall Rockies and takes his first creel of golden trout. This trout fishing is all charm: the slow ride into the hills as the sure-footed mountain horses pick their way along the trail, giving you time to watch the stiff-legged bounds of a big-eared mule deer spooked by your passing; time to watch the soaring flight of a golden eagle over the cliffs, and silence in which to hear his hunting scream from half a mile away. And given time enough, you break over the last divide to see the sapphire gleam of a tiny lake snugged in between rocky walls. If the sun is still high enough you will have time to pitch your canvas and make camp before the evening rise. If not, the goldens will be on hand next morning, when the tall crags along the ridge are beginning to cast long shadows over the mirror face of the lake.

147

The
BASS

SMALLMOUTH
Black Bass

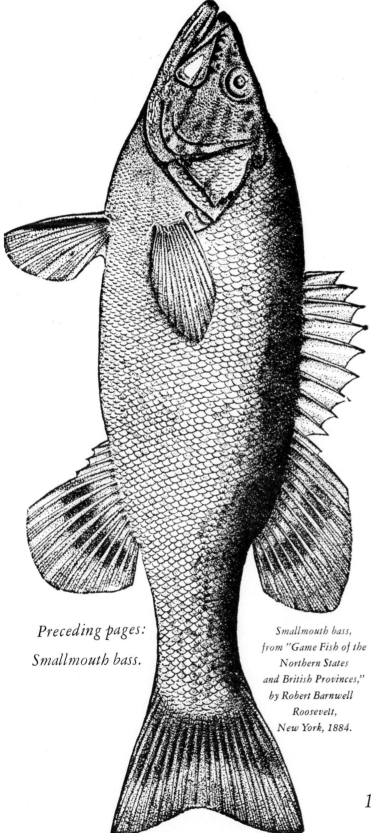

Preceding pages:
Smallmouth bass.

Smallmouth bass,
from "Game Fish of the
Northern States
and British Provinces,"
by Robert Barnwell
Roosevelt,
New York, 1884.

On the west shore of the lake lay a huge boulder of rough granite, half submerged and far larger than the long row of rocks forming the shore line. The sun, on this late May afternoon, cast a long shadow from the boulder out over deep water. Microp lay in this shade, finning restlessly, watching for signs of life to appear in the shallows. He was hungry now, after the long fasting of winter.

The thick mass of winter ice had disappeared only a short time ago. Its rotting crystals had pulled away first from the rocks and the tumbled masses of dry-ki to clear the shores. But Microp had not moved from his deep-water hideaway under a waterlogged stump until the ice had broken into shards and drifted into the main body of the lake.

Now, as the sun dropped toward the pointed spruces lining the western shore, Microp moved out, together with some smaller bass, into the depths of the lake. Schools of smelt were starting to riffle the surface. The little group of smallmouth bass cruised just under the surface until, a quarter of a mile offshore, they came upon a clutch of the tiny, slender, silvery fish feeding on plankton.

Microp and his fellows charged into the smelt from below, scattering them wildly, sending a spray of a dozen or more erupting from the surface. The bass fed savagely on the little fish, slashing and churning at the rear of the moving school. But as dusk settled the smelt went down into the deepest water and the bass, whose hunger had been sated for the day, moved again toward shoal water.

While the days passed and the weather became warmer, Microp, goaded by the mating urge, searched for a spot for his nest. He moved to the east shore of the lake where the sun beat down most strongly, looking for a small expanse of fine gravelstones among the rocks. He found the proper place at a rocky point running out fifty yards from shore. The water was about four feet deep and nearby was a dark hole that would be a haven in emergencies.

After circling the spot several times, Microp turned to the business of nest building. In this clean, rock-lined Canadian lake it was not an arduous task. Hovering over the gravel bottom, he fanned away a light coating of silt with a few sweeps of his broad, powerful tail. A twig that resisted his sweeping was picked up

150

in his leathery jaws, carried to the edge of deep water and dropped. In an hour the bed was about two feet in diameter, the cleared space showing as a light spot among the dark rocks of the bottom. Microp moved off then to find a mate.

Within another hour he returned to the nest area, driving ahead of him a fat, dark female bass, about four pounds in weight. She came reluctantly. Microp herded her like a collie with a wayward sheep—cutting her off as she headed away toward the lake depths, bullying her ahead of him with his blunt nose, nipping at her flanks until she rested over the nest.

After a time the female swam slowly around the nest, circling it several times. Eventually she dropped down to rest on the bottom, lying almost on her broad side, with Microp hovering above her. Suddenly she became rigid. Microp's fins quivered expectantly, his gill covers lifted and closed in a faster tempo. Below him, the female responded to his action. Her rigid body began to tremble slowly, then to vibrate rapidly. Her fins fluttered. A string of eggs was extruded from her vent. Microp sank quickly to her side, emitting a tiny cloud of milt to cover the eggs.

The female rose from the nest and drifted away, unheeded now by Microp, who was circling the nest excitedly. He came to rest over the spawn, fanning gently with fins and tail. A strong sun beat down through the clear, faintly amber-colored water, warming the clean gravel, and with the warmth life began within the eggs.

Microp tended the nest for two weeks, watching warily for intruders. Only once did fear drive him into the dark hole of water near the point. A hunting osprey, on an early morning search for chubs along the lake shore, spotted Microp near the nest. The fish hawk hung high above the lake, his pointed wings holding him steady as he studied the bottom. Microp fled at once into the depths, but the osprey, no match for five pounds of smallmouth bass, beat his way slowly toward the head of the lake where the inlet stream, flowing over a sandy delta, offered him easier hunting.

By mid-June Microp's family had become perfectly formed bass about a quarter of an inch long. They left the nest and he saw them no more. Now, still feeling the militant ardor of his parenthood, he was ravenously hungry. He spent his first day away from the

*Float fishing in autumn
on a river in the Missouri Ozarks
provides top-drawer angling.
Smallmouths are active
in cool weather and respond well to
small lures. Below:
Angler sharpens hooks of a
light casting plug.*

nest chasing small minnows in the shallows. He picked up several dragonfly nymphs from rocky crevices and sucked in a few gray millers from the surface. He was thus busily engaged when he was alerted by a bug, somewhat larger than the naturals, alighting with a soft splash close to the point of rocks by the edge of the deep water. It rested briefly within the small circles widening from its point of contact, its tiny, fat body looking succulent and juicy.

Microp's reaction was prompt. A quick flirt of his tail brought him within striking range. The bug struggled feebly as though trying to rise. Microp rushed it, seized it in a great boil on the surface that carried at once, visibly and audibly, to the angler. A quick lift of the rod checked Microp as he headed for deep water to swallow his new find. Stung and surprised by the restraint, Microp burst through the surface, head shaking, gill covers flared. His big mouth opened wide and the hook, barely pricking the horny edge of his lower jaw, fell free. Microp re-entered the water with a splash, righted himself, and was swiftly away into deep water to ponder the frightening event. This was his first experience with food that fought back.

The angler's chagrin matched that of the bass. He turned in the bow of the canoe to face the guide before retrieving the limp fly line. "Man, that was a bass! Best one all day, I'd say!" The guide nodded prudently, then pointed up the shore with the paddle. "Should be another about that big up along the next shoal," he said. The loss of the bass was shrugged off. More than a dozen belligerent smallmouths had already been taken and released that afternoon, some almost as large as Microp. Nonetheless, angler and guide both knew that five-pounders were not easy to come by at any time.

The big smallmouth kept to deep water for the next day or two. The shallows along the shores were already becoming uncomfortably warm, and as the heat of July bore down from clear skies Microp spent more and more time in the cooler depths, feeding on small bait minnows—chub and smelt—which also liked the coolness of the thermocline during the summer. At daybreak, however, after a chilly Canadian night, he felt no discomfort working the edges of grassy coves and alder-screened bays where he might find a big moth still fluttering on the water near shore, or a frog kicking along from one weed patch to another.

When the lake level sank from lack of rain, the bass stayed in the deep holes, moving through channels from hole to hole during the summer. He traveled with many others of his kind in search of food—now almost exclusively minnows. A favored spot for evening feeding was a deep channel between a long,

timbered point and an island. There a cool-water stream broke from the heavily forested mainland, carrying a never-ending supply of brook minnows seeking the lake's bounty of small insects.

The channel, four miles from Microp's spawning ground, was also known to fishermen. When the pale red glory of the Canadian summer sunset cast its glow over the lake, a skiff or two could always be found anchored near the channel—near enough to cast bait over it, far enough away so that a hooked, fighting bass would not disturb its feeding mates.

With a dozen smallmouths weighing three pounds or more—Microp did not consort with smaller bass— he came into the channel near sundown, moving steadily from the deep bay in the lake where he had spent most of his summers. He knew the route well and could follow the channel easily by sensing the cooler, brook-fed water it held. He knew also that small chubs hid in the long grass growing from the bottom. He poked about in the weaving grass, flushing out chubs as he went. Some were grabbed by his fellows, some fled back to the grass in terror, where Microp clutched and swallowed enough, after turning them headfirst, to fill his big pouch. As the sun slipped behind the tall evergreens on shore, he moved out of the grass into the clear path of the channel. He was

sated, but still pugnacious enough to take more chubs.

A fat one now swam before him, lazily moving across the channel, twisting feebly as though another bass had struck and then released it. This was a challenge that Microp could not resist. He came to the minnow, now nearing the surface, swung below it and grasped it solidly. He dropped to the bottom of the channel to mouth it leisurely.

Suddenly he felt a tug, then a strong pull that turned him back up the channel. Shaking his head, he broke for deep water in a rush, feeling the strain become heavier as he swam. He felt, too, the sharp prick of the hook buried in his tongue. It drove him to the surface and beyond in a wild leap. The action drove the hook point well in, past the barb. He would not shake this one loose.

Desperate now, he rushed through the bottom

Below: Rocky, cliff-bound streams where waters are cool, pools deep, are ideal haunts for smallmouth bass.

Left: Anglers test an old-mill stream in eighteenth-century painting by George Harvey.

Leaping strike—and rush—
of a taking smallmouth is always a
pleasurable experience.
The six-pound bass (below left)
approaches maximum size
for north country.

Right: Punt fishing,
from "The Angler's Guide,"
London, 1815.

grasses, feeling the vibration of the singing line through his head. He could not free himself from the strain. Again he jumped, throwing a couple of chubs from his gullet as he did so, trying to vomit bait, hook, and all. Twisting and turning below the surface again, he emptied his stomach completely, the bait minnow in his mouth tore free, leaving only the torment of the hook.

He tried to swim away from his relentless adversary, but the line that cut through the water beside him restricted his movements and turned his head as he did not want it turned. He forced the fisherman to feed him a hundred feet of line, against the steady drag of the reel, but it was not enough. Microp was weakening. In his last full-strength drive he tried to rub out the hook against a boulder in the bottom, but the rough granite did not take hold. Frustrated, he turned toward the pull of the line and felt an instant of relief. But only an instant. The angler retrieved his slack, forcing the fish toward the top. Microp now saw the skiff for the first time. He dived under it, hoping to find security beneath a rock ledge or a fallen log. Still the line pulled him out into open water. He made for the bottom grasses, pumping down the rod tip until it was buried in the water. But the spring of the rod was inexorable and exhausting. Microp turned once on his side, quickly righted himself, and made again for the shelter of the boat's bottom.

He drove headlong into the meshes of the wide-mouthed landing net. Churning furiously and resentfully at this last degradation, he lashed the surface with his powerful body until the guide lifted him into

the air—the first time he had left his element other than under his own power and by his own choice.

The guide dealt him a solid blow over the eyes with the bone handle of his hunting knife and pulled him gently from the net. "Guess you'll be saving him for mounting, Doc," he said, with no query in his voice. "This is the best one of the season for both of us."

He stretched Microp out on the paddle blade. The broad tail hung over the tip and the strong, dark bars over his cheeks stood out prominently in the fading light. His final action—always in character—was a quick, aggressive lift of his spiny dorsal fin in a last spasm of defiance.

Of all the axioms of angling, none is more comforting than that attributed to the twelfth-century Persian poet, Omar Khayyám. Freely translated, it reads: "Allah does not subtract from man's allotted span the hours spent in fishing." Considerably more recent, but equally famous, is Dr. James Henshall's pronouncement on the black bass: "Inch for inch and pound for pound, the gamest fish that swims." If both sages are correct, the man who fishes for bass is surely blessed.

Henshall, although he did not make a distinction, certainly was referring to the smallmouth, *Micropterus dolomieu,* a truly American fish with a fighting heart. *M. salmoides,* the largemouth, is more widely known in America and has fine game-fish qualities, but when all factors are weighed the smallmouth must be said to exceed him.

157

*The late Doug Haines with
a beautifully barred, heavy smallmouth
taken in the White River district
of Ontario, Canada. This deep, clear,
rock-bound lake is
choice habitat of this species.*

In his own way the smallmouth is a handsome fish. He is somewhat more slender than the largemouth, but has a wider tail. When hooked, he jumps a bit more readily and oftener, bores deeper, resists longer. He does his last fighting in the landing net. To a man who has taken many smallmouths the image of the fish is one of bravado and belligerence; he has a character reminiscent of the Spanish fighting bull. There is no delicacy of form or action in him. He is sheer power in dark armor.

Curiously, bass were slow to achieve game-fish status.

Even today other species take precedence in some areas. In eastern Maine, for example, which offers some of the finest smallmouth fishing in America, bass are largely ignored by the local anglers, who prefer to go after trout and landlocked salmon. Since the three fish frequently inhabit the same waters, the fishermen wait until the best part of the trout and salmon season is finished before turning to the bass. I admire trout and salmon as much as the next man, but to overlook the bass seems to me unjust and unrealistic. I think bass have given me more action per hour spent in angling than any other game fish.

The first real champion of the black bass as a game fish was Dr. Henshall. Noting that trout and salmon were becoming less numerous in the 1860's, he predicted that the day would come when the bass would be recognized as America's premier game fish. He also said that as soon as proper tackle was developed bass fishing would move to the "very forefront of angling effort." A hundred years later one can say he was not very far wrong.

The two species of *Micropterus* are closely related

members of the sunfish family and often are found in the same waters. If a geographical separation can be made, it is that the smallmouth is the northern black bass, the largemouth his southern cousin. There is considerable overlapping of range, however. Smallmouths may be found in the Deep South and largemouths far up into Ontario, Canada.

Originally, the smallmouth had a more limited range than the largemouth, although it could not be said to be cramped: the Upper Mississippi and its eastern tributaries to the Allegheny range, the St. Lawrence drainage, upper New York state, and Lake Champlain. Extensive transplanting was begun about 1850, when it was discovered that the fish were rugged enough to survive transportation by rail and able to adapt to wide variations in water types and temperatures. Today their distribution runs from New Brunswick, Canada, across the southern belt of the Dominion to the Rockies, and then south, almost as far as the Gulf of Mexico. The smallmouth may be said to like somewhat colder water, water perhaps a bit cleaner than that tolerated by the largemouth; it is a good fast-water fish.

Both are co-operative enough to permit you to choose your angling method. They respond readily to the fly rod and its small lures, as well as to the heavier stuff tossed with a spinning or bait-casting rod. They take trolled lures and every conceivable natural bait, whether still-fished or cast. Finally, if you want to meet them on the simplest terms, they will go for a chunk of pork tossed over a weed bed with a cane pole. Each method, of course, must be applied in its own time and place.

To take smallmouths with any degree of consistency, you must have knowledge of the fish in its specific waters, and this may vary enormously. In northern, deep-water lakes, the fish stay in the shallows only for a brief period in late spring and early summer. Hot weather always finds them in the cool depths. Normally, they are daylight feeders, but the reverse is true in the heavily fished, warmer waters of the South, where bass become night feeders during hot weather. Bass are highly sensitive to heavy fishing pressure, speedboat racing, water skiing and other summer nonsense. It does not take much of this sort of civilized activity to convert a bass into a nocturnal prowler.

159

Barbel fishing, from "The Complete Angler," 1825.

The smallmouth loves rocks and clean gravel, and seldom strays far from deep water to feed. He will hide near a submerged log or stump near the shore line when looking for food, but this lie will always be near a spot deep enough to give him protection, say, eight feet or more. The smallmouth does not like mud bottoms or heavy weed growth, if he has any choice in the matter.

In summer fishing, rocky shoals offshore in deep water are favored spots. Once a bass fisherman locates an underwater shoal or rock pile, he may take fish with a deep-running plug or with natural baits—and he usually keeps the location strictly to himself.

The smallmouth is generally a deep feeder, for the obvious reason that he spends comparatively little time in shallow water. Still, if you can catch him on the surface with a fly rod or light-lure casting tackle, you will have the finest bass fishing there is. When the fish are working in the shallows along shore, during the early weeks of the season, their reaction to a surface bug or popper is startling. A smallmouth is no lure follower. If he decides to smash at a top-water bait, he does so promptly and positively—usually before the bait has been retrieved more than a few feet. This makes accuracy in placing the lure extremely important.

His speed in taking a surface lure is matched only by his speed in ejecting it when he discovers it is not food. He is extremely perceptive about this, more so than any other game fish. An angler's reaction time must match that of the fish if he expects to hook many rises. It is nearly impossible to strike too soon when the bass explodes under bug or plug. By the time you see his rise, he will have either taken the lure or rejected it. He might miss it, but rarely. A mature bass takes with precision. His cavernous mouth and large, flaring gill covers suck the lure in when he operates this equipment all at the same speedy instant.

Smallmouths are great travelers. They may move miles in search of food. In the St. Lawrence River, tagging experiments show that smallmouths commonly travel ten miles or more up and down the river in a week or less. In my own experience, I inadvertently "tagged" a smallmouth and recovered him later some distance away.

One early July evening I was casting a small live frog at the mouth of a spring brook coming into the Canadian side of Spednic Lake, New Brunswick. After a few casts along the edges of a log boom, I struck a heavy fish that took as the frog hit the surface. I set promptly with the limber spinning rod and just as promptly the light, braided nylon line snapped. Checking the line I discovered that it had been scorched (probably by a cigarette) a foot or two above the six-foot leader. The bass was now trailing the leader and a short piece of line.

Two evenings later I was working over a channel between two islands. I was using a small surface plug and had taken three or four bass feeding on minnows. Again I had a heavy surface smash from a big bass and this time fought him to the canoe. I tired him thoroughly, since I was not keeping fish and didn't want to net him. As he came along the side, gasping, I ran my thumb into his mouth and lifted him by the lower jaw, which seems to stun a bass long enough for the hook to be worked free. Sure enough, my leader and a piece of braided line, with a scorched end, hung from the corner of his jaws. I extracted both hooks and slid him back. There is no doubt that it was the same fish that had taken my frog at the mouth of the brook —some four miles away!

160

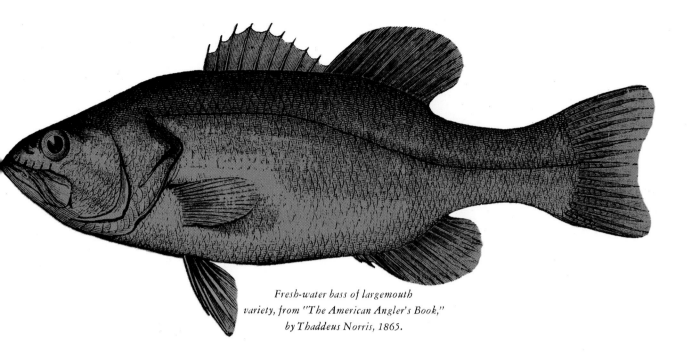

LARGEMOUTH
Black Bass

No one can ever accuse the largemouth bass of failing to live up to his name. For his size he has the biggest mouth of all fresh-water fish, and he works hard to keep it filled. This endears him to the angler who seeks to fill the mouth with a tempting lure or bait.

The largemouth also has done his part to fulfill Dr. James Henshall's prediction about the place of black bass among American game fish. And he is very nearly ubiquitous. He is at home in every one of the forty-eight states, and even in the fiftieth, but not, I think, in Alaska.

As to his surroundings, nothing discourages a large-mouth. You can drop him into a noisome mudhole and somehow he seems to survive, either through sheer courage or complete ignorance of what makes a good habitat for fish.

The best thing about the bigmouth bass—just another of his many local names—is that he provides good fishing for many thousands of anglers. Countless farm ponds have been created primarily to support this fish, and he thrives there, too. It is difficult to think of a location in the United States that is not within a few hours' distance of bass.

Ever since the black bass species were recognized—and it was not easy to pin them down, judging by the array of scientific names they have borne over the past century — the largemouth and the smallmouth have created a certain confusion among inexperienced observers. They are, of course, similar, but the differences are sufficiently wide for a veteran fisherman to identify either one at the first jump.

First, the matter of color. The smallmouth is darker than the largemouth, as well as of a different hue. The smallmouth is black or brownish, the largemouth has a greenish tone. It must also be remembered that there may be variations within each species depending on where the fish has been taken.

Both species usually are darkly striped. The smallmouth may have several stripes running vertically to his length. In the largemouth, the stripe may be absent, but where it appears it is broad and runs horizontally the length of his side.

The heads also offer several identifying differences. The smallmouth's upper-jaw line extends only to the center of his eye—*never* beyond. The largemouth's *always* extends beyond the eye. The smallmouth often has five bars radiating backward from the eye; the largemouth has none. The smallmouth has fourteen to eighteen rows of scales across the cheek, the largemouth never more than twelve. Finally, the dorsal fin of the largemouth has a division between the spiny and soft portions, the smallmouth's dorsal always has a distinct connection between the two areas.

No angler can say he has found the best technique for taking largemouth bass. The cosmopolitan tastes of the fish and his incredible adaptability to many types of water offer an angler the widest possible choice in method. Furthermore, the largemouth has no scruples about spending much of his time in fairly shallow water. If there's a fallen log, a rotting tree stump, or a bunch of lily pads anywhere in largemouth waters, the odds are favorable that a bass or two will be hiding in the vicinity, usually out of the direct rays of the sun. Once you have located your fish, you can approach him —as you can the smallmouth—with almost anything in the bait or tackle box.

Heavy fishing pressure in bass waters has made the fish more sophisticated in the past twenty-five years. The great, outlandish wooden baits that scored heavily some years back no longer fool a big bass, except possibly at night or in wilderness country. For like the brown trout, the largemouth bass can be classed as a game fish of civilization. The best largemouth waters are readily accessible and well worked. Successful angling for bass demands thorough knowledge of the locality and flexibility in fishing methods.

When I was a youngster living in farm country, bass already were becoming educated. For years the "killer" on the shallow, warm-water lakes was the "Decker plug," a fat, heavy, surface lure that spewed water from a propeller head when retrieved rapidly. It had indeed been a killer in its time, but it had been tossed too often and too carelessly on our bass waters. Bass were beginning to ignore it.

Like other bass fishermen, I worked the Decker plug. Yet, no matter how carefully I dropped it ahead of those big bass which fed so savagely among the weeds and lily pads, it simply scared them away. Of course, I also

In the South, largemouth bass run in sloughs lined with dense waterweeds.

tried live baits, although without enjoyment or success. The big lunker bass continued to feed within easy reach, their dorsal fins exposed as they came into the shallows, almost every summer sunrise. Diffidently, I thought that perhaps a fly rod might make a more delicate approach, if I had the right lure.

My only heavy fly rod was a crude, jointed steel Bristol, quite strong enough to handle a big bass, I felt. I could not get much distance on a cast, but I was prepared to rely on a quiet approach. For a lure I chose a cork-head feather minnow in brown and green, which was the only lure recommended for bass on the fly rod that I could find in the tackle shop.

With the feather minnow tied securely to a stout gut leader three feet long, I was certain I could hang onto a fairly heavy bass. I waded out from the marshy shore of the pond just far enough to reach the edge of the lily pads where I had seen the bass.

The day was not ideal. The sun beat down from a pale-blue July sky, unhampered by clouds. The pond simmered in the afternoon heat, glassy smooth, with

no sign of life, except for the dragonflies darting over the lilies. It would be better, I told myself, if I could wait until sundown to try the new lure, but my evening farm chores would prevent that. A few more steps and the warm water was above my knees. Now I could put the awkward little minnow fly right on the edge of a pocket with a sidearm toss of the rod.

The lure spatted on the calm water about thirty feet away, close to the pads. It rested there in a tiny, widening circle momentarily, then I raised the rod and wiggled it toward me. It moved about a yard before disappearing in a quick swirl. I struck quickly and mightily, and was fast to a bass. He was not big. Maybe a pound, I thought, as he jumped clear and I had a look at him in the bright sunlight. He bored for the safety of the pads, but I checked him easily and skidded him over the surface until he came within reach. I lifted him out by the lower jaw, extracted the single hook from his leathery tongue and strung him on a piece of clothesline at my belt.

It was no trouble to take bass on that little feather

Hooked largemouth leaves his habitat in a boil of water, a shower of spray.

*Shore-line casting with top-water
lures (pages 164 through 169) is the sportiest
technique in bass fishing.
Lure is retrieved slowly and carefully,
the bass follows
and takes with a heavy swirl. Once hooked,
the fish leaps to throw the
angler's lure, providing sport right
up to the gunwale.*

minnow. The fish, in fact, were wild about it. As I waded along the shallows, it seemed I was raising a bass every three or four casts. It may not have been that easy, but I certainly had action. I missed a number of rises by being too slow on the strike with that clumsy rod. Yet I hooked at least half of my catch for no other reason than because the fish rose so enthusiastically. These largemouths took the lure so deeply I had little to do except keep them clear of the weeds.

In three hours or so, I had twelve bass on that piece of clothesline—one of them a four-pounder—and had released a few small ones that would not have exceeded a pound each. At that time, I was not given to releasing fish, but the dozen I kept were all I cared to haul on the three-mile walk home. I was happy at

having achieved a big catch, but perhaps even more for having solved a fishing problem more or less on my own. I knew of no one who had taken such a string of bass from that pond, or, for that matter, who had ever taken bass on a fly-rod lure. Nor anyone who took bass from that particular pond during the bright, sultry hours of a midsummer afternoon.

The point is that I was dealing with bass that already were lure-shy and, perhaps, line-shy as well. In those days the plug caster used a black silk line of at least eighteen-pounds test, and this was rigged directly to the plug with a small snap swivel. The idea of a small, delicate top-water lure fished on a gut leader was new for that water and even for that time.

Perhaps just as important was the novelty of the lure itself. Game fish often respond hungrily to a new design of lure—at first. Then, as its novelty wears off, its effectiveness decreases, and, in time, it may be discarded for one of the more durable favorites.

Since that first day with bass on a fly rod, I have been a confirmed bass-bug fisherman. The peculiar excitement of this fishing is, like dry-fly fishing for trout, in the rise. Because the fish must be hooked instantly, he usually gives you a good show on the surface from the very beginning of the battle. Even trout and salmon fly-fishermen can find charm, subtlety, and spirit in fly-rod bug fishing for bass.

In heavily fished waters the feather-light bass bug seems to deceive wary bass more readily than any other surface lure. In fact, it is not unusual to find bass so

167

shy that even the small bass bug will be more effective if first dropped on a lily pad or bounced off a log before it hits the water. This suggests that the little lure has fallen to the water accidentally. Largemouth bass can be frightened easily by any unnatural movements of the lure.

The largemouth must be respected for his militant response to artificial lures. This alone places him among the top game fish. I don't believe that since those boyhood days I have ever found it necessary to fish for largemouth bass with any lure other than an artificial, whether the fish were surface feeding or out in deeper water. I cannot say the same of the smallmouth; there have been times on certain waters when I was forced to fish with natural bait to take a few fish. Perhaps this is not everyone's experience, but I am sure most bass anglers will say that the largemouth is truly cooperative about taking artificials—in a wide range of types, sizes, actions, materials, and colors. The variety of lures that purport to take bass—and usually do—is staggering. Although I have been closely associated with the tackle business for more than thirty years, I'm sure I have not seen more than half of the lures used for bass in that time.

The well-equipped bass fisherman has much the same approach to selecting tackle as the trout fisherman. He prepares for every possible vagary of the fish's mood in specific waters, at specific times in a season, and even to the specific hour of the day. The feeding depth of largemouth bass may range during any one day from the surface to thirty feet down. The character of the lake, the variation in its bottom, its crop of food, its vegetation, the clarity of its water, and the amount of natural cover it affords, all affect where, when, and how the bass will feed.

Angling logic dictates that fish must be approached at the level where they live and feed. Surface-feeding bass will take plugs and bugs of various sizes, with some variety of action and color. (Actually, I am not convinced that the color of a surface lure makes much difference to a bass, since he sees only its underbelly, which has less variation in color than does the body.) Going deeper, when bass are working in water up to ten feet in depth, a variety of diving, wobbling plugs is needed. For deep-lying fish in hot weather, sinking plugs are required, and this line-up must be augmented by plugs of several sizes and in several colors. (In underwater lures I believe this *is* significant.)

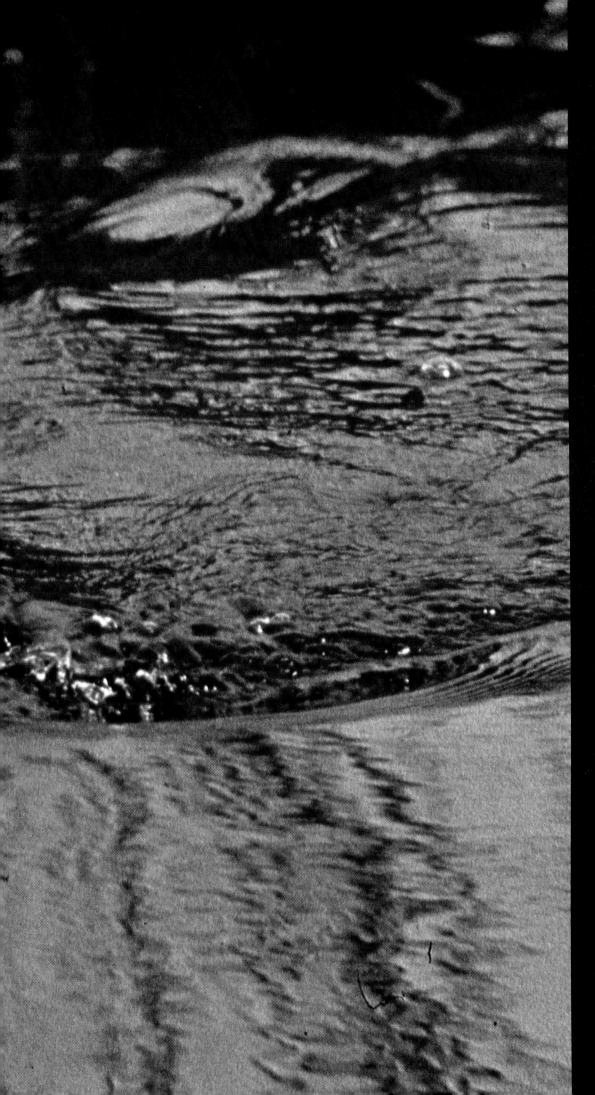

Huge mouth and militant spirit of the largemouth bass spur him to attack the largest and gaudiest of wooden baits.

Floating logs at edges of deep water are favorite largemouth hide-outs.

Just *what* these colors should be is another question, answerable only on the basis of local conditions—food, water coloration, and many other factors. Certainly it is true that bass in different bodies of water have different color preferences. In one lake it may be yellow, in another green, in another red and white. Only sound local knowledge and much fishing can determine this.

Color alone won't catch fish. It is also important that the angler "work" his lure properly. The mood of the fish at the moment must be considered and evaluated. At or near spawning time, bass are belligerent and will usually smash at any small object coming near them. Later in the season, when the bass are more wary, a surface lure must be placed precisely and retrieved slowly to give the fish time to look it over while deciding whether it seems good to eat.

In one Catskill lake where I have done much bug fishing, the bass absolutely refuse to follow a moving bug. The lure must be dropped within their striking range (within their window of vision) and left motionless on the surface. It may lie there for a full two minutes before a bass will rise slowly, look it over, and charge it. Twitching or moving the bug on this lake is taboo. The bass either are frightened by the movement or too lazy to take up the chase.

On another small lake, about twenty miles away, the largemouth make different demands on the fisherman. Here the best fishing is in the first hour after daybreak

Big Dardevle spoon is more properly used to lure pike, but largemouth will take it.

with a diving plug fished about one foot under the surface. I took a friend of mine there for his first trip on a sultry July morning, when mist was rising from the dark water between the stumps and lily-pad patches just as the eastern sky glowed pink.

I had taken many big bass here on a certain pike-scale finish diving plug. I was already rigged with one and I had given one to my friend. As my guest he was given first crack at a bass moving at the edge of lily pads, near deep water. His first cast went beyond the fish, as it should have. He reeled it back directly under the tiny ripples left from the last feeding boil. The bass should have whacked it, but he did not. My friend apparently was giving the plug an exaggerated, unnat-

ural action by reeling in too fast. He had no better luck with the next three or four fish and somewhat sheepishly asked what I thought he was doing wrong. I suggested that he slow the retrieve. He did, but the bass would not take. He surrendered his turn to me.

Using the same plug, I took a three-pounder on the first cast. Then two more, slightly smaller, on the next few casts. Before the fish stopped feeding, we had handled sixteen bass; he had taken only one. This fish hit the plug as it lay motionless on the quiet water while he picked out a backlash.

My friend managed to impart an acceptable rhythm to his retrieve before the end of summer, and from then on took bass as well as I did. Perhaps it had some-

*Three-pound bass, like
the ones at left, usually put on the biggest
show but sometimes throw
the lure, as above.*

thing to do with sonic vibrations. I'm sure I don't know.

Bass, largemouth especially, sometimes can be induced to smash at a lure in anger if they can be riled rather than scared off. Careful casts above or alongside a fish may be infuriating enough to make him slash savagely at the nuisance. Often, if it's a surface lure, he will knock it high into the air. Just as often, if you should hook one of these angry bass, you'll find him foulhooked over the nose or under the chin. I suspect that these fish have no intention of eating the lure. They smash at it to kill it or get it out of the way.

Whatever the reason, you will find that bass are rugged individuals. When you locate a big one in a good stump or log hide-out, you can expect to gain his attention, time after time, if you stalk carefully and cast accurately. A bass usually stays in one of these refuges until he is taken. And most likely, when you have conquered one bull bass in his lair, a cousin will be lurking there the next time you come along. A good lie for one big bass will be a good lie for others, if the water level and natural shelter remain unchanged.

The largemouth is a forthright game fish. He usually will meet you on your own terms, but sometimes he's moody enough to make you employ your full bag of tricks. I like best his spirit of recklessness in belting a surface lure and his solid determination to put on a good show in the air. He may wait in hiding like a fat cat watching his prey approach, but more often than not he is a bulldog in his attack and in his singleness of purpose. It is easy to echo Dr. Henshall's prediction that the bass will be America's number one game fish for the foreseeable future.

175

White Bass, Yellow Bass, Rock Bass—Bluegill & Crappie

Neither the smallmouth nor the largemouth are true bass. Although we always permit them their popular name, they are actually members of the sunfish family. Of true bass, there are but two species important enough to mention: the white bass and the yellow bass. The rock bass is simply another member of the sunfish group.

The white and yellow bass and a dozen or more members of the sunfish family that includes bluegills or "brim," and crappies, all masquerade under the ambiguous title of pan fish. The title is apt enough, for all of these fish are of frying-pan size and spend a short time in this utensil before being consumed by people who know good food when they see it. But it's

likely that the name pan fish was bestowed by anglers whose major interest was in big fish—musky, pike, steelhead, and the like—and who felt that the little fellows were beneath their dignity.

Nonetheless; while pan fishing is a gentle sport, somehow akin to bird watching, it can produce fast action at times and is something to fall back on when the bigger game fish are out of sorts. For the young fisherman, pan fish furnish an apprenticeship in angling, and in later years a proving ground for tackle and technique.

Now, having justified the existence of pan fish in angling terms, we can get to the nub of the matter: fishing for pan fish is fun. There's no use pretending

A deep, quiet pool,
sheltered by a rock ledge is choice lie for
sunfish. All members of this
family love to gather in low water.

Right: Gentlemen anglers
try their luck on an English stream,
from Henry Alken's
"National Sports of Great Britain,"
London, 1821.

that they engage in tackle-testing battles. They don't. Nor is it much of a strain to match wits with them. The pleasure in fishing for them is that they always are there, wherever fish are found.

Some species have seasonal "runs" that excite fishermen for miles around. I remember getting into a heavy traffic jam late one afternoon in the Upper Mississippi Valley as we were heading for the north country and musky. When we finally were forced to stop, I asked the driver ahead what was causing the holdup.

"White bass running in the river," he said. "They're ketchin' 'em like mad below the dam a few miles up." As indeed they were, we discovered, when we reached the spot about an hour later. The banks were lined solidly with fishermen for half a mile below the dam.

Every possible type of tackle was visible in the ranks, from long cane poles to bait-casting rods. Silvery fish were either flying through the air or flopping on the surface as they were reeled in. It was a carnival.

A good many of these white-bass pan fish were of respectable size, big enough to open many a trout fisherman's eyes. Two-pounders were fairly common, with most of the fish averaging about a pound. The bigger ones fought well against the anglers with light tackle but, under the circumstances, light tackle created some problems in fishing etiquette. There was little room to play a fish without crossing another angler's line. The fish hit so furiously it was simply a matter of "throw in, hang on, and haul."

These white bass and their relatives, the yellow bass, are native to the entire Mississippi Valley and are widely distributed in many of the large lakes. The white bass, in particular, has taken over in many lakes as the most important sport fish. Creel census checks on some waters show that white bass make up about half the total catch of all fish species taken.

The two basses are distant relatives of the salt-water striper and resemble him somewhat in fin arrangement and markings. The fresh-water bass are broader fish, however, and look almost identical, except for color. The white bass is dark gray to black on the back, with bright silvery sides, and a white belly. His stripes are less distinct than those of the salt-water striper. The yellow bass is really yellow—in some areas he is called the gold bass—and has a dark olive-green back. His stripes

179

are dark and distinct, and those appearing below the lateral line are always broken, or "interrupted." Thus, his scientific name, *Morone interrupta*. There are other distinguishing characteristics, but these will serve. Few fishermen care whether they catch white bass or yellow bass, as long as they are plentiful.

The white bass is a surface feeder when he is "running," the yellow bass is much less so. Both species are avid minnow feeders. The white bass, more than the yellow, varies his diet with insects and small crustaceans. As with all pan fish species, both fish travel in schools. When you find one you are likely to find a thousand. Yellow-bass fishermen usually troll deeply with a small lure or fly-and-spinner combination until a fish is taken, then they drop anchor on the spot to contact the school. Invariably, more will be taken at once. The method and lure you choose are of less importance than finding the feeding school. They have the largemouth's insatiable and promiscuous appetite and none of his caution.

This can be said of all pan fish to some degree. The smaller members—rock bass, bluegill, crappie, for instance—are hearty biters. And some of these fish show amazing courage.

One hot July afternoon I was bug fishing for smallmouth along the rocky shores of one of the Thousand Islands group in the upper St. Lawrence River. The bigger smallmouth weren't taking. But "red-eye" (rock bass) were there—plenty of them—eager to rise at every other cast. The ridiculous thing is that I was fishing with a large hair bug and the rock bass were barely large enough to take it in their small mouths.

Sunfish are found practically everywhere in the country. The bluegill sunfish, probably the largest of the dozen or so members of the family, adequately represents the clan. He is a tough character for his size, which rarely runs more than a pound, and fights with all the determination of a smallmouth bass. He's a zealous guardian of his nest during the spawning time and attacks any large fish that comes too close.

Bluegills usually don't school up like other pan fish, but you often can find enough in a "hole" or "bed" to keep you busy catching them for several hours. They feed heavily on insects and are just right for taking on small trout flies and the lightest fly-rod tackle. On this gear they really fight. Bluegills very likely have provided more fly-casting practice and fly-fishing experience for beginners than any other fish. They can be taken whenever the water is warm enough to keep them actively feeding, which means from early spring until after the first frost.

Crappies are also in the sunfish family, and prob-

181

*Still-fishing in deep holes near
brush (top) produces good daytime results
with white crappie (above).
Top right: Black crappie, also called
calico bass. Above right and
opposite page: One-man float fishing, fly casting
from shore, and small-lure casting
in snag-filled waters will take all species of
pan fish, including bluegill (far right).*

ably are caught in greater numbers than any other pan fish. When they're feeding near the surface over deep water, usually near sundown, the catch of crappies may be stated in bagfuls rather than in numbers. This is a prolific fish and its introduction into many bass lakes, particularly those of the South, has doomed other species. The crappie gets along well in muddy-water lakes and competes successfully with catfish, carp, and other rough fish long after the bass have given up.

The crappie comes in two colors—white or black—and carries a multitude of names, depending on where he lives. The white crappie may be called a strawberry perch, a crappet, a suckley perch, or any of a dozen other designations. Black crappies are sometimes called

calico bass, black perch, or strawberry bass. Both species are often called goggle-eyes (which is also true of rock bass). If you want to be sure whether you are catching white or black crappie, the easiest way is to count the spines in the dorsal fin: no more than seven (usually six) for the white crappie and seven to ten for the black crappie.

Crappies prefer deeper water than other sunfish species and it may be that this has something to do with their large protruding eyes. They do not like direct sunlight and when they school for feeding on the surface it is usually at dawn, dusk, or on cloudy days. Daylight fishing is best in the deep "crappie holes" near submerged weed beds, fallen trees, and

other natural covers. If you are still-fishing in the bright sun, you may find that the school will move under your boat for its shade. At such times you may catch them by dropping the bait just alongside the boat, but not by tossing it even a few yards off.

All pan fishing is action, plenty of action. If you don't care to spend a week stalking a musky, or an entire day taking a brace of bass, pan fishing is for you. You will find some variety of this gregarious clan in every type of water: the big lakes and rivers, the tiny farm pond, the meandering "cricks," the great water-power reservoirs. And best of all, you can take them on your fanciest tackle and artificials, or on a cut pole, a hank of cotton string, a black hook, and a worm.

183

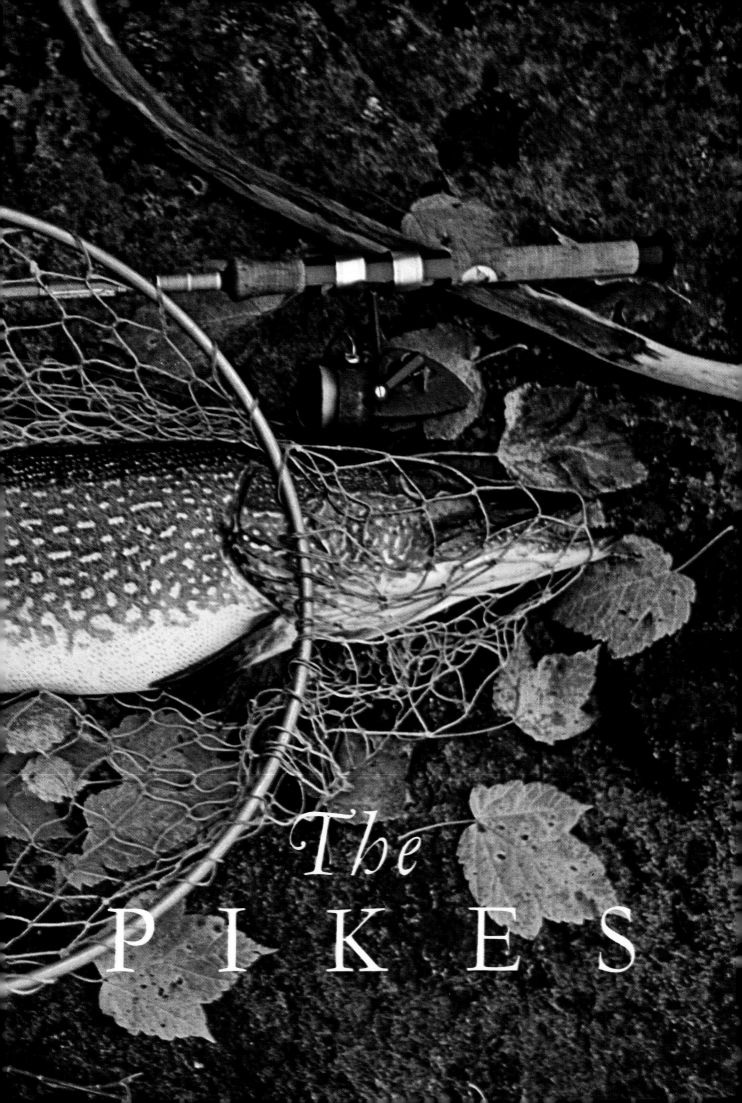

The
P I K E S

Preceding pages: Great northern pike.

MUSKELLUNGE

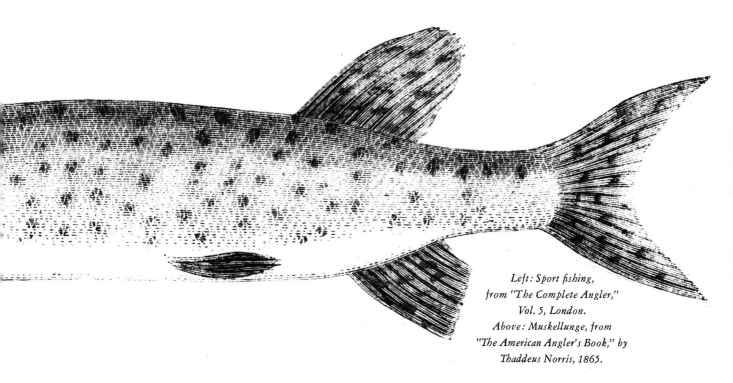

Left: Sport fishing,
from "The Complete Angler,"
Vol. 5, London.
Above: Muskellunge, from
"The American Angler's Book," by
Thaddeus Norris, 1865.

Blind ferocity cost Esox, the muskellunge, a full belly when he charged after a lone chub that was shuttling through the soggy branches of a submerged cedar. The chub escaped in a tangle of small boughs, and Esox did not see, until too late, the scattering gray shadows which had been a school of bigger chub following his intended victim. In a flicker of movement, the massed form of the school broke apart, each fish seeking safety from the marauder in the impenetrable thicket of treetop branches. Furiously, Esox gave chase to the darting chubs, his duck-billed mouth open, the tight rows of teeth exposed.

But not in time. He braked, swerved away, and came to rest with fins spread wide, his long head turned toward the sanctuary of the succulent minnows.

Esox was hungry. For many months, while his Canadian lake was mantled by a thick slab of blue-gray ice, he had taken little food. In his wintering grounds in a deep channel of the lake, smaller fish were not abundant during the soporific weeks of sub-zero cold. Much of the lake life that formed his regular diet was buried in the mud, hibernating until spring, and the few active schools of bait hid in shallow water.

When the ice left the lake, Esox had spent himself

Turbulent surface action is given
to the lure by the author, as he makes the
retrieve. Big musky strikes
savagely, leaps clear in a writhing
jump, re-enters headfirst.

in spawning over the weedy shallows in the casual manner of the pike family, then abandoned the females to search for food. He had roved above the weed beds beginning to sprout from the muddy bottom and searched among the stumps and logs near the shore line, but the hunt was not good. The water had not yet warmed enough to bring on the schools of pan fish. Coming one morning to the mouth of a small creek, he had managed to seize a pair of suckers as they headed into the moving water toward their spawning grounds, but that was days ago. The chubs in the submerged cedar were his first chance for a proper meal.

Now Esox was alert. He lay quietly along the length of a log resting on the bottom, a few yards from the hide of the minnows. His dark, brownish sides and back blended well with this background. He could easily be taken for a piece of waterlogged timber floating a few inches off the bottom. Only his eyes, as large as a human being's, moved—forward ever so slightly, then back, then upward as he scanned every tiny movement within his range of vision. He was not interested in the dragonfly nymphs crawling along the bottom or the stray leech that moved sinuously from beneath the log and swam directly before his long snout. This was food for bass or lesser fish, of value only in that it might lure an acceptable victim within killing range of the musky. But no small fish appeared. Esox decided to move on.

A hundred yards farther along, Esox came to a jumble of dead timber that had been piled up by strong winds from the west. Logs lay crisscrossed on the surface, many with butts resting well up on the rocky shore. Esox drifted through the dark recesses under the logs, but no chubs showed. Lazily he poked his snout toward the deeper waters; there was a plop on the surface. A white-footed mouse had fallen into the water and was swimming for shore. A quick flirt of his tail brought Esox gliding under the steadily moving mouse. A hole opened in the surface, a wide pair of jaws enveloped the mouse. In a moment only a swirl marked the breakfast spot of the big musky.

By the end of June, Esox's lean flanks had filled. The water had warmed. The weeds, now grown to the surface, held scores of small fish within the musky's reach. He would rest passively in a small pocket, ready to snare from ambush. Nothing coming within yards of his gold-flecked eye was safe: suckers grubbing along the muddy bottom, yellow-sided bluegills flashing through light and shadow among the weeds, a small northern pike also on the hunt.

Along the shore near these hunting grounds, a black duck had successfully raised a brood of nine ducklings by herding them always within the protective shelter of the tall reeds growing in the marshy shallows. Often, in the evening, she led her family in search of insects, always single file, always out of range of big fish. But the largest duckling of the nine, more precocious than the others, was bent on going his own way. Many times the mother was forced to turn him back from deep water and nudge him, as he peeped loudly, back into formation.

One day, as the sun dropped below the marsh, the duckling paddled within range of Esox, who lay along the edge of a lily-pad bed. The great fish pushed his thirty pounds away from the pads and, charging to the top, clutched the bird in a bulging vortex of amber water. Barely a suck of sound could be heard as the fish drove downward with his prey, and only a few tiny feathers drifted among the pads where the starlike white blossoms already were closed for the night.

The next day, as long shadows stretched over the pads, another lively swimming creature came over Esox's window of vision. This was a brighter bird, although smaller. It was golden-yellow, with wings flashing rhythmically over the calm water at the tip of a widening V-ripple. Its dangling feet were curved and sharply tipped. To Esox it seemed to be easy prey. He gave chase, came to the lure, and engulfed it with an enthusiastic surge of spray.

As the hooks bit, the big musky ground down vengefully on the surface lure. Energized by a killing rage, his teeth sank into the soft wood of the plug. But the sting of the hooks was sure. He could not get rid of it. Furious, he jumped clear, swinging his long head and rattling his gill covers. The belly treble tore free, carrying with it a strip of soft tissue from Esox's upper jaw.

Author tangles at close range with a twenty-pound musky on a six-ounce, bamboo fly rod.

Again he leaped, but the dangling plug would not shake out. Esox dove, then, for the weeds.

He swung to the side and the weight against the line grew heavy. The fisherman held tight; the fish swam under full power. The line snapped suddenly at the wire trace and Esox swept away, trailing the plug. Fifty yards beyond, he tried once again to toss the lure by jumping clear, to the chagrin of the angler still reeling in slack line.

The yellow plug and its length of wire leader remained in the musky's upper jaw for two days. It caught on the weeds as Esox moved through his normal hide-outs, not paining him greatly, but hampering his freedom. Then, as he pursued a chub one morning, the free treble hook caught on a tough root of a tree stump. The chub fled into a dark hole, but Esox could not follow. He was snagged. He jerked his head in anger, in terror. He writhed, twisted, and rolled. The big hooks still held. Esox sulked, thrashed aimlessly, then gathered his strength for a final lunge. The hook tore loose under the power of his drive, leaving a long rent in his upper mandible.

The muskellunge passed the many hot days of summer in the screening cover of deep water. Sporadically, when a gray day brought murky clouds and rain from the east, he moved into the weeds nearer shore, but he no longer fed with enthusiasm. A pair of frogs or a small sucker kept him going for days.

By the time autumn's first frost tinged the tama-racks with yellow, Esox's appetite had returned. He cruised the edge of deep channels, terrorizing the bait schools, slashing in sheer meanness, killing more than he needed to eat. The lean days of winter were not far off and his survival instinct urged him to build extra flesh. He was less choosy now, more vigorous as the water cooled, and he challenged any intrusion of his domain by creatures of smaller size.

He was attracted one morning by the sight of an object passing overhead. It moved steadily, and Esox, suspicious and vigilant, watched it as it flashed by, throwing off rays of light like the silvery sides of a whitefish. He trailed it briefly, and as it seemed about to escape into a weed pocket, he charged it and clamped down fiercely on its hard metal side. Turning, he felt once again the bite of the barb, a long-forgotten sensation, far different from the soft resistance of a minnow's tender body. Again he rushed and leaped, jingling the spoon in the air as he came clear.

Now he fought a different fight. He did not rush for the weeds. He surged out into the clear, deep channel, forcing many yards of line from the reel. Failing to outrun the curbing tension behind him, he bored down, rolled, and twisted to tear the lure free.

For half an hour he fought the good musky fight. Twice he came within view of the boat, saw the shining curve of the gaff hook as it thrust toward him, and burst away in fear. There was no escape. He was free to rush away as he pleased, but only under growing

Angling for musky on light tackle is all action. On ten-pound line and spinning gear, author is forced to give fish his head.

pressure. Before long, he was powerless against the steady spring of the rod.

Joe, the Indian guide, held the gaff underwater as Esox came near. Spent, the fish did not protest as the hook passed up through his long under jaw, and he was hauled, flopping feebly, over the gunwale.

Muskies of the "Old Fighter" class invariably carry battle scars. If the fisherman's big treble hooks haven't left their marks on his jaws, there will be other signs of conflict: old wounds on his sides, frayed fins, a ragged edge on the tail, all suggesting that the fish has lived dangerously since he came from the egg. I have seen few large muskellunge that were unscathed.

This, of course, befits the temperament and character of *Esox masquinongy*. Frank Forester, in his mid-nineteenth-century classic, *Fish and Fishing in the United States,* wrote that the musky "is the boldest, fiercest, and most voracious of fresh-water fish; and there is none, unless it be the Great Lake Trout, that can offer any adequate resistance to his attacks." There is some doubt that Forester had, in fact, ever caught a musky at the time he wrote this; his meticulous anatomical account of the fish derived from study of a specimen preserved in spirits by Professor Louis Agassiz of Harvard. Nonetheless, his representation of the fish was accurate then and holds true today.

The musky's form is long, thick, and powerful, and he moves with the speed and deadly intent of a torpedo. His lower jaw is undershot, like that of a bulldog, and his cavernous mouth is well endowed with grabbing and cutting teeth. These features, together with his large eyes, give him an evil aspect that is quite compatible with his morose spirit and crafty nature. He is admirably equipped for attack, and skillful in defense. He is always difficult to lure, more difficult to hook, and sometimes impossible to land.

Yet in his fierce, wild way, the musky is a handsome creature. He is quite similar to the northern pike in body shape and fin arrangement, but pronouncedly different in detail. His long body is thicker and more powerful than that of other pikes. His body marks are dark on a light background, the reverse of the pike pattern of light on dark. The musky's colors, which may vary from deep brown to light green in different waters, are more vivid than the pike's and his markings are sharper. He has a metallic lustre—bronze, blue, and green—about his head, gill covers, and upper sides. And, unlike the pike, he has scales only on the upper half of the cheek and opercle. (The pike is fully scaled on the cheek, half-scaled on the opercle.)

The musky is a Canadian citizen by ancestry and evolution. His Canadian name is maskinonge, which derives from the Obijway Indian word *mashkinonje,* through the French *masque* (face) + *allonge* (long). Thus, "long face," which is true enough. In the United States, he is called muskellunge. Everywhere varied spellings are permissible: muskallonge, muskallunge, maskalonge, maskanonge.

He is a low-country fish and requires big water, both factors dictated by his appetite. High mountain lakes or small bodies of water would never supply the vast amounts of food fish he consumes. He also needs cover —great weed beds in which to sulk quietly while waiting for fish, frogs, baby muskrats, young waterfowl, or even other muskies, to stray near enough to trigger his attack. These conditions are found in the area encircling the Great Lakes and the St. Lawrence River Valley. In New York state, Chautauqua Lake is the original home of a subspecies, the striped, or "tiger," musky, whose name derives from his vertical bar markings. But the tiger may now be found in many other lakes, as well.

Muskies have been introduced into the Ohio Valley and a bit further south, but Ontario still has the best musky waters in size, number, and the essential quality of wilderness that keeps a musky happy—if there ever was a happy musky!

Even in these ideal areas, muskies are not plentiful. More than any other fresh-water fish they lead a "lone-wolf" existence. Finding a school of muskies is unthinkable. It sometimes takes days of searching to find even one, and locating him is only the first step of the campaign to capture him. Any musky you catch will be a trophy fish, regardless of his size.

The lair of these tigers of fresh water is usually a sunken weed bed, a thick pad of lilies or other water growth, a deep hole in rocky bottom, or a sand bar in mid-lake. Wherever minnows or small pan fish congregate is a likely spot to find a musky. He prob-

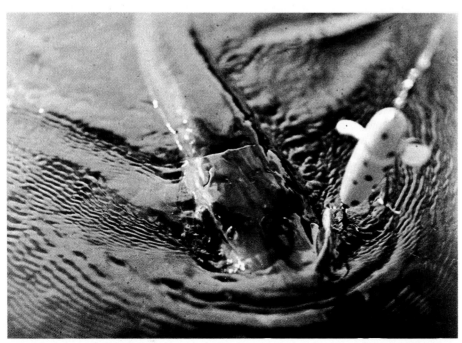

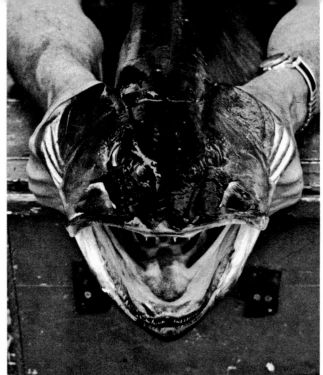

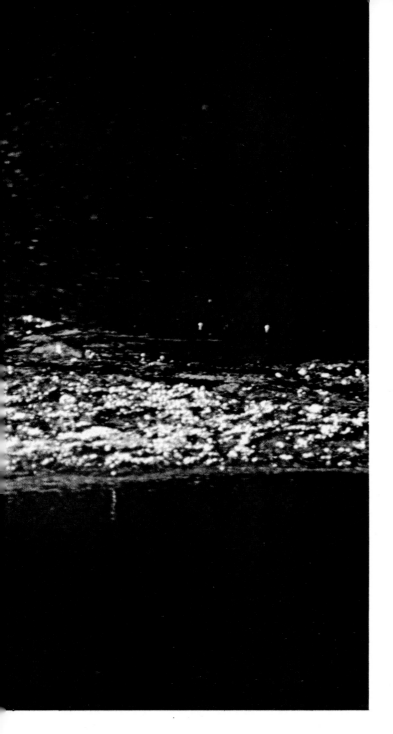

Onslaught of musky (above and
far left) taking surface
lure is spectacular, powerful. But spring of light
rod tires him, so that later (left) he
can be released. Toothy maw (above right)
leaves marks on Mud Puppy
(center) and other musky (below)

195

ably prefers a sucker to any other food. Stream inlets and outlets, where a faint flow of current attracts schools of suckers, are perfect places for a musky to lie at the edge of deep water, preparing for an attack.

More than other pikes, the musky shows great willingness to rise to surface lures. The explanation, if one exists, is that the musky is bolder than his cousins in showing himself on the surface and has no qualms about seizing any swimming creature that he can swallow. From an angler's point of view, this quality puts the musky in the top bracket of sport fish. I have taken a good many muskies on top-water plug lures. The savagery of their rise is always hair-raising.

The fish often follows a surface lure, creating a heavy wake, before taking. For the fisherman the suspense is agonizing. The powerful body pushes up a strong V on the surface. It comes closer and closer to the moving plug. Questions arise: Will he decide to grab the lure before it nears the boat? Should the retrieve be cut down to give the fish more time? (The latter seldom works.)

In the end, the fish makes the decision. His great, brownish shape may come into full view directly under the rod tip, with his baleful eyes watching first the plug, then your movements as you lift the plug from the surface. He may pause a moment or two, in full view, before he sinks from sight with imperceptible fin movement, or he may surge away with a great sweep of his tail, leaving first a wide hole in the surface, then a boiling surge of water that means a final exit. The crafty fish seldom can be lured again, once he recognizes the fisherman and the boat for what they are. Muskies get big by being fairly wise.

At certain times, muskies do a great deal of following without taking. Your lure, tossed over a weed bed and into his window of vision, may coax him out four or five times before he becomes bored and follows no more. But he is just as likely to smash the lure before it has moved more than a yard or two.

When a muskellunge takes, it is with destructive intent. The plug hobbles over the surface toward you. Then it is gone in a dynamic burst of spray and a mighty "thwack" of sound. You come back against the fish sharply, setting the hooks somewhere among that forest of teeth, hoping that at least one of the barbs has found a soft spot to catch and hold.

With the hook set, the musky dictates the fight. Throwing his weight against you, he makes his first surprised run. Then he bursts out in a shower of spattering drops and foam. His head shakes viciously, his gills show bright red, his saurian jaws grind down on the lure and its stinging hooks. Still pinned, he tries another furious jump. If the hooks remain with him, he runs swiftly for the nearest weed bed. If you can check him before he reaches this sanctuary, you have a chance. Thwarted, the fish will switch tactics. He rolls. He twists. He winds yards of your wire leader and line around his long, supple frame. If your luck holds, the coils may slip off when he charges ahead on his next run. If you can keep him away from weeds and snags, retain your hold with the hook, and restrain him in his full-power surges, you will, in time, bring him within reach, where you can slide the gaff into the V-pocket of his lower jaw.

Muskies are tough physically, as well as mentally. In catching all the fish shown on these pages, many were manhandled thoroughly before the guides and I could extract the hooks and return the victims to the water. Since I was using a light spinning rod and fly-rod tackle to get the most action from the fish, most of the muskies were completely whipped before we could get them into the boat. The bigger ones—up to thirty pounds—we gaffed through the lower jaw before lifting them into the boat to work out the hooks. This often took some doing when twenty-five pounds of fish were flopping frantically, yet all the fish survived. At least, we watched the lake day after day for signs of a dead fish and never spotted one.

One musky in particular—a handsome, striped fighter—came into the boat in full possession of his power. This fish left his underwater weed bed to follow my top-water Globe bait as I retrieved it briskly. Behind the plug the familiar V-wake of a trailing musky appeared, about fifty feet away. As the plug came closer, so did the push of water ahead of the fish. Now the lure was twenty feet from the boat, now ten. I reeled, lowering the rod tip, until only the two feet of casting trace wire connected the rod to the lure. And then the musky savaged the plug, throwing sheets of spray over me as I struck back at him. Stung, he jumped high and clear, and fell into the boat.

A twenty-pound musky fresh from his element and

tossing a free-swinging plug with an exposed treble hook just a few inches from a man's legs is a frightening sight. Worse, the fish thrashed into a cluster of rods, all rigged, that lay against a boat seat. He messed these up instantly, tangling plugs, lines, and rods into a writhing bundle. The guide, thinking quickly, began to thump him over the head with a paddle. About a dozen good licks quieted him down enough for us to go to work on him.

Our combined efforts finally got the plug free, and I gave the fish a heave out and away, glad to be rid of him. Stunned, he hit the surface and floated there on his side. This, I thought, is one fish that we will be bound to recover and save for lunch. But as we watched, one of his fins flickered and his tail stirred a bit. Finally, he righted himself and dove quickly toward the weeds. We saw him no more.

The enigma of musky fishing—what they will take and when—keeps an angler forever on his toes, employing many lures and baits in casting, trolling, and still-fishing. It is a matter of matching one's cunning against that of the fish, switching methods endlessly. Persistence in keeping a lure in the water where a fish can see it is the only firm rule in musky fishing.

The theory of "a big meal for musky" has for many years prompted anglers to try huge plugs and spoons, and these will take big fish at times. Yet the standard-sized bass plug takes as many big fish and many more of the smaller muskies. More comforting is the fact that the bass plug can be handled on lighter tackle and demands less arm power of the fisherman. For trolling, of course, there is no limit to the size of the lure that can be used if the rod and line is rugged enough to stand the strain. Big, flashy, revolving spoons, ahead of a bunch of gaudy hair and feathers, can be relied upon to attract the attention of the fish when the trolling is in fairly deep water, along submerged weeds and rock shoals.

Yet I hesitate to be too positive. The musky's response to lure or bait is essentially unpredictable, and so is his behavior when hooked. The fisherman must always be flexible and accommodate his tactics to the fish. For if ever you "freeze" on your reel handle—as many a good fisherman has done—your sole accomplishment for the day will have been to add to the education of another muskellunge.

Great NORTHERN Pike

Pike, by Bunny & Gold, reprinted in "The Complete Angler," Vol. 5.

There is much about the great northern pike to stir the fisherman's imagination, but too few fishermen realize this. They confuse him with the pickerel and ignore him if there is a chance for musky.

Yet here is a powerful game fish and a willing adversary that strikes avidly and indiscriminately at the angler's lure. There is no known lure—provided it is large enough—that the pike refuses to take. Spoons, spinners, plugs, and a host of natural baits are all grist for his toothy maw. There are no introspective pikes.

Besides his enthusiastic response, the amazing fecundity of his species and a devil-may-care attitude regarding his habitat, place the pike within easy reach of a great many anglers. Although he prefers the northern latitudes, his only invariable requirements appear to be two: an area well spotted with lakes, and enough food to satisfy his voracious appetite. This includes territories from the central Mississippi Valley, west to the Rockies, east to New York, and north to the St. Lawrence Valley.

Some of the largest pike come from the provinces of western Canada—Manitoba and Saskatchewan—and from far-western Alaska. But few anglers are familiar with Alaskan pike fishing, since the thousands of lakes in the tundra can be reached only by float plane. An hour or so by air from King Salmon via Northern Consolidated Airlines' bush plane carries the fisherman to a series of virgin pike-fishing waters, where I have caught countless big pikes by simply balancing on one

While great northerns are not
noted for above-water acrobatics, they
can put on a good show.
Naturally a shallow-water feeder, the big
pike often takes surface
lures, but prefers flashy spoons.

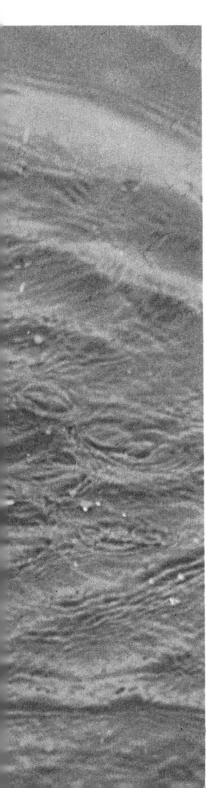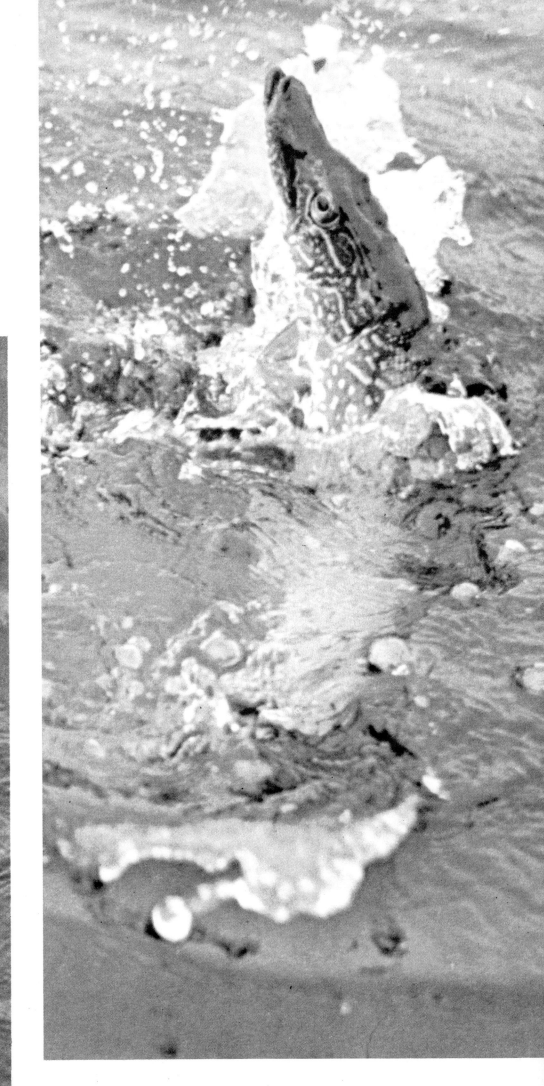

of the plane's floats and casting a red-and-white wobbler wherever there was water enough to hold fish.

For the *great* northern pike is properly named. He often grows to a weight of forty pounds or more, and twenty-pounders are not uncommon.

Still, in waters where pike and musky coexist, the interest in musky is always paramount. Muskies are a fish of legend in America. Those that reached a great age and size were called "old people" by the Indians, and today every north-woods fishing camp has its favorite stories about a stouthearted "Old Fighter."

The great northern, on the other hand, is much less esteemed. He is derisively called "jackfish" and "pickerel" in Canada, and both Canadians and Americans denounce him for feeding on small ducks and trout. Of this he is guilty, to be sure, although no more so than the prized muskellunge. I have even heard the pike branded as a poor fighter, but I have never known him to be one.

Quite the contrary, the great northern pike, scientifically *Esox lucius,* is tough and game. He is the fierce fish of the Old World, and as a creature of legend, he actually antedates the musky.

In 1497, in Europe, the famous Mannheim pike was caught. This fish was reported to be nineteen feet long and to bear an inscribed ring in his gills that gave his date of birth as 1230 A.D. The skeleton and identifying ring were preserved in the Mannheim cathedral for many years until some seeker after truth discovered that the skeleton had been considerably lengthened by the addition of extra vertebrae. The findings apparently had little effect on the tale, however, for the story of the Mannheim pike still persists.

Even Izaak Walton seems to have contributed to pike legend. Certain editions of *The Compleat Angler* describe a one-hundred-and-seventy-pound pike which was supposedly recovered after draining a pond near Newport, England. A printed report of the event says

Left: Close-up of hooked, fighting great northern shows the wide, duck-billed shape of his family's upper jaw.

that before the pike's recovery, a fisherman hooked the fish and was promptly jerked into the water by the great beast. The pike would have undoubtedly "devoured him also," the account says, "had he not by wonderful agility and dexterous swimming escaped the dreadful jaws of this voracious animal."

In Ireland, an editor of *The Fishing Gazette*, R. B. Marston, bored with stories of giant pike, offered a prize of ten pounds for any pike of fifty pounds or more taken in Irish waters. It was collected in 1923, when one John Garvin brought in a fifty-two-pound trophy.

The largest pike on record taken in North America was a forty-six-pounder that was killed in New York's Sacandaga Reservoir more than two decades ago. However, I have seen pikes far outweighing that one hanging from drying racks in Alaskan Indian villages. There, the fish are speared in the shallows during their spring spawning period, and are dried and stored for the sled dogs.

I remember one pair of great northerns I saw hanging from a pole in the village of Aniak. They were the property of the headman. As they hung with their tails barely clearing the ground, I realized that their dead eyes were on a level with my own—which made them some four feet, ten inches. At any rate, they were easily fifty pounds each. Certainly large enough to be inspiring. Still, American legends about pike have never kept pace with those of the Old World.

The great northern pike is a lean, supple fish. His lines are clean and designed for action, his body is strong. A large, flat head and wide duck-billed jaws mark his membership in the pike family, and, like his kin, he has the head of a marauder. His jaws are filled with needle-sharp, re-curved teeth and his eyes glare like a cougar's stalking a mule-deer fawn.

The pike is a fearsome predator, and his coloration is perfect for it. His back and sides are green, sometimes gray, and his sides are generously spotted with large oval blotches. He is almost invisible in his natural hide-out among the weeds and lily-pad beds in the shallows of a lake, where he stolidly awaits his prey. The sunlight filtering through these waters matches the mottling of his mantle.

His shape and fin arrangement closely resemble those of the musky and smaller pickerel, but the color of the northern's markings is the reverse of his relatives. The northern's are light on a darker background. Despite this distinction, however, the pike is often confused with the pickerel.

Genio C. Scott, one of our early American angling writers, may be responsible for some of the mix up. In the 1875 edition of his book, *Fishing in American Waters*, Scott groups both pike and pickerel together under the title "American Pickerel, or Pike." Conceding that the large "pickerel" found in the St. Lawrence River and other Canadian waters was called by some the "great Northern pike," he neatly sweeps science aside with the following profound statement: ". . . throughout twenty years' experience at taking pickerel, I have been unable to discover a very marked difference between the Northern pike and the pickerel south of the St. Lawrence." He then makes a weak attempt to account for the difference in size which exists between the two species: "All pike, after rising above the pickerel weight, and [that is] under five

*Light markings on
dark background distinguish the pike
from musky and pickerel.*

pounds, in England, are known as 'Jack,' probably named for a poacher named Jack Pike."

Obviously content that small pike are called pickerel and large pickerel are called pike, Scott goes on to compound his crime: "The meat of small pickerel is mealy, fresh and without decided flavor, when—because of its yellow color—it is called *dorée*...." Now the walleye appears, despite the fact that the walleye is not a pike at all. Unfortunately, this confusion left by Scott still continues.

Almost anything that moves can arouse the pike, no matter how outlandish the hardware. If the fish is hungry enough or angry enough, he will strike with abandon. At times, pike can even be taken on the fly, as long as the fly is a large bucktail or streamer.

I first met the great northern pike many years ago on Saranac River in the Adirondacks, just below Franklin Falls. I was casting a #2 bucktail over the heavy flume that drives along the rocky ledges south of the dam, hoping to raise a big brown, although I took none that day. As I worked my way down the long run toward quieter water, fishing the fly deeper and deeper with each cast, I felt a heavy fish take hold. I saw the long, white flash of his belly, as he turned in taking the fly. He was hooked solidly, and I could feel him shaking his head just under the surface. Suddenly the line and leader broke free with a snap. The fish disappeared, leaving me with a slack line.

When I examined the end of the leader—gut in those days—I noted a short frayed section. It had not pulled away from the eye of the hook as I first suspected, thinking I had tied it on carelessly. The gut was actually severed.

Still, I never suspected pike. I tied on a new bucktail and tried my luck again. A few casts over the deep pocket elicited another heavy surge. This time the fish rolled up so that I could see his duck-billed head and spotted sides. Again, I held fast. It was only a matter of seconds before the pike's teeth cut the gut.

I didn't really want a pike, but losing two flies to the fish riled me a bit. So I rummaged through my trout gear for a piece of wire. Finding none, I settled for a small Indiana spinner that had been mounted on a short wire shank. I clipped off the spinner with my gut cutters (not a wise practice, I admit) and rigged it between a new fly and my gut leader.

In another cast or two, I hung a heavy fish once more, and it took me fifty yards down the flume before I could hook him out by the gills with a makeshift gaff I had made from a crotched stick. Aided by the surging currents, the big pike battled well—as well as a brown, although he was, perhaps, a bit more logy in his rushes. I took a dozen more pikes that day, all three- to five-pounders, and I'd be a fool to say I didn't enjoy the fishing, even though I was not taking trout.

The great northern's fight is powerful and vigorous. Once he feels the sting of the hook and the restraint of the line, he churns the waters actively. As a rule, he gives up more quickly than the musky, but this is largely because the musky has a weight advantage. A musky will always outweigh a pike of the same length —unless the pike has just swallowed a small muskrat!

Actually, I have never noted much difference between the battle offered by a great northern and a musky of the same heft, if the two were taken on similar tackle from the same waters. Perhaps the musky is a bit more crafty or spectacular—he is almost surely a leaper, the great northern rarely so—but he is certainly no more courageous.

The great northern pike will come again and again to the lure, mouthing the drifting hardware in an angry attack, vying with the angler until he can no longer resist the constant presence of the rod. Even a fresh wound from the fisherman's hook seems not to discourage him. I have caught and released the same fish three times in a single day, fin-clipping him each time to be certain of my identifications. I once caught a pike that only moments before had fought a good battle with my fishing partner, finally sweeping away with my partner's big spoon. No sooner had he reached his weed-bed rest than I tossed my own spoon in that direction, and within a few casts, had him charging out to fight again. More than likely, this pike had not even paused long enough to regain his wind, for I landed him easily, pried out both spoons, and slipped him back into the lake to watch him head once more for his weedy haven.

The pike provides the stuff of good fishing: action, a satisfying thrust against the rod tip, and, often enough, the weight and drive to make you bark your knuckles on a spinning reel handle as the great fish rushes away with your lure or bait.

PICKEREL

Pickerel, from "The First Annual Report of the Commissioners of Fisheries, Game and Forests," New York, 1896.

Not much can be learned about pickerel and pickerel fishing by reading contemporary books and articles on angling. The little brother of the pike is studiously ignored by fishing writers. He is of insignificant size, no battler, and somewhat down the scale of food fish. To cap it off, pickerel are trophies only to the young. Mature fishermen, when they do sport with the tiny pike, are usually sneaky about it. They're after bigger game and catch pickerel only by happenstance.

For this, however, you cannot fault the pickerel. He happens to live in the neighborhood of larger, more sporting fish—bass, pike, trout, even land-locked salmon—and the competition is too great. Few pickerel ever reach five pounds in weight and only the chain variety can be expected to grow much above legal minimum size. The grass pickerel and banded pickerel are little guys that rarely grow to one foot in length.

The eastern, or chain, pickerel (at one time called "federation pike") is the only species large enough for consideration in angling. *Esox reticulatus* is his scientific name, and this refers to the network of dark markings on his sides, often chainlike in appearance. If this is not enough to identify him, a look at the gill covers will do it. The pickerel has gill covers completely scaled, both cheeks and operculum, and from top to bottom. There is a point in belaboring this matter of identity, since pike, pickerel, and musky are continually confused by fishermen.

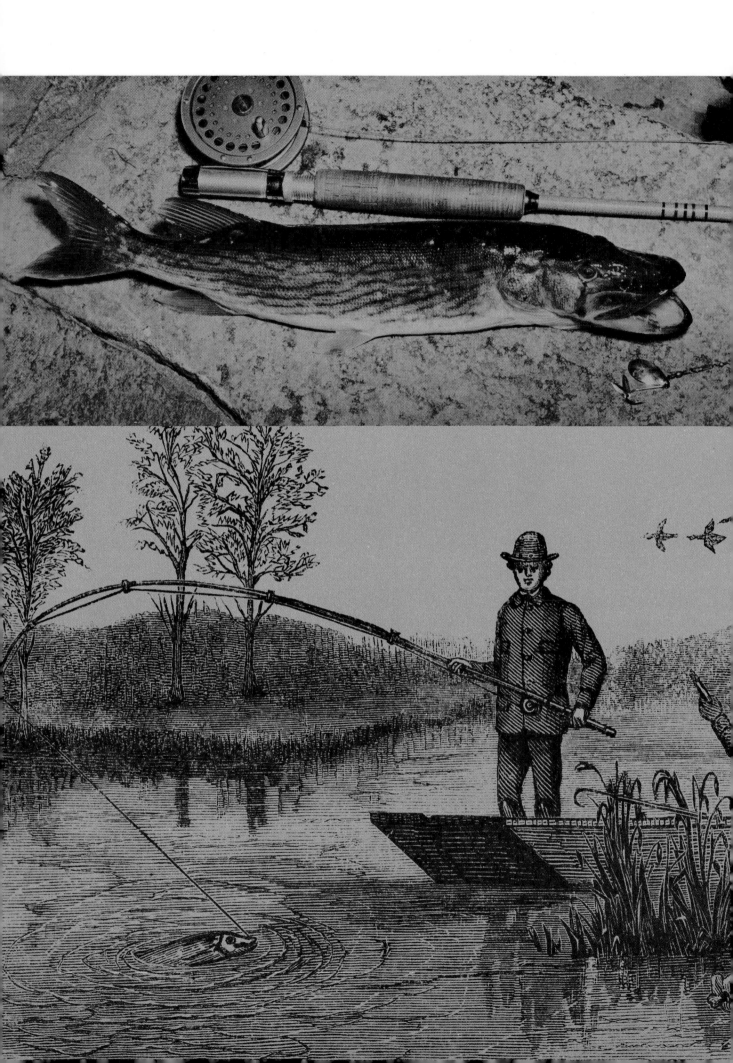

Everything said of the northern pike and the muskellunge applies to the chain pickerel on a smaller scale. The little pike is fierce, a free biter, a tyrant among smaller fish in his area. He is beset by ravenous hungers and his equipment for taking and devouring his prey is identical with the two larger pike species. His courage, lack of caution, or downright stupidity—I am not certain which—lead him to strike any small moving object within reach. In shallow, weedy waters, he will pester a bass-bug fisherman, for he rises readily to the surface in the shoals, chewing up delicate hair lures and frequently cutting through the leader with his teeth.

More than any other species, the pickerel is a boy's game fish. Most farm ponds and creeks in the East and Midwest have pickerel and their lack of fear of the fisherman makes them an attractive target for young anglers. The pickerel was the first game fish I caught, and I am sure this is true of many other boys, both on the farm and in the suburbs. Pickerel love a small, slow-moving creek, shaded by alders and willows, with a muddy bottom rich in vegetation. There are thousands of these streams in farm lands, and a young fisherman can pick the spot where he'll find a pickerel just by looking over the water.

I well remember stalking along the creek bank on hot June days, peering under the lily pads and in the grassy pockets to find the long, slender shape of a pickerel hanging motionless in mid-water, lying in ambush like a miniature musky, ready to dart from his hide after the first shiner minnow that passed by. Those pickerel were easy victims. I was armed, in those days, with a twenty-foot cane pole, rigged with a few yards of heavy, green cotton cord, and one of the black Kirby hooks that could be bought in almost any general store at the satisfying rate of fifteen cents for a full box of one hundred.

The black hook would be well covered with half a night crawler, while the other half trailed behind to give a provocative wiggle as it was drawn across the fish's nose. And if the long pole didn't wave too closely over the fish to frighten him, the fish would usually oblige by rushing out to the bait on the first pass. Then, as he slowly moved back toward his lie, he would chomp on it until the worm was well within his long mouth. Most often this whole suspenseful drama of seizure, return, and mouthing the bait could be seen from shore. When the worm finally disappeared, the unsuspecting fish was yanked up and out of the creek in one mighty heave.

With the first fish in hand, the rule was to take out the Barlow knife and cut a long strip of stark white skin and thin belly meat from his underside. This provided a skitter bait, somehow more satisfying to use and usually more alluring than the night-walking worm. And in the heat of summer, when the worms were hard to come by, a good substitute was a strip of rind from a side of bacon, thoroughly soaked to make it white and pliable. The tigerish little pickerels would grab this pork rind just as readily as a worm, but they were not inclined to hold it and mouth it for long. You had to hook the fish quickly, and this led to many lost strikes.

I suspect that skittering is one of the oldest forms of angling for pickerel. Robert Barnwell Roosevelt describes the method in his *Game Fish of the North*, in 1884, recommending both the belly of a yellow perch or ". . . a slip of the skin of pork cut into something resembling a small fish." Scott also gives skittering its due in *Fishing in American Waters*, in 1875, although Scott suggests the use of a small spoon (Buel's), mounted with red and white feathers, or a live minnow.

When I first fished for pickerel, I had never heard of either Roosevelt or Scott, but their methods apparently were common knowledge among country boys. The idea of gently dropping a fish-shaped bait in the weedy pockets of pickerel hangouts, and teasing the bait along with a tempting wiggle just under the surface, comes down to us as still the most effective method of taking these little fighters. Certainly, it gives the most sport in pickerel fishing.

Pickerel lie in small, tight spots in weed beds, among lily pads, logs, and stumps—and invariably in

"CAVEAT ENTERED."

shallow water. The light little bait, tossed with a long, flexible rod, can be placed in just the right spot over or near the fish. It sinks slowly, can be twitched a time or two before it fouls in the weeds, and then must be lifted out for another cast.

A spoon or plug usually will foul in the weeds on the retrieve, since with bait-casting tackle it must be reeled up to make the next cast. Also, a spoon must be kept moving quickly to keep it from sinking to the bottom, where it will catch fast. At times, pickerel just won't charge out for a steadily moving lure, although they do love the flash of metal as much as other pikes. Sometimes you must tease them, dropping the belly bait near them, then lifting it toward the surface, pausing again to let it sink, then giving it a few more twitches with the rod tip until the fish takes or you pick up for another cast.

A refinement of the ancient skittering technique which I have used for many years is fly-fishing with a fairly powerful rod—not for casting the fly, but to handle the fish when he thrashes about in the weed pockets or charges off for a tangle of tree roots. Here, the large bucktail fly with silver body replaces the pork rind or belly strip. And do not forget the safeguard of a few inches of wire trace rigged between the fly and the leader. The white bucktail (or yellow, or red, or any other bright hair) can be cast and fished just like the skitter bait and a great many pocket holes in weed beds can be covered readily and thoroughly with the fly rod, better, in fact, than with

other types of tackle. The fight of the smallest member of the pike clan becomes significant when fairly light tackle is used.

I have never cared much for still-fishing of any kind because of the lack of action. I like to keep working for the fish, casting, trying different spots, always hunting either for a hungry fish or a different approach that will get some attention. Yet I have had many good hours still-fishing from a boat for pickerel, using lively shiner minnows that made the bobber cork dance about until it was yanked under by the surge of a taking fish. The still-fishing method works better than any other when the weather settles down to the real heat of summer. Pickerel move out into deeper channels in the ponds when the sun beats down, and this is where you must fish for them. At this time, they are less likely to be goaded or enticed into chasing a fast-moving spoon or spinner. The idea of a small minnow swimming about in a limited area seems to appeal to a pickerel. He can study the little fish at his leisure, and then, prompted either by its helplessness or the stirrings of appetite, grasp it with a minimum of effort. Summer pickerel are as lazy as any other pike; their appetite falls off and they drowse in the shade of a weed patch as readily as a farm hand under a maple tree when the haying is done.

As with many other game fish, the bright sunlight of summer makes fishing for pickerel rather unsure. We used to wait for cloudy, rainy days before taking

off for the nearest pickerel pond, and our judgment was always confirmed. The fish come alive on a damp, cool day and keep your bobber dancing for as long as the minnows hold out.

Early spring and fall are the proper times to fish for pickerel. With appetite uninhibited and the sluggishness induced by warm water not yet upon them, the fish are most spirited and aggressive. They'll hit the big red-and-white wobbling spoons, a revolving, feathered spinner (or spoon hook), and almost anything you care to toss out. The pickerel's fierceness, despite his small stature, is astonishing. It's not at all unusual to hook and land a two-pound fish on a big spoon, only to discover that his belly already has been well filled by a smaller fish, its tail visible in your pickerel's gullet, as you work out the spoon's treble. And the smaller fish might well have been the bigger

fish's offspring. I once caught two pickerel on a big Dardevle: a four-pounder on the spoon and a foot-long fish, that appeared to have been gulped only a few moments before, inside him.

Not long ago, I hooked a fair-sized pickerel, about three pounds, on a half-ounce Wob-L-Rite. The fish offered only feeble resistance as I drew him in on light monofilament and a delicate spinning rod. I netted him, then lifted him out of the meshes by grabbing him over the gill covers. As he came out of the net with his deep yellow, chain-marked sides gleaming, I was somewhat disturbed by his odd shape. His belly was distended, which is not unusual with such a greedy fish. What was strange, though, was that he swelled out sideways, rather than downward. When I opened him I found within a bluegill sunfish as wide as my hand.

The
P E R C H

WALLEYE
(Pike—Perch)

Stizostedion vitreum is an awkward name, difficult to pronounce, difficult to spell—except for students of Latin with a deep interest in fish. It serves, however, an admirable purpose. From a hatful of many local names, it fixes precisely and with finality the identity of the walleye, a member of the perch family and a good North American game fish. The trouble is that the worlds of the biologist and that of the fisherman are far apart. Fishermen will continue to call the walleye a pike-perch, a blue pike, yellow pike, pickerel, jack salmon, *doré,* or one or another of two dozen names, depending on where the fish is being caught.

The French-Canadian calls the walleye a *doré,* a pleasant name that reflects either the golden-yellow color of the Quebec walleye, or its intrinsic value as a sport and food fish. You will get many opinions about walleyes in different quarters. On one misty morning, casting for northern pike in western Quebec, I snagged a five-pound walleye. Mike, my guide, netted him and lifted him from the water with a gleam in his eye. "Thees wan mak' a good lonch," he said.

Further north, only a week or two later, I fished a big, sluggish, dark river, winding through a murky evergreen forest. I was taking big squaretail brook trout on a small wobbling spoon. In the middle of a deep pool I hung a heavy, slowly moving fish. I pumped him up to the top and could see the yellow

gleam of his side. Another walleye. This time my guide, Jean, spat over the side of the canoe in disgust. "Sacré," he said. "Dat sonofabitchvalleye got no bizness here!" And he plucked the struggling fish from the water, ripped out the little treble hook, and tossed him far back into the spruce trees before I could protest.

There is universal agreement on the walleye as a delight for epicures, whatever else may be said of him. His flesh is firm, invariably pure white, and becomes succulent with gentle cooking. Its flavor is delicate and uniform, whether the fish comes from Lake Champlain in New York or the Yellowstone River.

Curiously, walleyes may either put up a spunky battle or simply allow themselves to be reeled in with

Pages 210-211:

Walleyed pike, or pike-perch.

Above left: Walleyes grow

fat in man-made lakes. This fish was taken

on baited spinner trolled

in Kentucky's Cumberland Lake.

Above: Waiting for perch
to take, from "The Complete Angler,"
Vol. 5, London.

213

Walleyes do not jump when hooked,
but splash furiously as they near the boat and the
fisherman's net. Their name
refers to their large, milky, luminous eyes, but in
Quebec they are called doré because
of their golden color.

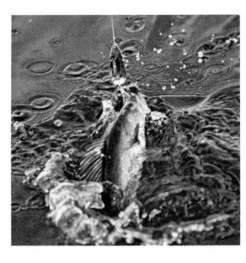
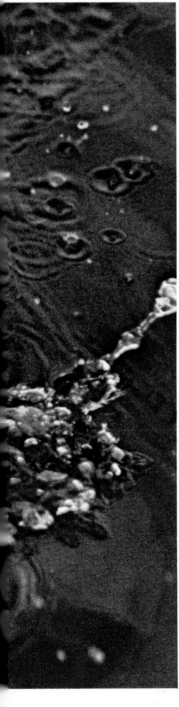

little more than a protesting wiggle. I have encountered both extremes.

Trolling after dark one warm evening on a Catskill lake, we were rigged with trolling triangles, half-ounce sinker, and June Bug spinner, trailing a pair of night crawlers—standard gear for walleye. I was rowing the skiff and had my short trolling rod stuck in a rod holder clamped to the side. On one pass near a swimmer's raft, over about twenty feet of water, my reel click sounded off. I grabbed the rod quickly and began to reel in. The resistance was heavy, but slowly I cranked away, feeling not a tremor of life. My partner turned the beam of a flashlight on the wire leader coming out of the water and lowered the big boat net in readiness. Still no protest from the fish.

Then the dangling June Bug spinner came clear and, below it, the bail wire of a white-lead bucket appeared. We had a chuckle over this as my friend unhooked the bucket and dropped it over the side. I picked up the oars, pulled a few strokes, then put my rig back to work after checking the bait.

On the next turn along the shore we again passed the raft and again my reel burred against some resistance. I picked the rod out of the holder, cranked steadily against a familiar heavy weight. My partner was now a bit impatient. "All right," he said. "Haul that bucket up here so that we can get back to fishing!"

In a minute or less I had the snag near the skiff. My partner turned on the flashlight and sent the beam directly into the gleaming, luminous eye of a big walleye. Now, at long last, the fish showed signs of life. He thrashed on the surface, sending my friend scurrying for the net. After a few hectic passes, he came up with a seven-pound walleye.

Again, on a warm, dark summer evening, I was casting a big streamer fly across a long pool lying under the old covered bridge at Downsville, on the east branch of the Delaware. I had already taken a three-pound brown trout and snagged another good fish that came unpinned as I tried to beach him over the stony shore. The big fly made an audible spat in the stillness over the pool each time I dropped it near the far shore. I would allow it to sink well, then lift the rod tip to bring it through the sluggish flow of current in the deep center of the hole. This I did many times before I felt the gentle pluck of a taking fish—

Overcast skies are best when angling for walleyes. The fish shuns daylight, is basically a night feeder. Walleyes are taken by slow trolling in deep water.

characteristic of the rise of a trout feeding after dark. I came hard against the fish, knowing instantly I was into a heavy one. He rushed off upstream, then gave in to the pressure of the rod, turned, and drove fiercely down into the dark, deep water under the bridge.

I followed him, playing him as carefully as I have ever handled a fish, working him into the shallows, where I could see him wrinkling the surface in the dim light reflected from the star-filled night. I decided then to play him well out, so I could strand him in the shallows and grab him over the gill covers without using the net. For I had grave doubts that my net would handle him and I did not want to use my little pen-light for fear of alerting other trout in the pool.

The fish resisted strongly, boring deep, cruising up against the current until he neared the spot where he had taken the fly. He fought the typical fight of a brown trout at night—deliberate but strong, not as sure of himself as he might be in the daylight. In the end, I led him out into a few inches of water, where I could barely make him out as he lay on his side. I reached down carefully and closed my fingers over his back, just behind the gill covers. Now I knew, without question and for the first time, that I did not have a trout. His back and sides were as rough as sandpaper, not slippery smooth as a trout's would be. So I lifted him out and carried him to the shelter of the screening brush on the bank before I beamed my light on him. It showed me an eight-pound walleye.

Over the past thirty years, I have not caught many walleyes—a few hundred, perhaps—but I have been fortunate enough to tangle with them in many different places and in many types of water. I think it can be fairly said that a walleye fights his best when he lives in a river. A river seems to transmit some of its vigor to its fish. It may be that life in the moving water builds more muscle, or that the search for food is more strenuous, sharpening the fish's movements and stimulating his reactions.

As a feeder, the walleye is distinctly different from other game fish. Endowed by nature with large, milky eyes, he sees as well in the dark as a prowling house cat, and nighttime is when he feeds most enthusiastically. It is possible to catch him by daylight, but mostly on dark, overcast days.

Like the lake trout, the walleye prefers deep water, although I have always suspected that it is not the cold temperatures of the depths that he needs, but the gloom.

And like all fresh-water perch, walleyes travel in schools. Where you find one, you will find more. The canny technique, when trolling in deep water, is to have on hand a small buoy rigged with a heavy sinker and enough line to reach the deepest part of the fishing area. When you hang a fish, toss the buoy over the side to mark the spot where the fish are congregating. Your choice of action then permits anchoring near the buoy and still-fishing with minnows, or trolling repeatedly over and around the marked location.

The walleye apes the smallmouth bass in his choice of water and bottom. He is not a weed lover, but a traveler over sand, gravel, and rock in clean, clear water. In feeding he resembles the lake trout: his diet is basically minnows and his dental equipment is remarkably like that of the laker. The walleye doesn't feed or live in water as deep as the lake trout, but he will respond to the same angling technique in trolling: the flash of a spinner or spoon, coupled with a natural minnow.

Under cover of darkness walleyes usually will leave the deep water of a lake or the deep river channels to forage for bait minnows near shore or over shallow bars. In the northern limit of the walleye's range—in southern Canada—it is usually possible to take the fish by casting a surface or near-surface diving plug along the shallow ledges close to a drop-off.

In the St. Lawrence River a novel variation of the trolling method is most effective after dark. A bait-casting rod is rigged with a diving plug—a Pikie minnow, for example—and a small sinker is nipped to the casting trace about a foot ahead of the lure, just enough to keep it traveling under the surface. The angler picks a spot where the smooth glide of current passes over a rock-and-gravel bottom, not more than six or eight feet deep, before dropping into a dark channel, where the fish lie during the day. With the coming of dusk, the fish rise from the depths to cruise the shallows at the head of the channel.

The boat, with outboard motor set to equalize the speed of the current, is run over the shoal with just enough line released to put the lure over the feeding area. Then, slowly, the fisherman trolls across the width of the run, back and forth, covering the shoal water with the plug wiggling its way along the bottom, just upstream of the break into the channel. That this method is effective was clearly demonstrated to me one evening in the Thousand Islands when my wife, fishing with VanCampen Heilner, took a nine-pound and a six-pound walleye from a flat riffle just above the Canadian Span.

Each section of walleye water offers enough variation in fishing method to keep an angler on his mettle. In the Delaware River, for example, the best bait is the lamprey, trolled deep in the big eddies, behind a June Bug spinner. In the lakes of western Ontario, a deep-running plug, cast over sand bars and rock shoals, takes as many fish as one could want. And, in these northern waters, the walleye will often rise to a streamer fly, fished after sundown or on a murky day.

It must be said, though, that the walleye's tastes run more to natural baits—minnows, lampreys, worms— than to artificial lures. In daylight fishing, almost anywhere in the walleye's wide geographical range, the natural bait becomes a necessity for successful angling. In many lakes the favored food is yellow perch, since the walleye is not embarrassed by eating close relatives. And during the "eel-fly" hatch in the St. Lawrence Valley, walleyes gorge on this largest of May flies, the *Heptagenia*. This species comes on at night, in clouds as thick as a February snowstorm. For several days after the hatch appears, walleyes can't be tempted to take any artificial.

The characteristics of the walleye—night feeding, lying deep and somewhat inaccessible to the fisherman, a hesitancy in striking artificials, and an indifferent fighting stature—put him well down on the list of desirable game fish. But walleyes grow to a gratifying size. Five-pounders are common, and if you keep after this fish long enough, you may even tangle with a twenty-pounder.

The best times to go after the walleyes is in early spring and after the first autumn frost, although they can also be taken during the summer by those who are enthusiastic about fishing after dark. And together with the yellow perch, the walleye keeps the shanty villages busy and excited during the winter months, when an angler's only contact with a rod in northern waters is the short jigging stick, played thoughfully over a small hole bored in two feet of ice.

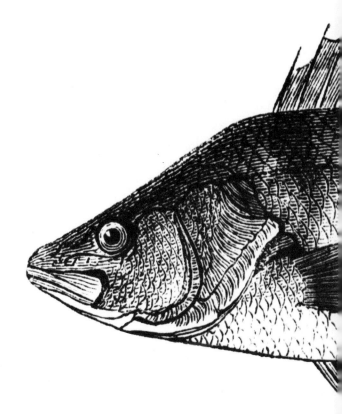

Yellow & White Perch

For many years I have spent at least one week in June on Palfrey Lake in New Brunswick, Canada, most recently at Arlie Day's camp. The June fishing there for landlocked salmon is often exceptionally good, and probably the best in North America for taking big, hard-fighting smallmouth bass on fly rod or light spinning tackle, using top-water lures. Nearby are some good brook-trout lakes and, of course, rivers famous for Atlantic salmon, which begin their first runs in late June.

I look forward with particular eagerness to this annual trip. In this old Canadian province, fishing has been a way of life for centuries. Its lakes, ponds, and streams have been well fished but, in the main, it is not crowded with anglers. The fishing is seldom easy, but it can be profitable if you stay with it. The challenge is far greater than in fishing the true wilderness waters, further north in Canada, where at times the fishing offers no problems at all.

Despite the fine salmon and bass angling at Palfrey,

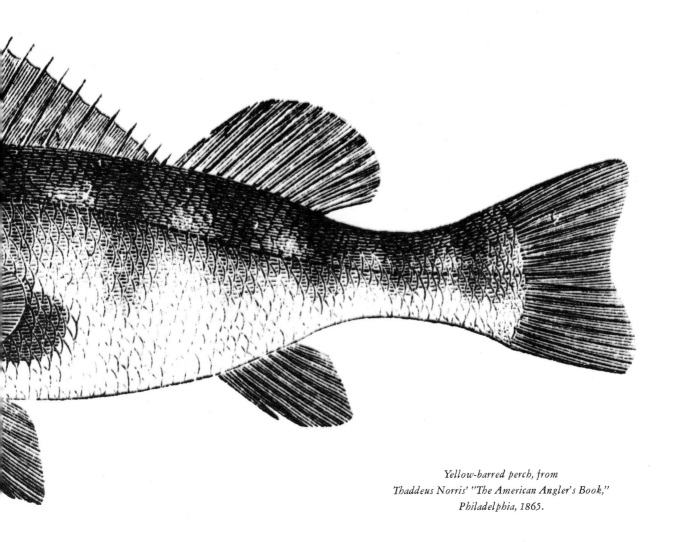

Yellow-barred perch, from
Thaddeus Norris' "The American Angler's Book,"
Philadelphia, 1865.

however, I also look forward to encountering one of the smaller species of sport fish in these waters— the white perch, which will appear on the table at breakfast each morning that I am in camp. I am not the dedicated fish fancier some anglers are, but I always have been partial to fish at breakfast. I am fond of small brook trout and grayling for the morning meal, will accept bass or walleye as well, but for tops in Canadian breakfasts I choose the white perch taken from a clear, deep lake. Palfrey can be counted on to produce a few for the table almost any day, and there are times when they bite so furiously that a few hours' catch yields enough fish to satisfy a man's craving for perch for more than a month.

These Palfrey Lake white perch are pure metallic-silver in color, bronze green on the backs, and, rather often, show deep blue or purple tints along the throat. They are handsome little fish, resembling the salt-water striper to some extent, with a similar arrangement of fins. Actually, the white perch is essen-

tially a salt-water fish, found in brackish waters all along the Atlantic Coast from Nova Scotia to South Carolina. They run up coastal rivers and eventually find themselves landlocked in a lake. This lake existence, I'm sure, puts them at their best in color and form, and, with good feeding, they grow to their largest size there. I have taken a good number running about two pounds, particularly in the late summer, after they have had months of good feeding in a quiet, northern lake.

White perch are a school fish. I have seen them early in the morning and at dusk, riffling the calm surface of a lake in great patches that must hold thousands of fish. At such times, if they are feeding on smelt or other minnows, you can take them as fast as you can toss a fly or a little wobbler over the school. Conversely, the school may kick up a real fuss on the surface, with many fish leaping clear all at once—and they won't touch a thing. Apparently, they play on the surface as well as chase bait.

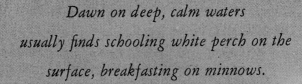

*Dawn on deep, calm waters
usually finds schooling white perch on the
surface, breakfasting on minnows.*

A feeding school of white perch is a terror when it catches up with a patch of minnows. The perch charge in, darting in fury from right to left, snapping and chewing for all the world like a school of bluefish attacking a half acre of mossbunkers. If you are on hand and can reach the fish, there is no limit to the amount of action you can have.

But these fish can be temperamental. A school will surface and begin to feed wildly for a few moments, and then stop abruptly. Or, it may stay up for an hour, or two, or several. Sometimes the appearance of the minnows will not even bring white perch to the surface. I have watched smelt and saw-bellies working over a good, deep-water hole with no sign of action from the perch.

When they are really feeding, white perch exhibit great aggressiveness in attacking large minnows. I have caught many perch weighing about half a pound that were loaded with smelt up to six inches long.

These were usually caught when I was trolling for salmon, using a long spoon or a big tandem-hook trolling fly. Occasionally, a small fish will come flopping in with the three barbs of a #1 treble hook wedging open his tiny mouth. It's not only remarkable that such a diminutive fish is so ferocious in feeding, but I have always wondered just how it can manage to take such a big hook all at once. Many times, you will feel the nip, nip of a white perch as he follows the moving lure—and he will often follow for a hundred yards—before he finally snags himself.

These fish are strong battlers for their size. When a two-pounder strikes savagely at your trolled streamer fly, it will be a moment or two before you are convinced that you are not fast to a small landlock or a smallmouth bass. Usually their frantic, rapid wiggle, transmitted through the line, will give away the perch's identity, however, before you see the fish.

Often you will find yellow perch in the same

220

Fishing from the riverbank, from "The Angler's Guide," London, 1815.

*Right: A page from
"A New Guide to the English Tongue,"
by Thomas Dilworth. Benjamin
Franklin, printer, Philadelphia, 1747.*

waters with the white perch, but the two do not min-
gle. Although the two species are confirmed minnow
and insect feeders, it is rare to find yellow perch feeding on the surface. These are deep-water fish,
fonder of underwater weeds, brush, and snags than
the white perch, which prefers open water and clean
gravel or rock bottoms.

Yellow perch are much more common than the
white. The yellows are found almost everywhere in
America except in the Far North, and they are a true
fresh-water fish, rarely encountered in salt or brackish
water. Like pickerel, yellow perch are the fairest of
game for young fishermen. They bite freely and often,
and have no inhibitions about taking bait on a hot,
sunshiny day. Yellow perch are "nibblers" rather than
strikers. If you are fishing with some form of natural
bait—worm, minnow, or grub—using a small float for
a bobber, a yellow perch will tantalize you a bit before
finally taking. The float will tip and wiggle, then stay

150   A NEW GUIDE

A Bird in the Hand is worth two in the Bush.

FABLE XII. *Of the Fisherman and the Fish.*

A Fisherman having cast his Line in the Water, presently
after drew up a Fish.

The little Captive entreated the Fisherman that he would
spare her (she being but small) till she was grown larger ; and
then she would suffer herself to be taken by him again.

No, no, replies the Fisherman, I am not to be so served :
If I let you go, I must never expect to see you any more ;
neither should I have caught you now, if you had known
there was a Hook within the Bait : And I was always of that
Temper, that whatever I could catch, I had rather take it
away, than leave it behind me.

The Interpretation.

Never let go a Certainty for an Uncertainty.

White perch (above) bear some resemblance to the salt-water striper in fin arrangement, and are often found in brackish waters, along with striped bass. These perch generally average less than a pound, but the occasional two-pounder can be a battler.

still for a few seconds. Then it will tip and bob again and again before it pops under abruptly in the age-old signal to set the hook.

The yellow perch is also a school fish. I remember, as a youngster fishing farm ponds, my friends and I often resorted to a sneaky trick to keep track of a moving school of perch. When we caught the first fish we ran a piece of light string through his lips, then tied a cork to the end of the string, giving the fish about ten feet of leash to drag around. Once he was turned loose he ran right for the school and stayed with it. We followed in our leaky scow, poling or paddling to keep up with the moving cork. Then, dropping our worms or grubs near the spoored fish, we could always take plenty of perch from the rest of the school.

Yellow perch are true pan fish. Most of them run

less than a pound and they make fine eating. My only objection is that they are tough to scale. I usually finish the job of cleaning by skinning the fish rather than fighting the leathery scales. White perch, on the other hand, scale easily when they are taken fresh from the water. I always keep a short piece of board in the boat so that pan fish can be cleaned and scaled promptly.

You can take yellow perch on all sorts of small lures: wet trout flies in gaudy patterns, small streamers, little spinners baited with worms, small minnows, tiny wobbling spoons. The only rule is to keep the lure small and keep it under the surface. And if you want really big perch, fish off a rock ledge or steep drop-off, where the water may be forty feet in depth. For these bigger perch, minnows are the best bait.

Anglers of scientific bent may wonder why I chose to include the white and yellow perch in this section

of the book, and why I did not put both species in the section on pan fish. I realize that biologically the white perch is not a perch, but a relative of the white bass and yellow bass. However, a white perch is always called perch—most often white perch, occasionally silver perch. The yellow perch is, of course, a pan fish and more properly belongs with the rest of those interesting small substitutes for game fish.

Yet, I did not want the walleye to stand alone in a special section devoted to the perch family. This might give him more distinction than he deserves, although in his own peculiar way he is a unique specimen.

And since this is a brief book on angling, not a scientific treatise on fish species, I have taken some liberty with science and grouped the walleye and the yellow perch—both of which are true perch—along with the white perch on the grounds of common sense.

The
WATER

T Y P E S
& How to Fish Them

A n g l i n g is compounded of many things. First, there are the fish. Without a fascination for the creature to be caught, no man will become an angler or stay one for long. At the outset, a fisherman may judge his success solely by the number of fish caught, the pound weight of the largest one, or the regard in which the species in his creel is held by more experienced fishermen. But in time he will establish his own values. He will learn that each fish has its own characteristics and capabilities, that each contributes to his fishing pleasure. The opinions he forms will very likely last him throughout his angling lifetime.

Secondly, the fisherman is spellbound by the tools of his craft. The rods and reels, the many types of lines, the endless number of flies and lures, in endless sizes and shapes, all have a mechanical and aesthetic appeal —and a talismanic quality that seems to promise success.

Then, as he catches fish, the angler becomes curious about the science and philosophy of his sport. He begins to study the literature of fishing.

At once he discovers that angling is a paradox. No two men seem to catch fish on the same baits or lures, and discord runs high in discussions of the best fly patterns and the best fishing methods. This can be a turning point in a fisherman's career. Often he is tempted to resolve the differences by trusting mechanics—by buying more tackle, by trying other methods. There is nothing wrong with this, except that angling has more to do with fish than with tackle, and that the tackle mechanic may become too obsessed with his gear to learn much about fish. A fisherman's techniques and the lures, flies, and baits he uses are less important than where and how he applies them. This means he must know the waters in which fish live. The angler who does not know what goes on beneath the surface of a river or a lake is not well grounded in his sport.

All angling practice is based on the willingness of a fish to feed. The successful fisherman offers the fish something it thinks is good to eat, and at a time and place when the fish *wants* to eat.

This simple formula becomes enormously complicated when the fish's element is considered. For although most fresh-water game fish have extremely varied appetites, the decision to feed or not to feed is

Preceding pages: A valley river in the West.

dictated by a complex of physical factors in the water itself. Changes in stream levels, changes in water temperatures, which influence the oxygen content, variations in the color of the water and its clarity, its hardness or relative softness, all affect what a fish feeds on, as well as when and where he feeds.

All fish are uncomfortable in water with a low oxygen content. When fish are uncomfortable, they do not feed. Their first consideration, therefore, is to find a spot in the lake or stream that carries at least their minimum requirement of oxygen. The minimum varies with the species. For instance, trout need the most oxygen, largemouth bass much less. As water temperature rises, it releases its oxygen, ergo, most game fish head for deeper water or spring holes in the summer— or seek the shade of trees or heavy aquatic vegetation.

Water with a good supply of lime encourages the growth of vegetation and plankton. Plankton supply important, often vital, food for the minnows game fish feed on. Vegetation releases the necessary oxygen. A fertile lake which grows good vegetation also grows good fish. If such a lake has sufficient depth—thirty feet or more—over a large part of its bottom, it is ideal for a continuing supply of fish.

A fresh-water angler usually begins his fishing education on a small stream, perhaps a small pond. There is an intimacy about small water that has its own charm, probably because a man can come to grips with it more readily, can learn in a short time what it holds, or at least enough to catch some of its fish. A mountain trout stream is a good beginner's laboratory, since there is no part of its tiny pools, rapids, and pockets that cannot be explored. The fish and the insect life can be watched and studied, the good lies covered with fly or bait, and the effect of flowing water on the fisherman's manner of tempting a fish can be resolved. This is learning to "read the water."

M o u n t a i n   B r o o k s

T h e   b e s t thing about small, rocky brooks —I am thinking of those less than twenty feet wide— is that it is possible to cover all the water with a minimum of wading, to fish every pool or run without changing position, once the right spot for casting has been chosen. The angler's big problem in fishing small streams is to keep from frightening the trout. This often means fishing from your knees after a crawling approach along the banks. And, since nearly all brooks of this type are shaded with trees and brush, you will use the sidearm cast for much of the fishing, although for most fly-rod casters this is more difficult to control than the overhead cast.

Small brooks are most readily fished with a light fly rod. I believe that it is not necessary to use one longer than seven feet. A rod of this length throws a fair amount of line—forty feet or so with a sidearm cast—and is easier to handle in close quarters than a longer rod would be. I am also reasonably sure that every method of fishing that can be profitably explored on such small streams can be done with the fly rod. A spinning rod, however short and light, does not do as well. Spinning lures are not as easy to place accurately on short casts as a fly or bait on a fly rod. Most spinning lures are also too heavy and too large for practical use on small waters. Only extremely skillful handling will keep them from snagging on the bottom or on mossy rocks at every cast. If you feel that a spinner is necessary to attract fish, a light Colorado blade fished from a fly rod will be as effective as heavier stuff.

In working a small brook, the fisherman always should move upstream. Since a fish lies facing the current, the approach from the "blind spot" directly behind his tail makes a close stalk possible without frightening him into cover. Then, again, the tails of the runs and pools can be covered first. A fish raised and hooked at the tail of a pool can be led quickly downstream and away from the pool, and the angler will avoid scaring off the other fish.

And in such small waters no reach is so long that it cannot be covered by an upstream approach. A bait as tender as a small angleworm can be flipped upstream for thirty feet or more by first allowing it to drag in the fast water below you, to create tension enough to flex the rod for the upstream flip. The dry fly, of course, is fished upstream as standard practice, and it is no real problem to fish a nymph or wet fly by upstream casting. In the normal course of fishing these sunken flies, the straight downstream drift is usually effective. Then, if it seems desirable to impart some crosscurrent motion to the sunken fly—to suggest emerging, swimming

nymphs—it can be done by making a quartering-up cast, fished out by holding the rod parallel to the bank and by stripping line to give the fly the desired crosscurrent movement.

In the small brook, when the water is clear (and most often it is), the trout easily can see almost every object that passes near. It is seldom necessary to fish deep, for a fish does not have to move far to take the fly. The exception is after a freshet that clouds the water; under these conditions a worm is a good bait. At such times, fish take best when the bait moves just over the bottom, where they are feeding on nymphs, worms, and other food carried along by the rise of water. Casting the worm directly upstream allows it to drift down naturally in the current, without drag on the line, allowing it to fish just over the bottom. In very high water, a bit of lead must be added to get the bait down. A good stream bait fisherman always carries a supply of sinkers of different weights, changing these to suit the fishing depth as he moves along the stream, fishing pockets, pools, and runs.

The good lies of fish in a small brook can be detected at a glance. The deep spots hold the fish, and this does not necessarily mean only the pools. Every spot in which the rocky bottom is hidden from clear view, either by the depth of the water or the broken flow of current, should hold a fish. In small brooks a trout's lie is of limited area and he seldom moves from

The upstream approach won't scare fish.

this spot. It may be only a square yard or so, but he maintains this domain until he is caught or until a change in stream conditions forces him to move.

This provides much of the charm that small brooks hold for fishermen. The confines of the stream pinpoint the good lies. And when you take a fair trout from such a lie, another is sure to move in shortly, usually within a day or so.

Trout in a small brook rarely choose to lie in the fast riffles, unless there are sizeable stones on the bottom to break the flow of water. Then, a fish will often lie at the apex of the V formed by the flow after it breaks around the rock and re-forms downstream. Here a trout can wait in relative comfort and see clearly all food life carried toward him by the stream.

The more obvious good lies conform to a pattern: cover for the fish, current flow not too fast, and food readily available. The cover can be a small rock ledge, a mossy boulder, a crack between stones, or a submerged log. It also will have an adequate depth of water—enough that the bottom cannot be seen clearly.

The pleasure in fishing small brooks is that the trout are not periodic feeders. They keep at it more or less throughout the day, taking many types of insect life as they come to the surface. The shade over the streams also helps to keep these waters fairly cool, and, thus, encourages feeding during daylight hours.

A fly-fisherman can reasonably expect to raise fish periodically throughout a day, not only because the fish feed continually, but because they seldom are selective. Small-stream trout are always on the lookout for drifting insect life, and it's likely that you will find a dozen different forms and species of trout food in every fish you take. These are the trout that often can be "pounded up" by repeated casting over a good spot with the dry fly. Any standard, high-floating fly will do.

Meadow Creeks

The meadow creek is often sluggish, with deep, dark pools overhung with willows or cottonwoods, where largemouth bass, suckers, and pickerel live together in amicable toleration. Less often, it flows lazily through bottom land. Its shelter here comes from tight stands of alders, its bottom is sand

Depth of water in pools of a mountain river conceals fish (top right), while angling in clear, high mountain lakes is best over deep water (lower left). Fast, open mountain creek permits easy fishing (lower right).

and gravel. This can be trout water, if its source is nearby mountain springs, and almost always it is small-mouth-bass water.

Angling over a meadow creek broadens a fisherman's knowledge far beyond what he gains from mountain brooks. The lies of the fish will be more varied. There certainly will be some areas of fast water where fish may lie in the V behind submerged or exposed boulders. There will be depth enough in the pools to conceal a fish and give it some sense of security. The banks at the bends often are undercut. Upended trees lie along the banks, the trunks, limbs, or roots that are submerged forming deep, dark caverns. A swirling eddy will bore a deep hole in the sandy or gravel bottoms. All these are pockets in which to look for fish.

Years ago I used to fish a slow, meadow stream about thirty feet wide with soft banks lined with alders, screening the deep places. It was a clear, cold, spring-fed stream with a smooth bottom of sand and fine gravel. There was little vegetation to change the flow of current or to hide a fish. On a clear day, with the sun high overhead, it was possible to see minute details in that stream bed with the help of Polaroid glasses. And although the stream bed teemed with insect life —caddis, burrowing May-fly and dragonfly nymphs— it was unusual to spot a trout, and then it was always a little fellow.

I knew there were big trout, both browns and brooks, in this stream. The opening-day fishermen always gathered a few on worms, when the water level was high and the water cloudy, as most meadow streams are in early April. But after the water level receded and the stream cleared up, few fish were taken. I often

229

Best fishing in the small meadow creek is in the deep, shaded areas.

wondered where the trout could hide, and spent many hours looking for them.

By pure chance, I happened to pass this meandering creek one evening early in May, as I drove home from a trout stream further up in the mountains. When I crossed the bridge, a cloud of May flies hit my windshield. Eggs carried by the females splattered and ran down the glass in yellow streaks. I pulled off the road and walked back to the stream with a pail, to rinse away the sticky stuff.

As I dipped the pail, a great bulge of water broke from the surface of the smooth glide just above the bridge, beneath the overhanging tips of some alder branches. At first I thought it was a surfacing muskrat, but within a few seconds the big roll and the widening rings came again, sending wavelets to lap against the banks. It was almost dark, but I could see that this was a big fish, and in this stream it had to be a trout. I returned to the car and rigged up, tying a large Bivisible dry fly to the leader.

I sneaked back under the bridge. The big trout kept rising systematically, gobbling the hatching duns from the surface with hungry sucking noises. Large March Browns were coming down the stream literally in patches, and this trout was taking them without caution or restraint. I could see his nose poke above the surface as he sucked in the flies. I moved to within a dozen yards of the fish before dropping the fly over him with a sidearm cast. He had just risen as my fly

touched the surface, so he ignored it—and the next few floats of the fly over him.

There was still enough light for me to see what he was taking. If single flies came over him, he would not rise. But if a tiny cluster drifted down, he was up and taking with a series of audible smacks. I watched until the next little group of three or four, floating close together, came toward his lie. I dropped my Bivisible in with them. He rose surely, solidly. I lifted the rod just enough to take the wrinkles of slack from line and leader, then felt him, heavy and surging, as he rushed upstream for a few yards. He swerved in toward the bank, tugged a time or two, and the broken leader flipped back toward me against the tension of the rod. The contact had lasted three or four seconds—that was all.

By this time it was too dark to find out what he had fouled me on. But a few days later I returned to look over the situation, and to find the hidden branch, tree root, or log he might have turned around to put breaking pressure against the fine gut. I never did find it, but I found his home: a muskrat hole about a foot below the surface. He had dived into this without hesitation after the hook pricked him.

Nor did I ever take that trout. A friend of mine, after I had tipped him the hiding place, raised the fish on a big dry fly, all hackle and tied to a stout leader. He caught him feeding in the same spot, used the same system to bring him up, then hauled his two-foot length down under the bridge, where the trout could no longer reach the security of his muskrat hole.

This was the clue to finding the big trout in this stream. The banks were honeycombed with muskrat holes and there the trout hid, waiting only for a good hatch to bring them out. At dusk, as the clouds of fluttering duns and flopping caddis flies rode the surface, the big browns would come from the banks, take a feeding station a yard or two away, and gorge on the hatch. Thereafter, I caught many fine trout in that creek. I never fished except to a rising fish and, after getting in the right position, seldom had to make more than a single cast to get the hook into one. Considering the number of fish hooked, I did not land many on my light dry-fly tackle, but I had some memorable encounters with huge fish, larger than any I have ever taken on a dry fly.

Catching fish from these slow, fairly deep meadow streams is a task of first locating the fish, then finding their feeding times. I know of several where the feeding of the fish is just as critical as it was with the muskrat-hole browns. One in particular is a stream holding big brook trout in extremely deep holes, where it seems to be impossible to bring up a fish to a fly, or to sink it deeply enough to reach one. Yet each one of these deep holes is fed by current dropping quickly over a sand bar lying just a foot or so below the fast water. At dusk, when the hatches of May flies begin to show on the surface, the big trout move up from the depths to lie over the bar, gulping flies greedily as long as the hatch lasts, and in open water so shallow that any sizeable fish would shun it in daylight.

I suppose that some of these big trout can be taken on bait or on a heavy spinning lure, but the stream is restricted to fly-fishing. This is just as well, since you can take the big squaretails readily on a big Gray Wulff dry fly once they come over the bar to feed.

In deep, slow water the movement of the current must be studied before making the first cast. And unless a big hatch of flies is on, the fish will lie on the bottom of the holes with no interest in coming far up for food. The water entering these deep pools usually churns downward, carrying with it the food the fish need when they are taking underwater life—which is for most of the year. I find that in fishing the wet fly, upstream casting gives the fly time to sink far enough

to gain the fish's notice. On a slack line it comes to him naturally, just as a real insect does. Bait fished the same way also makes the most natural approach to a fish, if it is dropped well upstream of the hole, in the incoming current, then allowed to sink and drift along freely—as though unattached to leader and line. Laying a long, pretty, straight cast over deep, quiet water may inflate the ego, but it won't produce many fish.

Mountain Rivers

When Charles Cotton cannily observed that stream fishing is done at three basic levels he was oversimplifying the situation. His theory was sound enough with reference to a fish's feeding habits, but it stopped short of present needs simply because we know more about fish and have better equipment to explore new ideas.

As I stated earlier, Cotton said: "I shall divide Angling for Trout or Grayling, into these three ways. ... That which we call Angling at the Top, is with a fly; at the Bottom, with a ground-bait; in the Middle, with a minnow, or ground-bait." In our day we may explore all three levels with proper fly-fishing, as well as with baits and many lures. Cotton, unfortunately, did not know about the dry fly—true top fishing—but his "Angling at the Top" would compare with what modern wet-fly fishermen call fishing a "fast" fly. His "Middle" ground we fish with the wet fly, nymph, or streamer, and his "Bottom" with the weighted nymph or some form of imitation caddis worm.

Cotton well knew that three different feeding levels exist in most large streams and he coped with them in his own way. We have learned that changes in water levels, temperature, and clarity may influence a rise to the surface, bottom feeding, or mid-water activity. The presence of desirable food at each level prompts the feeding activity of fish, and the degree of insect activity is the direct result of variations in stream temperature, water clarity, and sunlight, or the lack of it, during the normal periods of insect emergence.

Few fishermen consider that the flow of water through a pool or run divides itself roughly into three layers, each traveling at different speeds. The top level moves fairly fast, the middle level a bit faster, and the bottom level slower than either because of friction over stones, gravel, or whatever. In clear water you can actually see the differences by following the movement of small bits of matter in suspension. To the fisherman this is significant because it gives him some clue concerning the speed at which a fly or bait should be fished in order to attract the attention of a fish at a particular level.

Obviously, this three-layer division of water can only be observed in rivers, or sections of rivers, where the flow is moderately fast. In rapids or broken "pocket water," the currents have no uniformity at all. In slow-moving water, there is little difference in speed among the three levels. But mountain rivers provide the opportunity to explore the three-level technique.

On big rivers a man is forced to "read the water," first to find the fish, then to make the taking presentation of fly or lure. The wide stretches of a big stream present far different problems in locating fish than do small brooks or meadow creeks. The fish are not confined by a limited water area, nor do they need to look for hiding holes under banks, tree roots, or logs. In a big mountain stream the banks are usually swept clean and clear, leaving bare, rocky shore lines during most of the fishing season. The angler must find his fish in the open reaches of the stream.

One of the best old-time wet-fly men I ever knew picked his good lies by looking for "black water." These are the deep spots in the stream, not necessarily pools, but deep runs and glides where depth makes the water look darker to the wading angler's eye. The security a trout, or any game fish, needs to feel is given by depth and this is most often found squarely in the middle of a big river. Wading then becomes extremely important to the fisherman. He must get far enough from shore to reach the fish, and close enough to the lie to present the fly or lure at just the right angle.

The study of currents is most important on big rivers. Granted that we see the long, dark strip of water which indicates a deep run, where will we find the fish? And this means feeding fish, for there is a marked difference between the lies of feeding and resting fish. Three different areas offer good feeding stations: the edges of the fastest water coming into the run; the lower end of the fast flow as it breaks

Quiet, shallow, weedy lake is ideal water for pickerel or largemouth bass (top left). Rock-bound pool in brook is good dry-fly spot (top right); typical wet-fly water can be seen at bottom.

into the quiet water, and the very tail of the run, just before it breaks over into the next bit of fast water— *provided* that there are some sheltering rocks on the bottom large enough to offer "breaks" in the current.

Since good angling practice is largely common sense, based on the feeding of fish and their comfort level, the feeding stations described conform to two factors: availability of food and a modest flow of current that a fish does not have to fight strongly. As the fast current breaks down into the run it leaves a patch of quiet water on either side (often a back eddy, with reverse current). A fish lying on the inside edge of the quiet water can remain there with minimum effort and watch for food being carried into the run. When a fish rises to a fly drifted down through this fast water he invariably charges toward the middle of the run, suggesting that he is working from the outside, watching and feeding toward the center. He is less likely to rise to a fly cast and fished through the quiet water on the sides of the fast flow.

The prime feeding station in such a run, however, is at the tail of fast water. Obviously, the food supply carried in is at the maximum and has slowed down enough to give the fish a chance to see it clearly. This slowing of the current is also a more comfortable situation for the fish. If there are some fairly good-sized boulders lying on the bottom to break the speed still more, this is the best feeding station in the run. There's depth enough for cover, a moderate flow of water, and a choice supply of food.

As a rule, the tail end of such a run is the least

productive of the three feeding stations. Larger fish will not lie there normally because of the shallower depth. But a good hatch of surface flies or emerging nymphs will often bring fish down to this spot (again, if there are some bottom rocks to break the flow) where the fish can pick up flies leisurely in relatively quiet water. Normally, this is a choice spot after the sun has left the water and the stream has darkened a bit. Most game fish, trout in particular, are chary about feeding in shallows where the sun can reveal them.

Deep, quiet sections of this typical run may hold many big fish during the day, generally the biggest in the run. But these fish usually are resting and not to be had—although an odd one may pick up a bait dragging over the bottom. When these fish feed they move from the quiet water to one of the three typical feeding stations. Thus, fishing with any type of artificial fly or lure over the deep, still water of a pool or run is rarely productive.

With the fly, it is possible to explore the two upper levels of a run of this type, but rarely the bottom level, because the speed of current will not permit the fly to sink to the bottom. But the two productive levels can be covered with the dry fly, fished over the three feeding stations, or the wet fly or nymph cast up and across and then fished over the lies with some cross-current action. This is "Angling at the Top," as described by Cotton. Fishing the middle level, which, incidentally, is the most productive of the three in this type of water, involves getting some depth to the fly or nymph before it comes to the fish. A level line or a heavy torpedo line of the sinking type will help to put the fly down, but the important move is dropping the fly far enough upstream to gain depth by the time it comes over the fish. The fly is fished on a natural dead drift, coming to the fish as either a drowned insect or as a free-floating nymph readying itself to break free from the shuck, prior to emergence.

A most effective method of fishing the sunken fly may be used when the fish are rising to nymphs swimming up from the bottom toward the surface, where they break out rapidly. In this technique, the angler takes a stand opposite the feeding station (rather than downstream from this spot), then makes the up-and-across cast, well above the fish. The fly, carried by the current, sinks down well, perhaps two or three feet

deep. As it comes to the fish, it is "kicked up" toward the surface by a lift of the rod tip to tighten the line, and a swimming movement is imparted by a quick, fluttering motion of the wrist. This is not easy to do, since a real study of the currents must be made to determine the depth that can be achieved on the drift, as well as their effect on dragging the line. Flies tied on extra heavy hooks, or with weighted bodies, are almost a must for fishing the "rising" nymph this way.

Fishing the fast-water rapids and "pockets" of a big river offer another change in method. This is productive water in warm weather, because the churning effect of rapids mixes a maximum supply of oxygen in the water and keeps the fish active. Finding the good lies is not too difficult. A glance over the rapids, if you have waded closely enough, will show the dark spots that are pockets in the bottom, usually formed just behind a small, submerged rock. For you will not often find fish lying in fast water over a fairly smooth bottom. It takes a pocket, where the current breaks and slows over the bottom, to provide a comfortable resting place. Generally, you will raise a good fish from fast, white water and wonder how he could hold a feeding station in current flowing five to seven miles an hour. But if you wade out to that spot you'll find a hidden rock offering just enough projection from the bottom to break the fast flow and that is the spot your trout was using.

234

*Mountain rivers, like
these, call upon the angler for
the greatest variety of
fishing technique.*

*Upper left: Carcajou Pool, Lake
St. John, from "Angling Resorts," by Wakeman
Holberton, 1890. Above: View
on the River Wye, from
"The Complete Angler," Vol. 4, London.*

Farm Ponds

In general, the farm pond is simply the oasis of a nearby farmer who uses it to water his stock, irrigate his crops, and, perhaps, raise a brood of ducks. Often, it is also a school for beginning anglers armed with makeshift equipment, and sometimes it is the nostalgic retreat of an experienced fisherman.

Unpretentious as these waters may seem, they are the havens of both game fish and pan fish. Large-mouth bass lurk in some, and where bass are not available, pickerel, white or black crappie, perch, bluegill, "brim," and bottom-feeding catfish or bullhead may be found. In northern latitudes and mountain foothill country, it is even possible to take trout, but only if the pond is spring-fed. And numerically such ponds are rare. Pond water is generally too warm for the trout to live comfortably.

No rules about "small waters, small fish" apply to farm ponds either. It is incredible how large fish will grow in these environs when the food supply is good. I have taken bass up to seven pounds from ponds that were no more than an acre or two in size, but plentifully endowed with frogs, minnows, dragonflies, and the myriad of lesser animal life on which bass thrive.

Yet, in spite of the interesting sport they may promise and their availability, these waters remain relatively unfished by most anglers, who choose bigger waters to search for more wild or more wary adversaries than they feel farm ponds are likely to provide. At the same time, and ironically, many farm ponds are well able to withstand heavy fishing. A few near my home give up hundreds of pounds of big crappies every season without any apparent diminution of supply.

Superficially, there is little difference between one farm pond and another, whether the pond is nestled in rolling grasslands, or in a patch of well-furrowed countryside, or deep in a wooded wilderness. The singularity of each pond lies in the character of its water, a factor which can vary greatly, depending upon its source. Water flowing freely over granite rocks to its destination bears little resemblance, chemically, to water which seeps slowly to an open pond through beds of limestone soil, and the chemical differences resulting in each instance directly affect the

quantity and quality of plant and animal life in the water. Thus, indirectly, they affect the fishing, and make some knowledge of very elementary biochemistry important to the angler.

Where there is an insufficient amount of small plant and animal life, fish will seldom be found. This is true for two reasons:

First, the natural life cycle underwater depends upon minute plant and animal organisms—sometimes called plankton—to provide sustenance to minnows and insects, which, in turn, are food for the bigger fish. The cycle is completed when wastes and decaying matter are released into the water by the larger species, ultimately fertilizing surrounding soil and providing nourishment for new plants and microorganisms.

Second, inasmuch as farm ponds are fairly shallow

Fine breeders of bass, pan fish, warm-water species, farm ponds are relatively easy to fish.

and exposed to the direct rays of the sun for the greater part of each day, their waters tend to be warm and incapable of holding enough oxygen naturally to sustain life. A rich plant life, both beneath and on the surface of the water, producing oxygen and freeing it through photosynthesis, is needed to offset this deficiency, and to permit the fish to live comfortably. Underwater plants are particularly vital, since the oxygen they produce is released directly into the water.

Once you have found a healthy pond, working it is not especially difficult and rarely dull. The pleasures to be had in small waters are twofold: you can use your lightest tackle and surface lure, and you can expect the action to be **vigorous and constant**. Pond fish are remarkably unsophisticated because they receive little pressure from knowledgeable sportsmen.

Whether it is curiosity or hunger that moves the fish to attack, they do so with both carelessness and vengeance, sometimes fouling your line or snapping it, before you can subdue them.

For the most part, pond fish, both large and small, feed in the shallows, near the heavier growths of weeds, permitting the angler to wade along shore lines (where the bottom is not too soft) to stalk his fish. It is relatively easy to cast from the shore to any number of the pond's most productive areas. The task lies in bringing a big fish in from this position. Chances of snagging the line are far greater than usual since a fish must be led through the weeds to net him.

Here the most rudimentary type of fishing craft can be helpful. A tiny, square-end punt, less than ten feet long, weighing no more than fifty pounds, and made

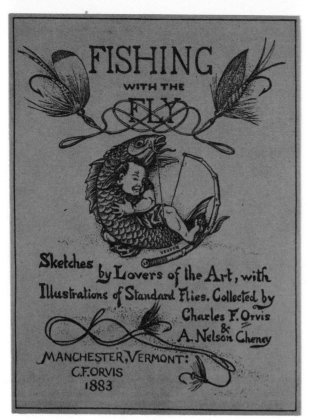

Frontispiece from
C. F. Orvis' "Fishing with the Fly,"
Manchester, Vermont, 1883.

likely to be roused by some type of top-water artificial bug (larger sizes for bass, smaller ones for crappie and bluegill). Somehow, however, I have always felt that these little ponds should never be fished with a lure that is too large. A big spoon or plug seems incompatible with the surroundings, and its splash upon the surface of a quiet spot will, I think, probably frighten more fish than it attracts. Yet, I am sure there are fishermen who will differ with me, and no doubt with good reasons.

There certainly will be occasions when a big fish breaks loose from a small lure and escapes in a tangle of weeds. At such times, the angler wishes he had used more rugged tackle. But the only concession I have made to this sort of situation is to fit a stout leader to the hair bug when I am going after bass. Often a big fish will work free if you slack off the pressure and allow him to make his own moves.

As in other angling, you will not land them all. Still, it's comforting to know that in the small pond

of plywood, is serviceable for two men and light enough to carry where it is needed. In addition, it can be homemade for about the cost of a fair fly rod.

A one-man rubber raft also works well for farm-pond fishing. It can be back-packed for half a mile or so without too much discomfort, and will permit you to cover all areas of the pond readily. There is even a device known as a fishing float which is ideal for this type of angling. It is nothing more than an inflated rubber tube fitted with a pair of wader-type legs.

Actually, it is better angling to fish the shore-line hide-outs and feeding spots from a point somewhere toward the center of the pond. And the use of a small craft makes it possible to probe weed beds and lily-pad clusters which are normally out of casting range of the wading angler.

In general, farm waters are fished with bait—usually by neighboring boys using a float and worms. This elementary approach works well enough for taking bullheads and perch, some crappie and bluegills, but it probably will fail to stir the pond's larger residents and more choice trophies.

In shallow environments bigger game is more

Still baiting for pickerel, from
"Fishing in American Waters," by Genio C. Scott,
New York, 1869.

238

a fish lost can frequently be engaged on another day. It's likely that a sizeable fish won't move far from a favorite feeding ground, even after he has been hooked and has broken away several times.

During a period of three weeks' fishing, I once hooked a large bass near a submerged stump in a small pond near my home. He promptly dove back into his hide-out, fouled the leader around a tree root, and snapped himself free. On three successive trips, he repeated the same maneuvers, before he moved at last into open water and gave me a fight on more equal terms. Curiously, I landed this six-pounder on the same fly-rod bug I had first raised him to—a minnow-type hair lure. Apparently he did not learn that a hair minnow was dangerous even after being hooked three times.

Of course, a good deal of successful farm-pond fishing lies in the way you approach the fish. Fish in small waters become alarmed quickly, and once frightened off, a choice specimen may be hard to attract again. Accurate casting also is essential, so that the best lies can be carefully combed.

In each instance, the lure must be worked slowly. Sometimes the merest twitch will bring a rise; then with little or no forewarning you will find yourself battling an angry fish. The presence of plankton in good pond water also tends to cloud it and forces the angler to give the fish enough time to see and take the lure. One reason why surface-lure fishing can be so effective under these conditions is that it creates a wake and ripple that can be detected by a feeding fish.

Best of all, farm ponds can be fished almost the year around. The ice leaves quickly in the spring and the shallow water warms rapidly—usually weeks before it does in large lakes and streams. Pan fish can be engaged almost immediately after the thaw, and since the water is rarely deep enough for fish to lie low during warm spells, fishing can be somewhat productive straight through the summer. Only the heavy frosts of late autumn finally put an end to the activity.

The farm pond is less subject to the whims of nature than are other bodies of water, and its various fish are, for the most part, willing to co-operate, once you learn their optimum feeding times. These inevitably come during the first hours of daylight and the last hours of dusk.

Warm Water Lakes

Warm water lakes vary so widely that few generalizations can be made about them. They range from the deep (ten to fifteen feet) to the extremely shallow, and from the naturally formed to the man-made. In addition, they differ in the color and clarity of their waters, in the materials which compose their bottoms, and in the quantity and character of the vegetation beneath their surfaces.

Probably the only all-inclusive statement that can be made about warm-water lakes is that of the many bodies of still waters in the United States, they are by far the most numerous. And it should also be said that where these waters are fertile and the food supply is good, the angler will find interesting sport. The proper lure can raise anything from a largemouth bass to a great northern pike.

The first task of an angler on warm waters is to learn how to determine their fishing potential. Scientists can determine the productive capacity of a body of water by analyzing its lime content. The higher the percentage of lime, the greater the amount of carbon dioxide and the larger the supply of oxygen; consequently, the more abundant the lake's plant and animal life.

Obviously, not many anglers off for a week's fishing are anxious to pack a carbon-dioxide kit with their tackle or to carry out extensive chemical tests once they arrive at their destination. Nor is such an analysis necessary. A fisherman well grounded in the essentials of his sport can decide rather positively whether or not a lake will provide good fishing simply by noting the color of its water and the size and quantity of its underwater weeds.

Clear, cool water, as I mentioned earlier, is capable of retaining the greatest amount of oxygen and of providing the richest supply of waterweeds. As water warms, however, its ability to hold oxygen diminishes, and as it clouds or darkens, the abundance of its underwater plant life decreases.

Brown waters do not permit the sun's rays to penetrate deeply enough below the surface to nourish plant life there. And without a substantial amount of waterweeds constantly oxygenating the water, the oxygen

Fishing in the warm-water sloughs of the South.

content becomes dangerously low—often too low for fish to live comfortably.

A knowledgeable fisherman takes such considerations into account when he chooses his lake and his method of fishing it. Where water is extremely murky, for instance, he will not try to raise fish much beyond a depth of twenty feet; if he did, his efforts probably would prove fruitless. In very dark waters, twenty feet is about the maximum depth the sun's rays can reach.

The clarity of the water also affects the choice of the lure and how it is cast and fished. Spoons of copper or gold finish or naturally colored plug baits which do well in clear water will not be satisfactory in brown or clouded water. A flashy lure of shiny silver or nickel plate, or a red-and-white plug that can be spotted more readily does better.

Also, clear waters require less pinpoint accuracy in placing the lure and fewer casts to cover lies well. To raise a fish in brown water, on the other hand, the lure must strike the water within inches of a hide-out or feeding station, and it must be retrieved slowly to give the fish time to see it and to decide whether or not to

240

take it. And in fishing "blind"—that is, casually covering an expanse of shore-line weeds—the next cast in dark waters should hit no more than a few feet from the last.

The shallower warm-water lakes are perhaps the easiest to fish, but they have their disadvantages. While they offer fewer deep holes in which fish may lie, thus driving choice specimens toward shore-line shallows to hide and feed, their fish are also more sensitive to seasonal changes.

Fish in these waters often lurk at depths no greater than six feet in the early part of the season; therefore, a surface lure cast with either a fly rod or a spinning rod and retrieved slowly and carefully over the surface is best. Normally it will rouse both largemouth and smallmouth bass, pickerel and northern pike, and any of several species of pan fish. In lakes where the pike species predominates, a skitter bait, or its artificial counterpart in a spinning-streamer fly combination, will be more effective.

Fishing the shallows can be tricky, and most warm-water lake fishing will involve this. It is never easy to work an underwater lure in weed- and snag-filled waters without hanging up on every cast. And all too often the fisherman is forced to use a lure he can handle easily rather than the one which best suits his target.

As temperatures rise in summer, the oxygen content of the water decreases, dulling the appetites and the responses of the fish. Usually, for much of this twelve-to fourteen-week period, all game fish and most pan fish retire to favored shady lies and give up feeding during daylight hours. Then, fishing is most successful when the sun is off the water. When skies are dismal, promising a spit of rain, or at the crack of dawn, before the sun first strikes the water, or even after sunset, when surface water is cooling and a few fish begin to take top-water insects, are the choice moments.

One shallow warm-water lake in my neighborhood consistently produces good largemouth bass in the first two hours after daybreak, but it is virtually impossible to raise fish at any other time in the summer. Not until autumn brings crisper days do the fish resume daylight feeding—and then only when the direct rays of the sun are not playing on the surface.

Sometimes a man-made warm-water lake will provide daylight fishing at the height of the summer, but only if you can locate the channel of the dammed stream bed that forms the lake. Water in the channel generally is cooler than the water in other parts of the lake and fair fishing is possible near the inlet source. For the most part, you will be forced to still-fish with natural baits in these areas, although a sinking plug, permitted to touch bottom before being retrieved, will also work well.

A fairly large, full-flowing inlet stream feeding a quiet, shallow lake also can be tried successfully during otherwise nonfishable hours. In such cases, deep fishing in the inlet channel is the most profitable. Besides increasing the angler's pleasure in hot weather, these feeder streams add to the oxygen content of deep, still water where plant life is inadequate. The force of the stream carries its mixture of oxygen well out into the center of the lake. Since stream water is normally colder than lake water, and therefore heavier, the stream water sinks and oxygenates the lower levels.

Many warm-water lakes are resort lakes, where heavy surface activity—swimming, boating, water skiing—discourages feeding fish and sends them in search of cover. In such environments, the angler must wait until the commotion has subsided before he can seek out a fish. He will find his best fishing hours are after dark or in the dim gray of dawn.

In the deeper warm-water lakes, early season fishing is most productive along shore lines, both where the bottom drops off fairly quickly and where considerable weed growth offers protection to the fish. When summer warms the surface waters, the fish move to deeper areas, particularly those rich in broad-leaved weeds. Their hideaways can be located by trolling with a lead-core line and a feathered-treble spoon, but not without considerable frustration. You'll hang up on the weeds soon enough with this rig. Another method of finding deep-lying fish is to drift slowly over their retreats, when the sun is high overhead, and search for the waterweeds below with the aid of Polaroid glasses, if the water is clear enough to permit it.

Whatever method you employ—the fly, the bass bug, or the spoon—fishing on warm-water lakes is done at a slow tempo, in keeping with the leisurely character of these waters and the logy movement of their food life. The reactions of both game and pan fish are adjusted to such rhythms, and the lure which deviates least will probably catch the most fish.

Mountain Lakes

N o t w o fresh-water lakes are quite alike. Their depths vary enormously. Each has some differences in the type of bottom, the quantity and variety of its vegetation, the clarity of its water, its lime content, its proportion of oxygen, and so on, ad infinitum. But one particular type of lake is invariably a good producer of fish. This is the clear-water lake having appreciable depth for its surface area, a recognizable feeding shelf, and a scattering of bays or coves well supplied with underwater weeds. This I generally envision as a mountain lake, since it is a type that is characteristic of mountainous country, although lakes of this general description are most certainly found elsewhere.

The salient feature of the mountain lake is that its waters divide into three distinct layers during the major part of the angling season. Each of the layers present different comfort levels for fish, in both temperature and oxygen content, thus giving the key to where the fish can be found and where they will be interested in feeding.

The annual ritual of "turn-over" and stratification begins after the ice leaves the lake in early spring. Until the moment the ice breaks up, the temperature of the surface water, just below the ice, will be thirty-two degrees. Below the surface, the water temperature rises as the depth increases, so that at the same time along the bottom, it will be at about forty degrees.

With the breakup of the ice, the warming rays of the sun and the action of the wind begin their work. The surface water becomes warmer (although it does not reach forty degrees), and being denser, begins to sink toward the bottom. Wave action helps mix the water. In time, usually within a few days, all the water in the lake reaches thirty-nine and two-tenths degrees, at which temperature water is at its maximum weight, or density. During the "turn-over" period, the cold-water species—landlocks, brook trout, and lakers—are most likely to be feeding on the surface.

After a week or so of intense sunlight, the lake begins its summer stagnation period. Gradually the temperature of the surface water rises above forty degrees.

Since warm water is lighter in density than cool water, a layer called the epilimnion is formed along the surface. This layer may be fifteen to twenty feet deep, and the temperature within it will vary only a few degrees. Its surface may reach seventy-five degrees, while the underside of the layer will have dropped only to about seventy. The thickness of the layer varies with the depth of the lake, as compared with its surface area, and with the clarity of the lake water.

Directly below the epilimnion, the thermocline establishes itself. This is the important area for the angler. In terms of temperature and oxygen content, it is the most comfortable level for all fish species. The thermocline layer may vary from ten to forty feet in depth (or thickness), depending on the type of lake. But the important factor is that its upper level will be at seventy degrees or less. At the bottom of the thermocline layer, a sharp drop in temperature takes place—down to about forty-five degrees.

From this point downward, a third layer forms. This is the hypolimnion, in which the water again stabilizes itself at the maximum density point of thirty-nine and two-tenths degrees. This layer normally holds insufficient oxygen to support fish in comfort, although there are some exceptions in waters where deep weed growths provide additional oxygen.

The three-layer stratification in deep lakes is maintained throughout the summer period. It breaks up only when fall weather cools the surface water and wave action again mixes up the layers to bring about a uniform temperature of thirty-nine and two-tenths degrees. This is generally constant until ice forms over the lake. The fall "turn-over" brings the fish toward the surface once more, and is largely responsible for the good fishing we have in early autumn.

Although the layering of lake waters may seem to be purely academic in an angling book, it explains why some fishermen will take fish during the "off" months of summer when most others do not. It becomes obvious that if you are fishing for the cold-water species—salmon, trout, smallmouth bass, walleyes—your efforts will be wasted fishing through the

Fly casting is effective
at mountain-lake inlets (left), but
trolling takes more
fish in deep water (below).

Above: After long portage to the
Racquette River in the Adirondacks, from
"Angling Resorts,"
by Wakeman Holberton, 1890.

*Most high mountain lakes are suited
to different species of trout, depending upon
oxygen content of the water.*

upper warm-water level of these lakes. It is rare that any of these species will move through water at a temperature much above seventy degrees, and rarer still to find them feeding there.

I experienced a perfect example of this during a summer trip I made to a Canadian lake. Landlocked salmon was the target. As everyone knows, the best landlock fishing is in the spring, during the period of the "turn-over," when the fish are near the surface. But I was in a mood to experiment, since I knew the lake and the location of all the deep holes.

When I arrived in mid-July, not a salmon had been taken for more than two weeks, either on a fly or by trolling with lures. Since I had never fished this lake during hot summer weather, I decided to spend some time with the thermometer to locate the thermocline. Within an hour on the first morning, using a metal-cased thermometer and a graduated line, I learned that I could reach a temperature of sixty-eight degrees at a depth of fifteen feet—the top level of the thermocline. At thirty feet the temperature showed a sudden drop to forty-five degrees, suggesting that this was the thermocline's lower level.

For trolling at between fifteen and thirty feet, I decided to use a lead-core line without any additional weight. By trolling near shore until the lure hung up on a rock, I could check the running depth of the lure when I retrieved it. After a few such trials, I learned that with one hundred and twenty feet of line and the proper throttle setting on the outboard, I could troll at a depth of twenty feet. I then went trolling, with gold-pearl Side-Winders in the one-third-ounce size.

Within a quarter of an hour my guide and I hooked the first salmon, a handsome fish of about three pounds. Before the dinner hour we had handled eight good fish, all better than three pounds. This was the pattern for five days of fishing, for a total score of eighty-two fish landed, many more than one hundred hooked. After the first day's success, the

word got out and more salmon fishermen moved into the lake. None, so far as we could learn, took a fish, since all were fishing the top with trolled streamer flies. It was absolutely essential to troll the lure at least fifteen feet deep, and, conversely, no use at all to troll deeper than thirty feet, which we learned after much experimenting with longer lines, added weights, and varied trolling speeds. The fish fed actively only within the limits of the thermocline.

The difference in temperature between the salmon's feeding level and the surface water became obvious with each fish we netted. The shiny, smooth bodies were quite cool to the touch and the contrast became startling when I held the fish in one hand and dipped my other hand into the lake water along the boat's side.

Trolling is certainly the easiest way to reach thermocline depths in fishing the big lakes. Yet this level of temperature extends to the bottom not far from shore lines, and makes casting with a sinking plug or spoon quite profitable if rock shoals or weed beds can be located at thermocline depths. Most of the deep-water mountain lakes have a definite feeding shelf well out from shore, at the edge of the deep-water

Wilderness Lakes

To rate as a wilderness lake, a body of water should be inaccessible by car. This immediately gives a fisherman two advantages: the fish are unsophisticated because of light fishing pressure, and chances are that the lake is far enough north that it is not unfavorably influenced by hot summer weather.

The float plane puts most wilderness lakes within easy reach of a fisherman. The smaller, isolated lakes in mountain country are too risky for take-offs, so these are seldom fished at all, except by the man who has courage enough to paddle and portage the miles necessary to reach them.

There is abiding pleasure in having a lake all to yourself, to know that you are not following in the wake of another fisherman, or, perhaps, a dozen who may have scared hell out of all the fish. I am sure that the joy of wilderness fishing lies as much in the splendid isolation of the surroundings as in taking the fish. The mountains stand close guard, the water sparkles, the foliage was never greener. Fish, in such a situation, can become incidental to the fishing.

I know dozens of lakes with this sort of charm where the fish are brighter and cleaner than anywhere else, where their glorious wildness is eminently compatible with their habitat. I seldom can see a native brook trout without also seeing the lush greenery of a Maine spruce stand, or the brilliant scarlet of a tanager in Adirondack beeches. The musky to me means moose country, as dark and mysterious in its thickets as the fish itself, with little families of black ducks and evening flights of mergansers swooping low over stump-filled waters. And when I see a great northern pike, I can see, too, the broad, slow wingbeats of Old Zack, the great blue heron, as he lifts up and away from the marsh grass, disturbed in his fishing by my casting with a big red-and-white spoon.

An angler does not need to know much about fishing and fish to take his share in the wilderness. He is guided, inevitably, and his guide knows the good spots and when to fish them. In the north country of Maine the big squaretails are ready to give battle at ice-out time and for at least a month after. The fly is the thing — bright wet flies cast along shore-line

drop-off. If the bottom is rocky, this shelf is a natural area for landlocks, smallmouth bass, and walleyes. If it is weedy, look for musky, northern pike, and largemouth bass. And, if its depth corresponds to that of the thermocline, you are almost certain to find feeding fish — if your lure or bait finds the proper depth.

During the spring and fall "turn-over" periods, the fish in deep, clear lakes respond to the same angling methods you would use on warm-water lakes. You are likely to find the fish moving almost anywhere because of the cool temperatures and high oxygen content. It is the summer months that demand some careful thinking and experimenting to find the optimum comfort level of the fish. A stream thermometer then becomes an essential part of the tackle.

The problem of taking fish from big lakes is complicated by other factors during the summer — the movements of feed minnows, the presence of "bloom" — underwater plant life — in and on the water, the color of the water itself. Most useful, however, is the sure knowledge of where the fish are likely to lie and feed, and this is always a matter of finding that magic middle layer of water, the thermocline.

shallows or streamers trolled over deep waters. When the first May-fly hatches appear, delicate fishing with the dry fly is the order of the evening. When the summer sun warms the water, the inlet streams, with their cooler flow, attract the feeding squaretails, and these bigger trout will lie in the spring holes where a sunken nymph or small wet fly, fished deep, can tie you to a husky fish of at least three pounds. It is more a matter of where and when, rather than how, that produces the fish in wilderness waters—and this applies not only to trout, but to all game-fish species.

When considering wilderness lakes, it is impossible not to think of the magnificent waters of southwestern Alaska, where the great rolling sweep of tundra country is broken only occasionally by jagged mountain ranges. This is the land of unwary trout, grayling, and pike, where simply to be on the spot means catching fish. The pike, particularly, are voracious in the shallow tundra ponds and a bright spoon cast from shore or the plane's floats brings a vicious strike almost every time. The grayling will be just as eager for a small trout fly, spinner, or wobbler. But the rainbows probably will prove more circumspect since they come in to feed on salmon spawn.

The great lake fishing in Alaska is for mackinaws, or lake trout. These are on or near the surface all summer since water temperatures just do not become

warm enough to drive them down. To some degree this is also the situation in western Canada, in the country of big pike and lakers. The fish are almost always near the surface and seem to be forever hungry.

In trout country, during the entire summer fishing season, it is unthinkable to fish with anything but a fly rod. With this, you can troll a streamer fly, cast a wet or dry fly, or fish a deep nymph over the spring holes. Evening fly hatches during the late spring and early summer always provide top-water action. If the fish are feeding under the surface, you can sink a streamer or wet fly. There is no nonsense about spin-fishing or heavy trolling tackle in real wilderness trout waters. Therein lies their charm.

A man is not forced into fishing at the crack of dawn or far into the black of night to take fish from wild lakes. The waters are normally cool even during the summer, and action can be had during daylight hours—if not during the heat of the day, certainly in the cool of dusk. Feeding times coincide with the appearance of flies and schools of minnows when the sun leaves the water.

A wilderness fisherman is most often a trophy angler—or he should be. Fish are easy to take in wild waters and there is little excuse for killing more than a man can eat or than he would want to preserve for mounting. Without effort, I can visualize great fish

246

I have found in the hinterlands: big squaretail trout —sea-runs—from Beadle Brook, a tributary of the Miramichi in New Brunswick, Canada, which can be reached only after poling a canoe nine miles upstream; huge muskies from the Kenora district of Ontario; lusty northern pike near the village of Aniak on the west coast of Alaska; grayling, each crowding the world's record, from Priest Rock in Lake Clark in Alaska. A man needs only one of these to stir his memories of great fishing.

Perhaps it is improper to end a book on angling with a minor essay on wilderness waters, where all the lessons of fishing science and technique are least necessary. Yet a fish is a wild creature, forever meant to be wild, and nowhere is this primitive fact more clearly seen than in the wilderness lake, far from men and the works of men.

Catching a fish is a wholesome enterprise, but better still is the feeling of living harmoniously with the fishing environment.

Once, on a beautiful evening at the outlet of Nonphyanek Lake in Alaska, when the red ball of the sun dropping below the bluffs made gold rims on the clouds above, I hooked a giant rainbow. I sent the hair-wing fly across the smooth flow of current breaking from the lake waters and saw the surging boil as the fish took. He jumped clear and sparkling, be-

tween me and the sunset when the hook struck home, creating a halo of spray and glittering water drops. He made off down the slick of the current as I tried to check him against the music of the reel. But he turned, himself, and ran upstream under full power, into the quiet water of the lake, defeating his efforts by giving me still water in which to play him out.

In time, he came to me in the shallows, where I beached him. I reached down and raised him by the gill covers. I held him to the western sky, where the broad pink of his stripe blended with the rose-coral suffusion of the horizon. He must have weighed close to ten pounds, although I did not have the pocket scales to check him. He was easily three feet long. I put him down gently into the few inches of water at my feet. He struggled to stay upright for a moment; I grasped him by the wrist and pumped him back and forth to start fresh water over his gills. In a moment he grew strong again and pushed away from my grip with a firm thrust of his tail.

This was a fish I should have saved for mounting; I do not expect to catch a larger rainbow in my lifetime. But I was a long way from home and his home was here, in the darkening lake, in the water-lapped silence, amid the pulsating colors and great vitality of the natural world.

The memory of him, as he was, contents me.

Many northern, wilderness lakes
are available to the angler only by air, but
this is water for squaretails
in NewHampshire (opposite page), muskies
in Ontario, Canada (left).

Far left: "Camp Fire," by Winslow Homer, 1880.
Below: Frontispiece from "Fishing in American Waters,"
by Genio C. Scott, New York, 1875.

INDEX

Photography Sources

BAUER, ERWIN: *pages 172, 183* (lower right), *230, 236-237.*

BRAUN, HARRY: *pages 82* (right), *83* (lower left and lower right), *84, 136* (top and lower left).

BROWNING, BILL, FOR MONTANA CHAMBER OF COMMERCE: *pages 117, 123* (right), *126-127, 136* (right), *142, 143* (lower), *145, 146, 210-211, 224-225, 229* (lower left and lower right), *233.*

CANADIAN GOVERNMENT TRAVEL BUREAU: *pages 102, 130-131, 243* (lower).

CANADIAN NATIONAL RAILWAYS: *page 243* (top left).

CANADIAN PACIFIC RAILWAYS: *pages 97, 158.*

FIORINI, BUZZ: *pages 86-87, 108-109, 110-111, 112.*

FLORIDA GAME AND FRESH WATER FISH COMMISSION: *page 240.*

JOHN J. HILDEBRANT COMPANY: *page 206* (top).

KOLLER, LARRY: *pages 72* (top), *78, 78-79, 79* (top and lower right), *80-81, 95* (top), *98, 104-105, 121, 122, 123* (left), *134-135* (lower), *135* (top), *153* (top), *156* (top right and bottom), *182* (lower left and top right), *189* (top right), *229* (top).

LAYCOCK, GEORGE: *pages 116, 176-177, 180* (top, lower left, and center right), *182* (top left and lower right), *183* (left and top right), *212, 216, 222.*

MAINE DEPARTMENT OF ECONOMIC DEVELOPMENT: *pages 76-77, 79* (lower left), *91* (right), *227.*

MANITOBA DEPARTMENT OF INDUSTRY AND COMMERCE: *page 200.*

MCCORMICK, ROBERT: *page 220.*

MCDONALD, COLIN, FOR ONTARIO DEPARTMENT OF TRAVEL AND PUBLICITY: *pages 90, 191, 235* (lower left), *247* (left).

MERCURY OUTBOARDS: *page 141.*

NEW YORK STATE CONSERVATION PHOTOS: *pages 55, 178.*

NORTH CAROLINA WILDLIFE RESOURCES COMMISSION: *page 173.*

NORTHERN CONSOLIDATED AIRLINES: *page 106.*

NOVA SCOTIA FILM BUREAU: *page 235* (top).

OREGON STATE GAME COMMISSION: *page 147.*

SILK, GEORGE: *jacket and pages 2-3, 42-43, 46-47, 58-59, 61, 64-65, 68-69, 100-101, 114-115, 118-119, 125, 128-129, 132, 134-135* (top), *135* (lower), *138, 152, 152-153* (lower), *156* (top left), *162-163, 164-165, 166-167, 168-169, 170-171, 174-175, 184-185, 188, 188-189* (top center and bottom), *192, 194-195, 198-199, 202-203, 214-215.*

SQUILLACE, ALBERT A.: *pages 148-149.*

STATE OF NEW HAMPSHIRE, PUBLICITY: *pages 91* (left), *246* (right).

TENNESSEE CONSERVATION DEPARTMENT: *pages 180* (lower right), *209* (photograph by Paul A. Moore).

TENNESSEE GAME AND FISH COMMISSION: *page 155.*

U.S. FISH AND WILDLIFE SERVICE: *pages 83* (top), *137.*

U.S. FOREST SERVICE: *pages 93, 244-245.*

VERMONT FISH COMMISSION: *page 120.*

VISHNIAC, DR. ROMAN: *page 51.*

WULFF, LEE: *page 70.*

Sources of Prints and Paintings

COLUMBIA UNIVERSITY, PLIMPTON COLLECTION:
Thomas Dilworth, "New Guide to the English Tongue," printed by Benjamin Franklin, Philadelphia, 1747, *page 221.*

FRICK ART REFERENCE LIBRARY:
George Harvey, "Old Mill," *page 154.*

GARBISCH, COL. EDGAR W., COLLECTION: Winslow Homer, "Sunrise, Fishing in the Adirondacks," *page 95* (lower).

METROPOLITAN MUSEUM OF ART, NEW YORK: Winslow Homer, "Camp Fire," gift of Henry Keney Pomeroy, 1927, *page 246* (left).

MISSOURI HISTORICAL SOCIETY, ST. LOUIS: Sketch from William Clark's journal, Lewis and Clark Expedition, *page 82* (left).

MUSEUM OF THE CITY OF NEW YORK: Currier & Ives, "An Anxious Moment," *pages 20-21;* "The Trout Stream," *page 24* (top).

NEW-YORK HISTORICAL SOCIETY: Brown's "The American Angler's Guide," 1857, *page 144.*
Thaddeus Norris, "The American Angler's Book," Philadelphia, 1864, *page 208.*
Charles F. Orvis, "Fishing with the Fly," Manchester, Vermont, 1883, *page 238* (top).
Genio C. Scott, "Fishing in American Waters," Harper & Brothers, 1875, *page 120* (top).

YALE UNIVERSITY LIBRARY:
John Yonge Akerman, "Spring-tide," London, 1850, *page 44.*
Henry Thomas Alken, "The National Sports of Great Britain," London, 1821, *pages 38, 179.*
"The Angler's Own Book," London, 1867, *page 140* (lower).
Dame Juliana Berners, "A Treatyse of fysshynge wyth an angle," 1496, *pages 14, 15, 17.*
Charles Bowlker, "The Art of Angling," London, 1786, *page 181.*
Richard Brookes, "The Art of Angling," London, 1770, *page 33.*
Peter Comestor, "Historiaux de la Bible," France, c.1460, *page 10.*
"Dialogus Creaturarum Moralisatus," Gouda, 1480, *page 16.*
"Dry-Fly Entomology," London, 1897, Volume 1, *pages 49, 52, 53, 56.*
Thomas Gosden, "The Complete Angler," 1825, *page 160.*
Frederick M. Halford, "Dry-fly Fishing in Theory and Practice," London, 1889, *pages 66-67.*
Paul Hartwig, "Die griechischen Meisterschalen," Stuttgart-Berlin, 1893, *page 12* (bottom right).
Henry William Herbert, "Frank Forester's Fish and Fishing in the United States," New York, 1849, *page 23;* 1864 edition, *pages 88-89, 139.*
Wakeman Holberton, "Angling Resorts," 1890, *pages 234-235, 243.*
Austen Henry Layard, "The Monuments of Nineveh," London, 1849, *page 12* (center).
Gervase Markham, "The Young Sportsman's Delight," [1712], *page 28.*
"The Modern Angler," 1830, *page 24* (lower).
Percy Newberry, "Archaeological Survey in Egypt, Beni Hasan," London, 1893-96, *page 12* (top).
Thaddeus Norris, "The American Angler's Book," 1865, *pages 161, 186-187.*
Dean Sage, "The Ristigouche and Its Salmon Fishing," Edinburgh, 1888, *pages 74-75.*
T. F. Salter, "The Angler's Guide," London, 1815, *pages 143* (top), *157, 201, 221;* 1830 edition, *pages 27, 29, 30-31, 159.*
Genio C. Scott, "Fishing in American Waters," New York, 1869, *page 238* (lower); 1867 edition, *page 206* (lower).
Izaak Walton, "The Compleat Angler," first edition, London, 1653, *page 18* (top right); "The Complete Angler," London, 1836, Volume 1, *page 18* (left and lower right); Volume 4, *pages 62-63, 103, 140* (top), *223, 235* (center); Volume 5, *pages 151, 186, 197, 213;* Volume 6, *pages 92, 94, 107, 133.*

B